IMAGES
of America

MISSION BEACH

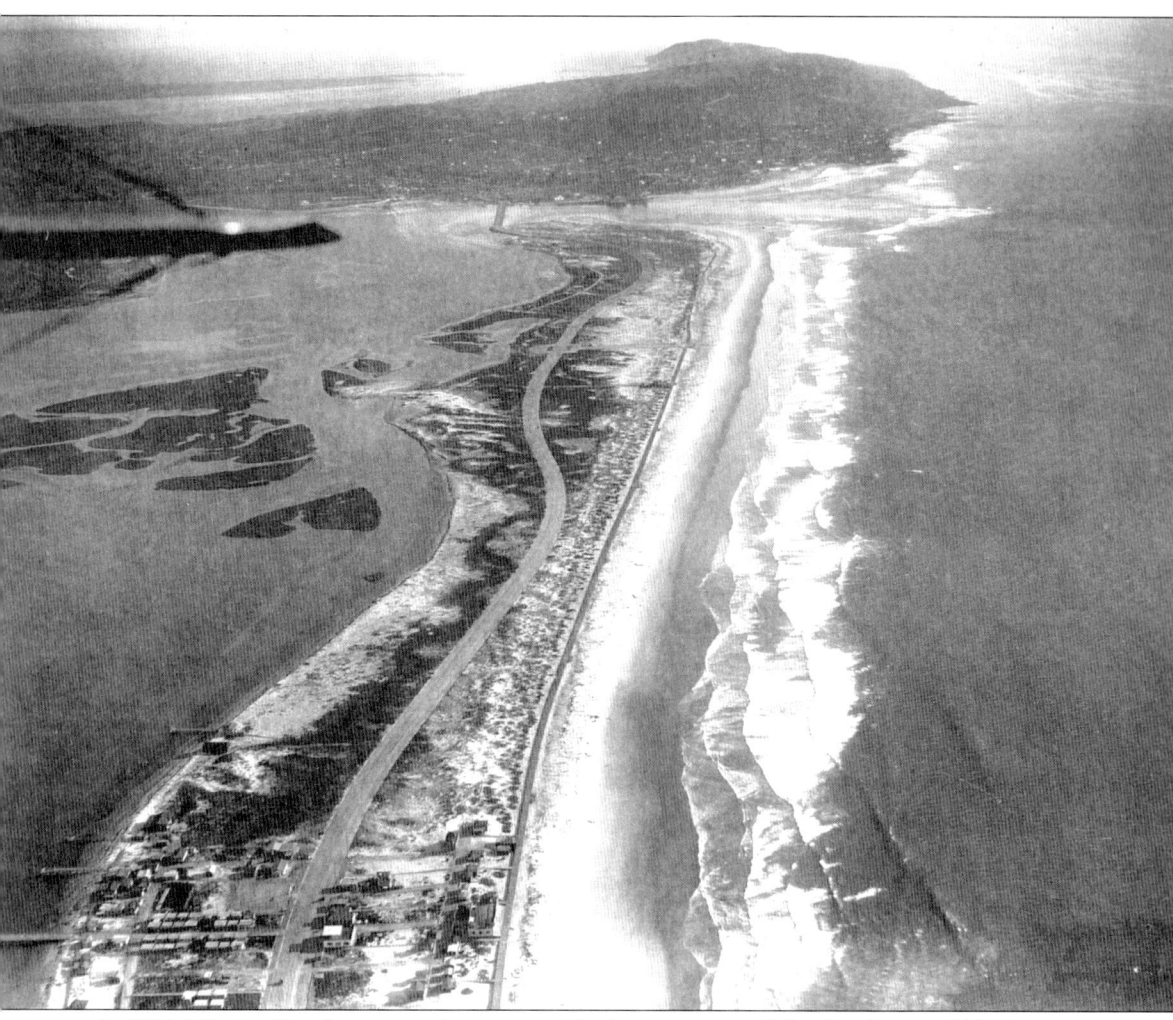

In 1916, Mission Beach was mostly empty, with the exception of the developing Old Mission in the foreground. On the oceanfront is Asher's Bathhouse and directly across on the bay, Asher's pier, cottages, and pool. In the background are Point Loma and the new bridge connecting Mission Beach with Ocean Beach to the south. (Courtesy of authors.)

ON THE COVER: Charles Lindbergh is test flying the *Spirit of St. Louis* over Mission Beach in 1927, prior to his history-making solo flight across the Atlantic Ocean to Paris later in the year. The Mission Beach Amusement Center with its centerpiece, the Giant Dipper roller coaster, is directly below the plane. Mission Bay is in the foreground, and the Pacific Ocean is beyond. (Courtesy of SDHS.)

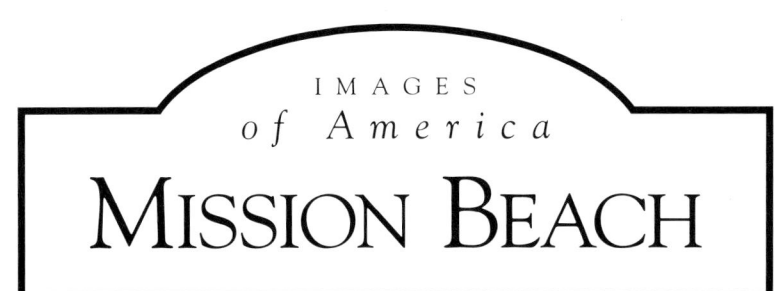

IMAGES of America
MISSION BEACH

To my good pals, Lily & Noal — Best wishes. Look back & enjoy!

Terry Curren and Phil Prather

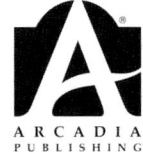

ARCADIA PUBLISHING

Copyright © 2007 by Terry Curren and Phil Prather
ISBN 978-0-7385-4785-5

Published by Arcadia Publishing
Charleston SC, Chicago IL, Portsmouth NH, San Francisco CA

Printed in the United States of America

Library of Congress Catalog Card Number: 2007924272

For all general information contact Arcadia Publishing at:
Telephone 843-853-2070
Fax 843-853-0044
E-mail sales@arcadiapublishing.com
For customer service and orders:
Toll-Free 1-888-313-2665

Visit us on the Internet at www.arcadiapublishing.com

This book is dedicated to all the Old Mission Beach pals who shared the wonderful experiences we had growing up in a very special time. Friendships that have lasted 60 or more years are rare and are a priceless gift. We are truly blessed.

Contents

Acknowledgments		6
Introduction		7
1.	The Early Years	9
2.	The Roaring Twenties	21
3.	The Lifeguards	39
4.	Belmont Park	57
5.	The 1930s and 1940s	69
6.	Mission Bay	81
7.	Old Mission Beach	105
8.	Later Years	117

Acknowledgments

There are many people who have been very helpful in the compilation of photographs, historical data, and information that has made this book possible, and we are grateful to each and every one of them. The picture credits show only a fraction of the people who have aided in the compiling of this history. Many of the pictures are from the authors' collections accumulated over a lifetime and include images from Union Title and Trust Company and Land Title Company.

Special thanks goes to Chris Travers of the San Diego Historical Society (SDHS), who was most helpful with her advice and her assistance in selecting special pictures from the SDHS collection; Debbie Seracini of Arcadia Publishing, who assisted greatly with advice, encouragement, and editing; Mission Beach Woman's Club and the Mission Beach Town Council for recommending us to Arcadia Publishing as authors for this book; Willie Skinner, who stepped up and provided us with a wealth of pictures and information, as well as steering us to many other sources; Anne Howe Mansfield, who opened her family photo albums and gave us access to many of the Mission Bay images; Duncan McFarland and Cleo Wright for their historical data regarding Charles Wright and the rock house; the staff of the California Room at the San Diego Public Library, who is always eager to help with any information requested.

Also, in no special order of importance, Don Crie, Suzy Suhre, Marshal Malcom, Steve Malcom, Norma Griffin, Bob and Dee Lange, Terry Polhamus Mendoza, Beach and Bay Press, Tom Lochtefeld, Lt. Nick Lerma, Roy Penwarden, Jackie Linstrom, Mary Willmont, Marilyn Brucker, and Mel Kirsner. We apologize to anyone who has been inadvertently omitted, and we also thank you.

INTRODUCTION

The story of the early development of Mission Beach is best told by its original developer, J. M. Asher Jr. The following is printed verbatim from a handwritten document that Asher provided to assist junior high school student Pat Donnelly in his research for a term paper c. 1945.

MISSION BEACH
J.M. ASHER JR.

Late in the year 1913 and early 1914, a strip of land, mostly sand dunes, located between the Pacific Ocean and Mission Bay, just north of Ocean Beach and bounded on the northerly end by Pacific Beach, was purchased in acreage from O. J. Stough, and the other "long time owners", by a Syndicate comprised of San Diego Business Men, including John D. Spreckles, M. Hall, the Rife Bros. Percy Goodwin, George S. Barney, and many others. The Syndicate Sub-divided this property into Blocks and lots, naming this sub-division, Mission Beach.

Early in 1915, J.M. Asher, took over the handling of Mission Beach, purchasing by Grant Deed several hundred lots, upon which Asher built a Tent City including Store buildings, a bath house, playgrounds with a concrete swimming pool, a Bayfront pier, side walks, surfaced streets and alleys, and many other improvements.

This venture led to considerable success and was the direct cause of the building of the present Mission Beach Amusement Center by the J. D. Spreckles Co. a few years later. That portion of Mission Beach that Asher purchased and improved is now known as "Old Mission Beach."

Asher also installed the original Gas & Electric system, and all water service, maintaining this service for many years.

The Parents and Grand Parents of many of the scholars now writing re various sections of San Diego, were known in their childhood and school days by Mr. Asher who was born in San Diego, Calif. over 65 years ago.

Mr. Asher well remembers the time when the present location of Mission Beach was the home of flocks of quail, many rabbits, lizards by the thousands, and also some "sidewinder rattle snakes".

Note: The base of Mission Beach, in many sections, is composed of boulders of considerable size and beautiful in color.

Before 1915, Ocean Beach, not Mission Beach, was San Diego's favorite beach of choice. In an era of the horse and buggy and a few early automobiles, Mission Beach was considered too long a trek, entailing a long roundabout journey north to Pacific Beach, westerly to the ocean, and then south to Mission Beach. The journey took several hours. Not only was Ocean Beach easier to reach, but it also had all of the attractions that drew people in, namely Wonderland, the oceanfront amusement park with a dance hall, food establishments, and rides for kids of all ages. Unfortunately, Wonderland was destroyed by a fierce winter storm in 1916.

In 1915, the Bayshore Railway Company erected a bridge connecting Ocean Beach to Mission Beach and built a streetcar line from downtown San Diego. The bridge, some 1,500 feet long and 50 feet wide, spanned the channel entrance to Mission Bay and provided much needed direct access for the streetcar and automobile traffic. The primary purpose of this new, easy access route was to promote the sale of Mission Beach real estate. The bridge also provided a great place for local fishermen to while away the hours, often going home with plenty of fish for the family meal.

By the early 1920s, Old Mission Beach, north of Santa Clara Place, was a thriving community, with new stores, many houses, and a growing population. Old Mission became the beach of choice for a growing number of people. It was at Old Mission Beach where young people from all the high schools and colleges in San Diego congregated up until the late 1950s, forging close friendships. It was a unique situation that so many people from such a wide spectrum of backgrounds, economic means, and geographical diversity could meet and share a lifetime of camaraderie. Even today, there is an annual gathering of these old pals, and the mailing list is still over 300 friends, even after more than 60 years.

J. D. Spreckles and a group of investors began the construction of the Mission Beach Amusement Center in 1924 at the corner of Ventura Place and Mission Boulevard, opening in 1925. The park consisted of a landmark roller coaster, the Giant Dipper, the largest wooden coaster on the West Coast, as well as a ballroom and a huge indoor, saltwater swimming pool, the Mission Beach Plunge. Filling out the amusement center were numerous carnival rides, arcades, food stands, and other attractions. The Mission Beach Plunge and the Giant Dipper have been designated as historical sites and are still in operation today.

The Mission Beach Ballroom hosted concerts by all of the major big bands and entertainers of the 1930s and 1940s, including Stan Kenton, Glen Miller, Artie Shaw, Lionel Hampton, and Nat King Cole. It was also the venue of one of the last of the marathon dance competitions, held around 1946.

The amusement center was owned and operated by Jack Ray in 1954. He changed the name to Belmont Park to associate it with other parks that he controlled. Today it is operated by the Wavehouse Corporation. Along with the building of the amusement center came the development of the southern half of Mission Beach, known as New Mission. Today that area is known as South Mission Beach, with the dividing line at Ventura Place, and everything north known as North Mission Beach.

In 1946, the Army Corps of Engineers completed a feasibility study and determined that the dredging of Mission Bay was a viable project. The massive bay redevelopment project began shortly after, transforming what was once a shallow, muddy, and debris-filled body of water into a totally usable water recreation and beach parkland. The dredging and shoreline was mostly completed by 1949.

Included in the development was a new bridge cutting diagonally across the bay, eliminating the need for the Ocean Beach Bridge. The O. B. Bridge was removed in 1951 and the channel deepened to accommodate large boats. Today Mission Bay has several fine hotels and restaurants, beautiful sandy beaches, world-renowned SeaWorld, and large, open-water areas and inlets that attract millions of visitors annually. It is enjoyed equally by the locals.

Mission Beach has seen many changes since 1914. Today there are very few vacant lots, and property values have skyrocketed. What was once a small, self-contained town with many young families in single-family homes has become more of a destination retreat for owners of high-priced condominiums. Mission Beach School has closed due to the diminishing number of young children. Many residents are seasonal, but Mission Beach is still the year-round home of many old-timers and quite a number of newer residents.

The beach lifestyle is different than any other. The people are friendly and relaxed, and the salty air is a natural high. Those of us who were fortunate enough to have grown up in Mission Beach have a lifetime of fond memories of having lived and played in the largest playground imaginable.

One
THE EARLY YEARS

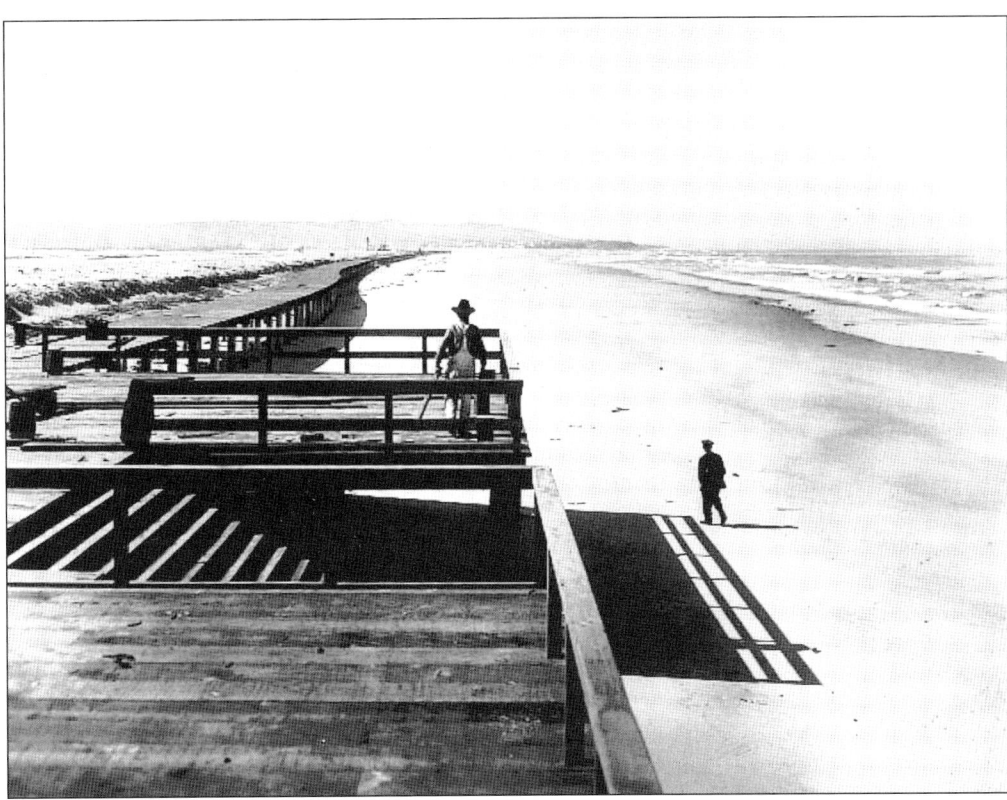

A carpenter is putting the finishing touches to a mile-long stretch of boardwalk in 1915. Traversing the sand dunes was an ordeal prior to the new boardwalk that eventually extended the entire length of Mission Beach, some 2.5 miles. The gentleman to the right is enjoying empty sand dunes and lonely beaches. Point Loma and Ocean Beach are in the distance. (Courtesy of SDHS.)

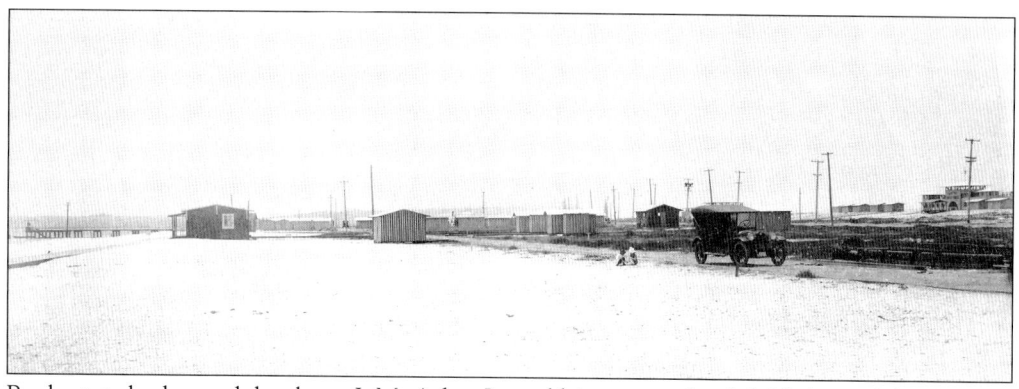

Real estate broker and developer J. M. Asher Jr. and his partner, Littlefield, first subdivided and sold land in Bay Park, overlooking Mission Bay. Asher then turned to Mission Beach. Looking south around 1914, J. M. Asher Jr.'s Mission Beach Tent City is visible. On the far right is Asher's Bathhouse on the oceanfront, and to the far left is Asher's pier extending into Mission Bay. The automobile is traveling north on Bayside Lane. (Courtesy of Willie Skinner.)

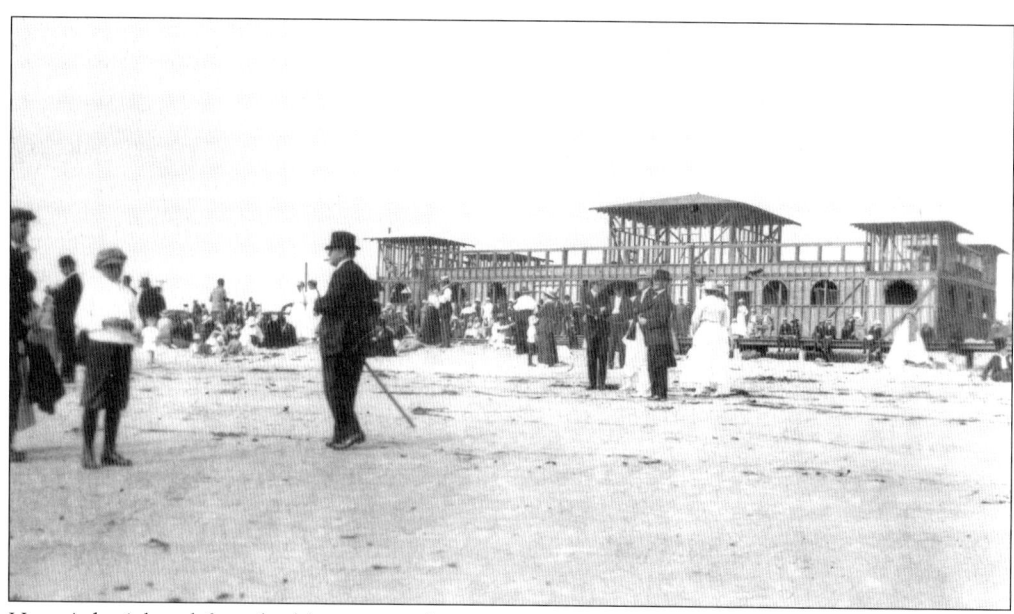

Here Asher's beachfront bathhouse is under construction in 1914. It was located between Redondo Court and Queenstown Court, the present-day location of a large condominium project. No bikini-clad women can be seen in this crowd! (Courtesy of SDHS.)

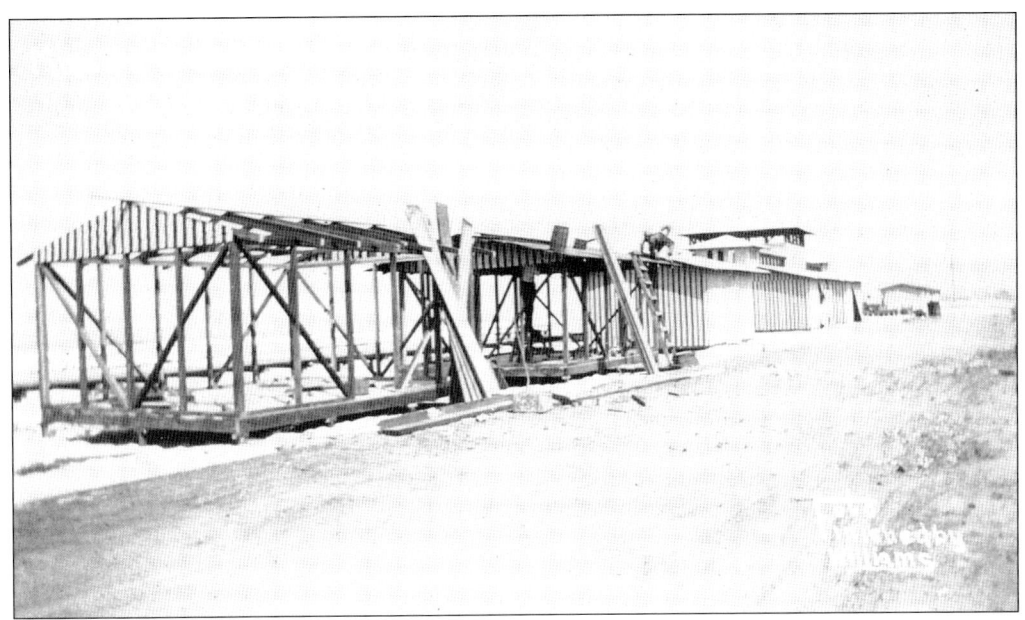
Construction of the tent city provided shelter and changing rooms for the public. The tents, approximately 12 feet by 15 feet, were available for day use and were also rented to those in the process of building their new beach residences c. 1914. (Courtesy of Willie Skinner.)

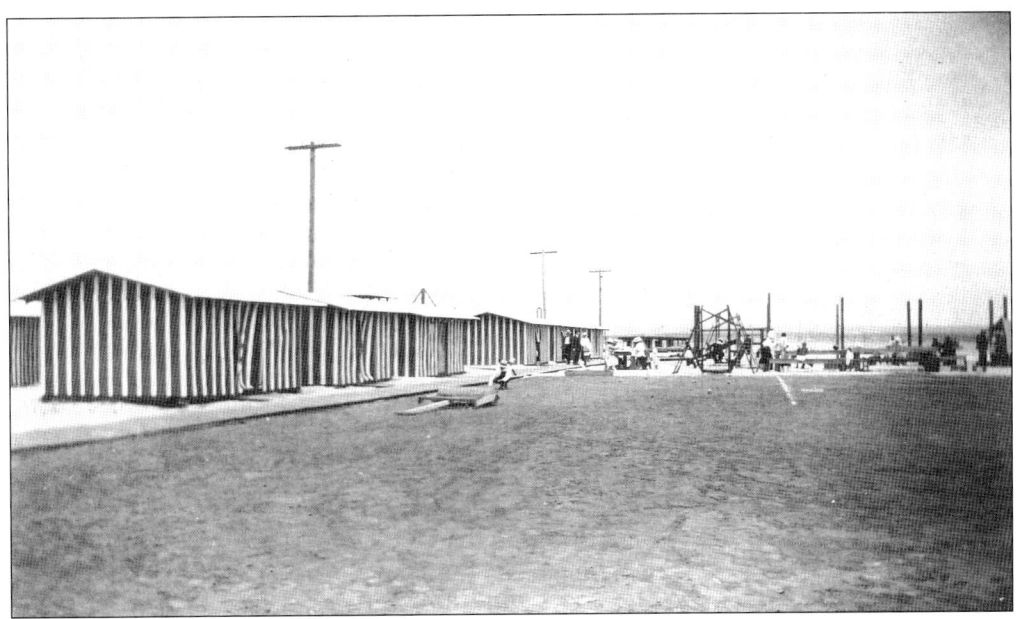
Looking toward the bay in this 1914 scene, Asher's tent city and the playground for the children are visible. Just beyond the playground was a small, shallow swimming pool. This pool was only in service for a couple of years before it was demolished and filled in. (Courtesy of Willie Skinner.)

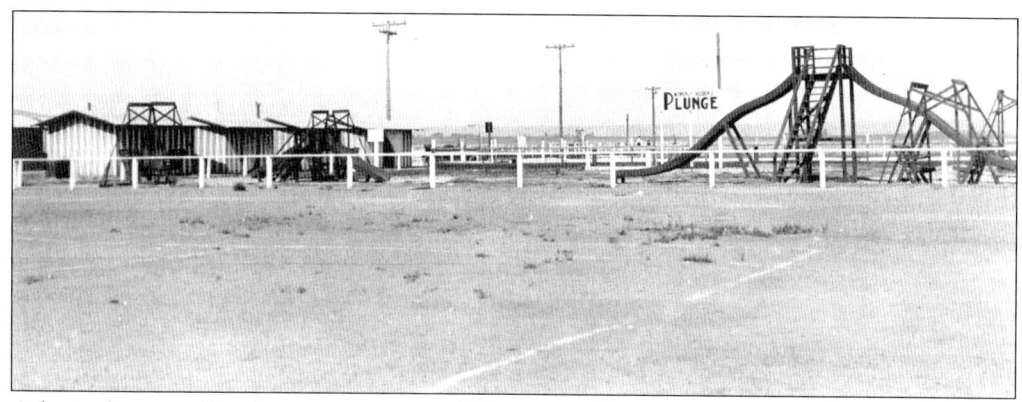

Asher's playground is adjacent to tent city. The swimming pool (also known as the Plunge) was just to the east along Bayside Lane. This swimming pool predated by 10 years, the large Mission Beach Plunge that was to be built at the Amusement Center in 1925. Crown Point is visible in the far background. (Courtesy of Pell Mell.)

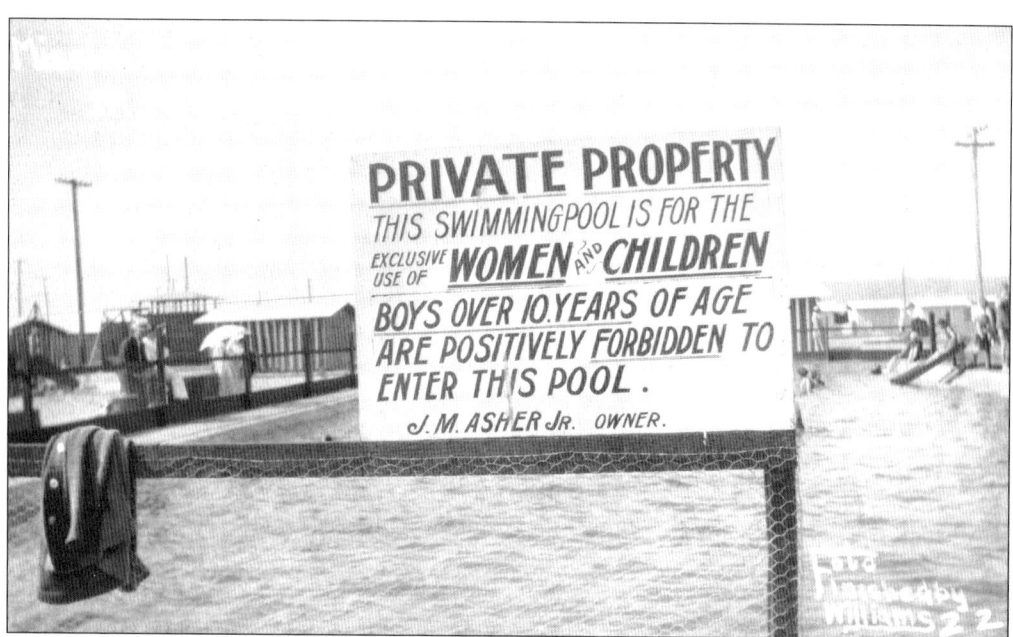

Asher restricted the use of the pool to women and children. It can only be assumed that boys over 10 and men were potentially uncontrollable when in the presence of bathing suit-clad women in 1914. (Courtesy of Willie Skinner.)

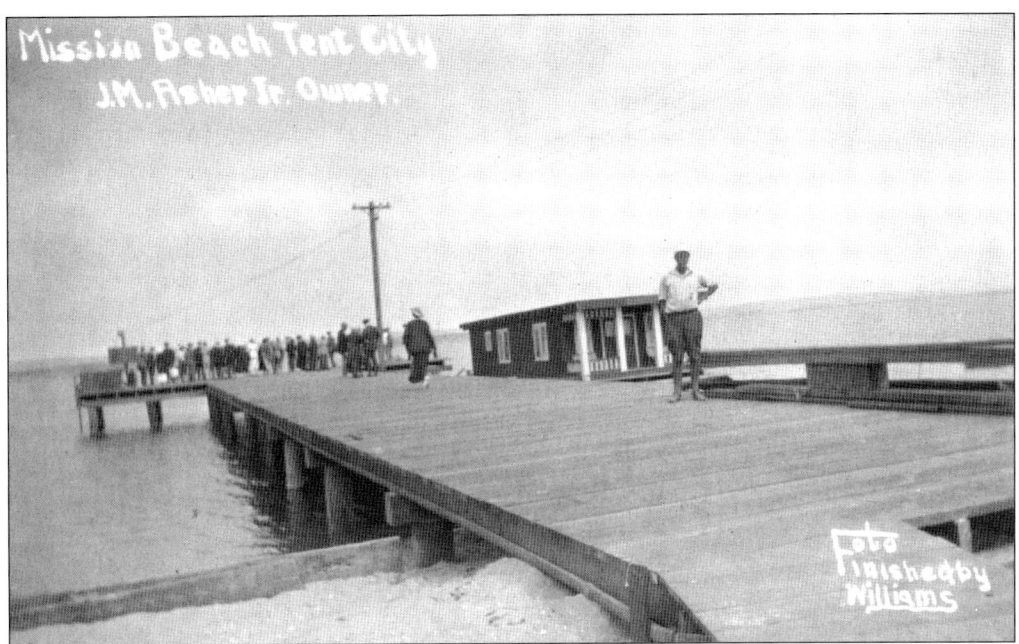

J. M. Asher Jr.'s pier, extending out into Mission Bay, was another attraction drawing people to the new community of Mission Beach. Fishing from the pier usually resulted in a good catch. The gentleman in the foreground is believed to be J. M. Asher Jr. c. 1915. (Courtesy of Willie Skinner.)

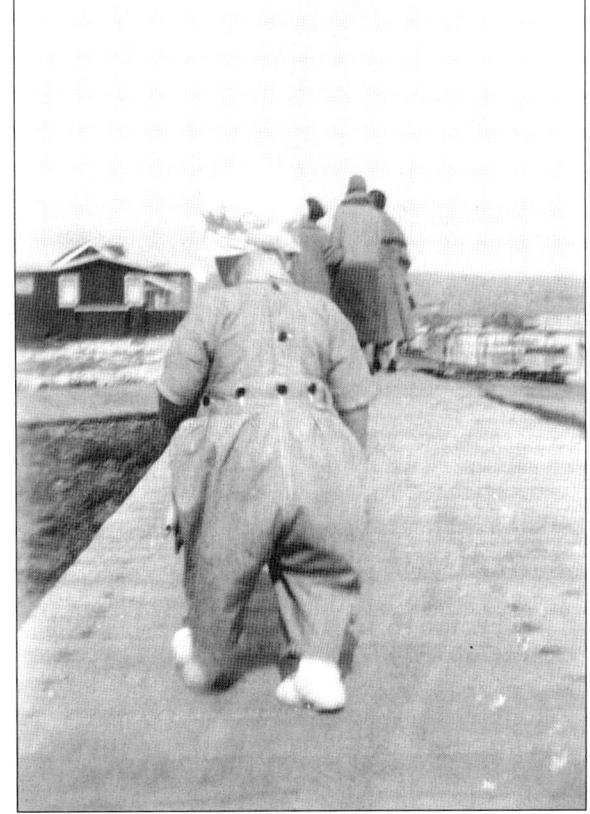

Hey, wait for me, mom! This young lady with the pretty sunbonnet is strolling along Bayside Walk, while the three women ahead are deep in conversation and seem to have forgotten her. The walkway is wooden, as well as the intersecting court on the left. Piers on the right extend into Mission Bay c. 1919. (Courtesy of Marge Harris.)

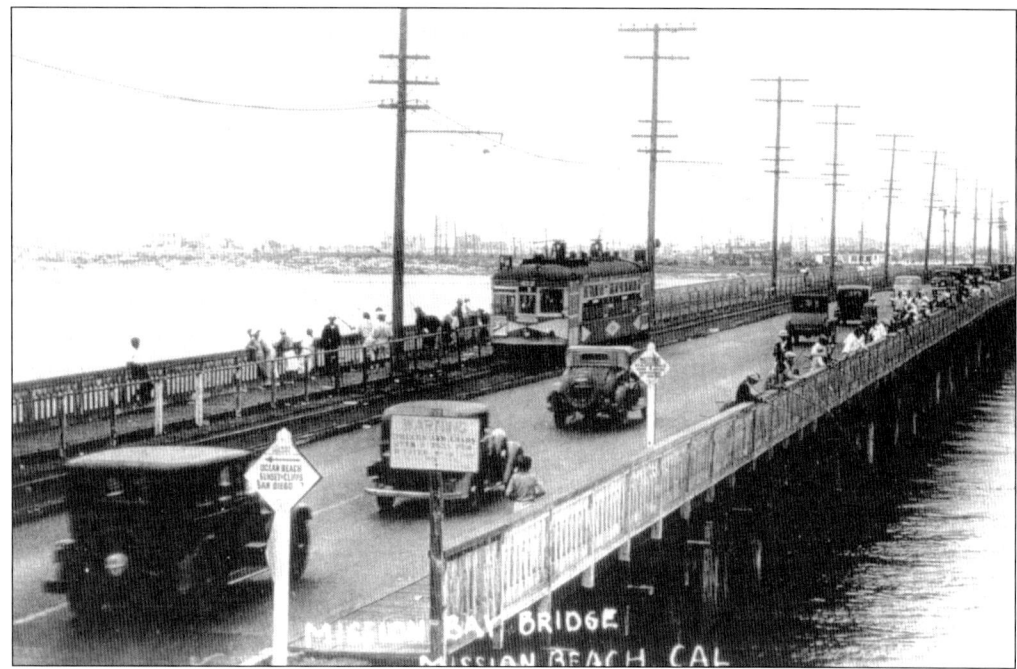

Before 1915, the only way to reach Mission Beach was a long trek around Mission Bay and through Pacific Beach. A bridge was built, connecting Ocean Beach and Mission Beach, by the Bayshore Railroad Company primarily to promote the sale of Mission Beach property. Trolley tracks were on the west side, and two traffic lanes were on the east. Wide walkways on both sides provided the locals great fishing opportunities, catching mainly halibut, flounder, bass, small sharks, and stingrays. Five-prong pole spears were also commonly used. (Courtesy of authors.)

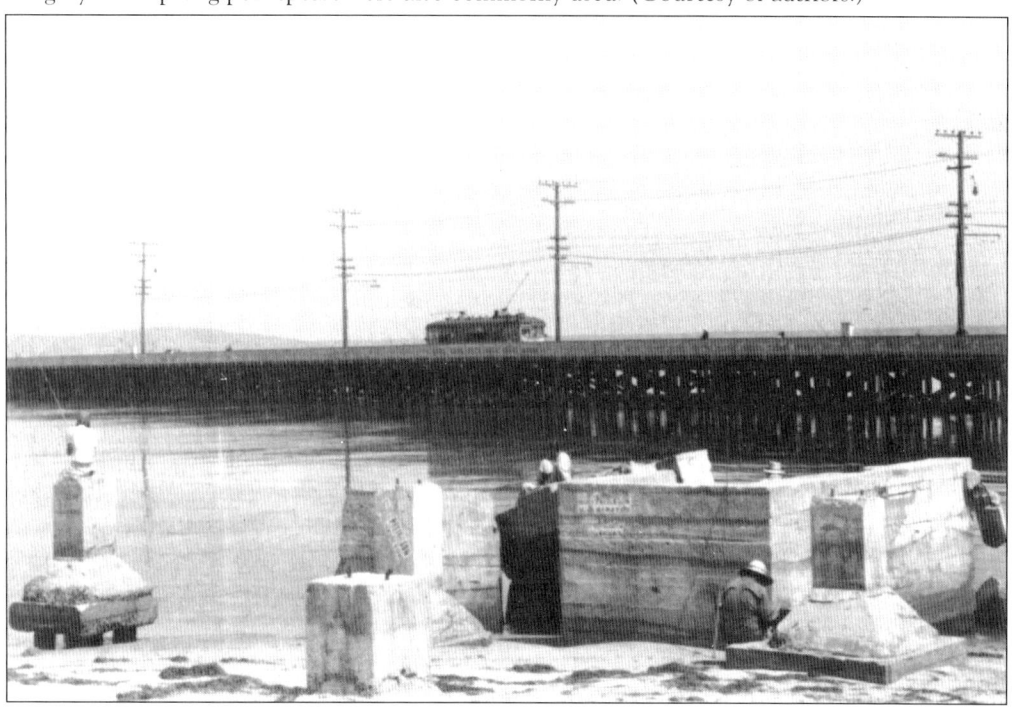

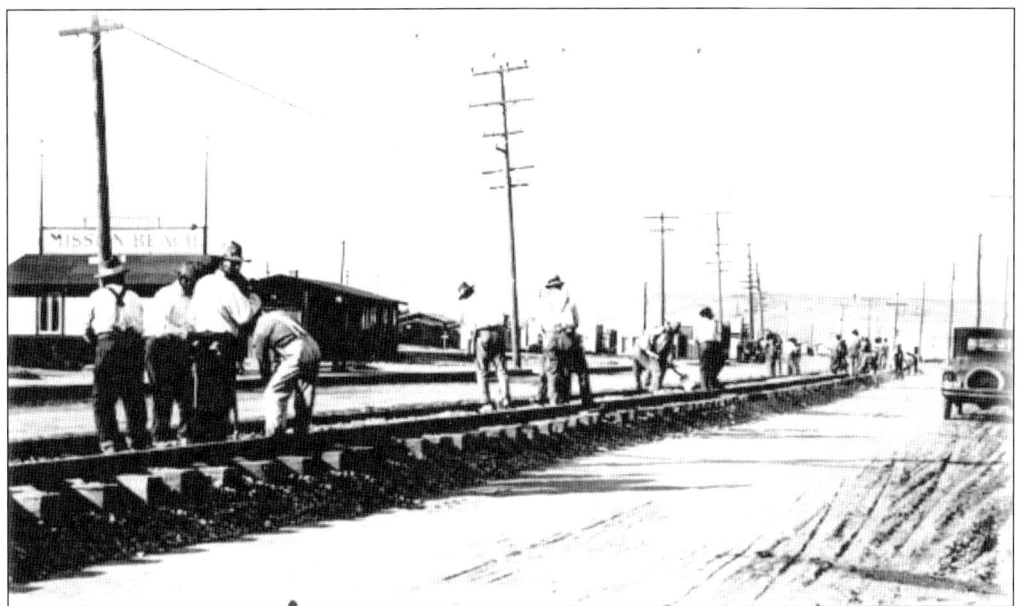

The streetcar soon followed the construction of the bridge linking Ocean Beach to Mission Beach. In 1915, the rails had been laid as far as Redondo Court, the center of the new development. These men are working around Pismo Court. Mission Beach is now primed and ready for development. The bridge is in, the trolley has arrived, and the sales office is open for business. All of north Mission Beach is for sale, and customers are selecting their favorite sites. Interior lots went for $450 to $500 and prime waterfront locations for as much as $1,000. (Courtesy of SDHS.)

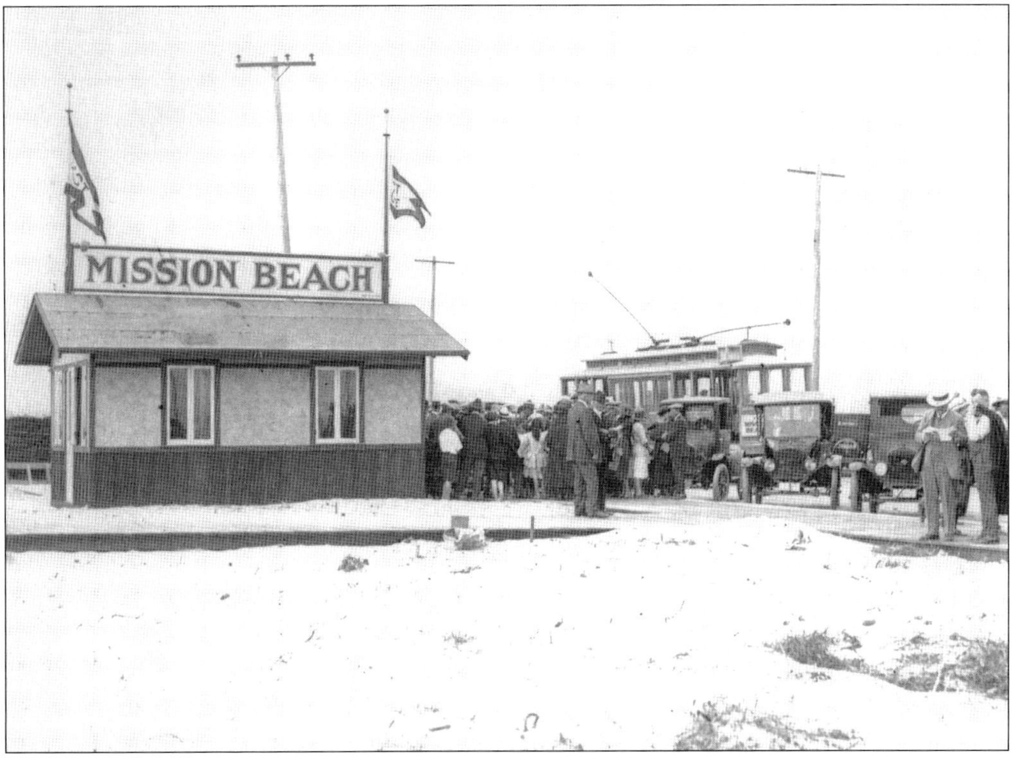

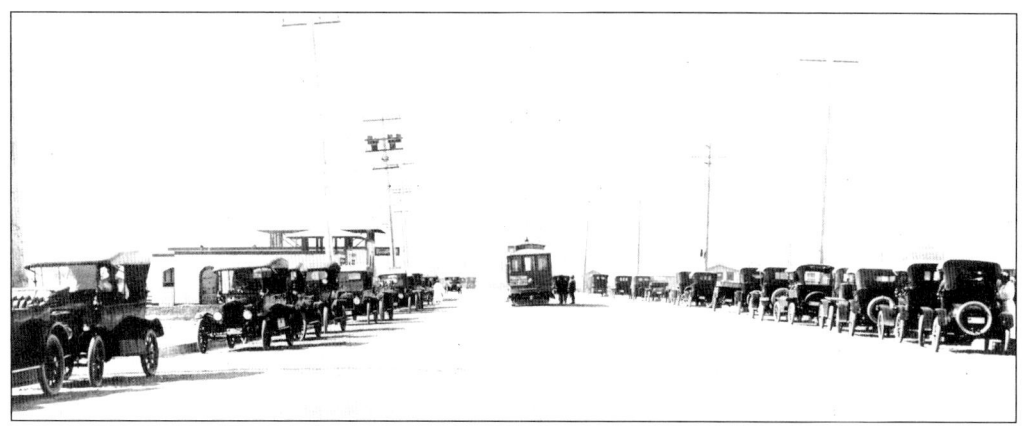

Business is booming around Redondo Court, the original terminus of the trolley line. The building on the left is the real estate office of J. M. Asher Jr., the original developer of Mission Beach. Parking space was scarce on July 4, 1916. (Courtesy of authors.)

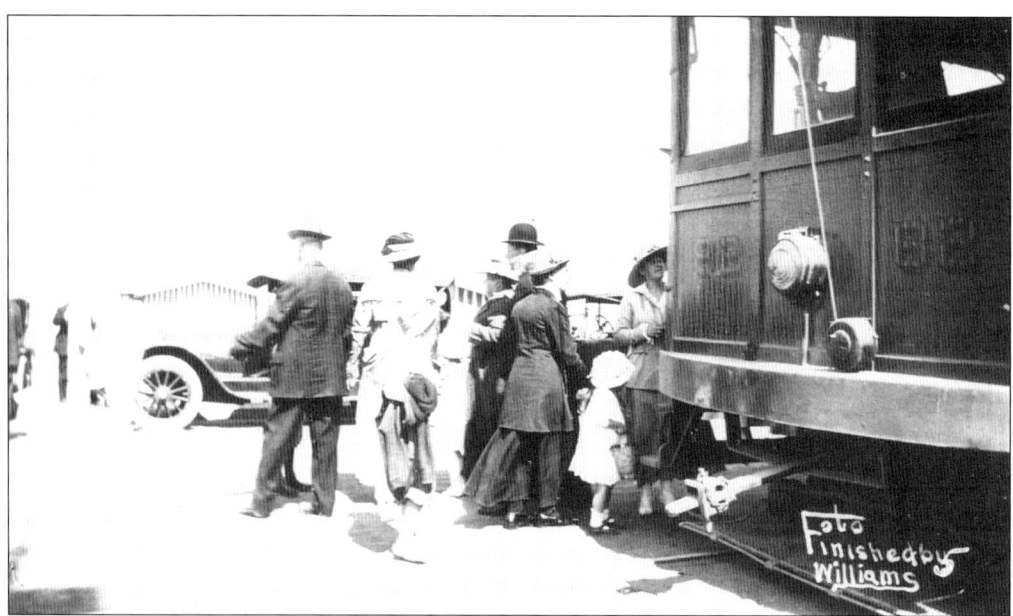

Men, women, and children rode the streetcar from downtown San Diego to Mission Beach. This was an exciting weekend outing for families in 1915 and 1916. Bathing attire could be rented at the bathhouse on the oceanfront for 25¢. (Courtesy of Willie Skinner.)

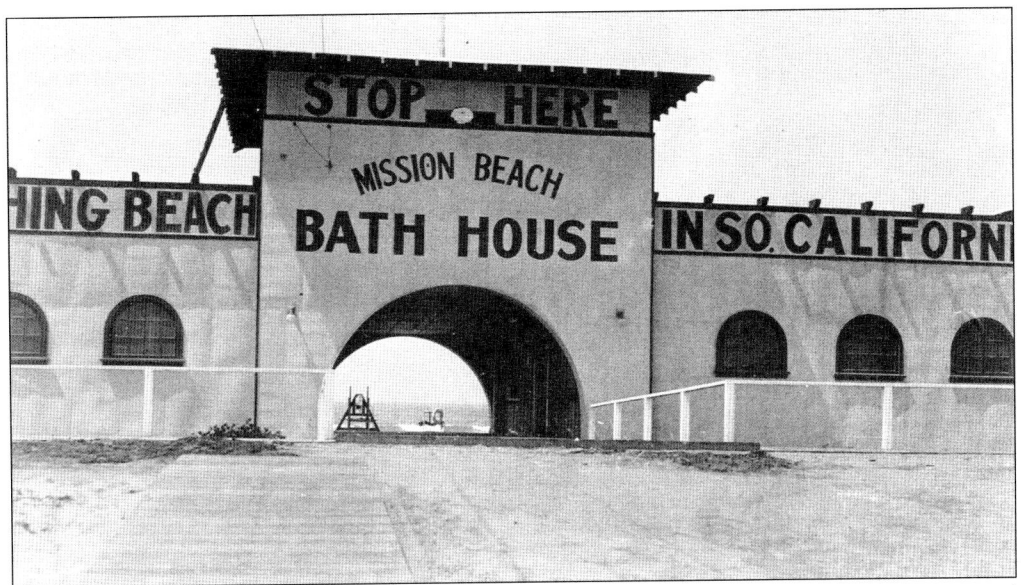

This view looks west through the main entrance of Asher's Mission Beach Bathhouse around 1915. Wooden walkways linked the oceanfront and the bay. This building, located between Queenstown Court and Redondo Court, lasted well into the 1950s, when it was demolished. The site was used for a parking lot prior to construction of condominiums around 1960. (Courtesy of Pell Mell.)

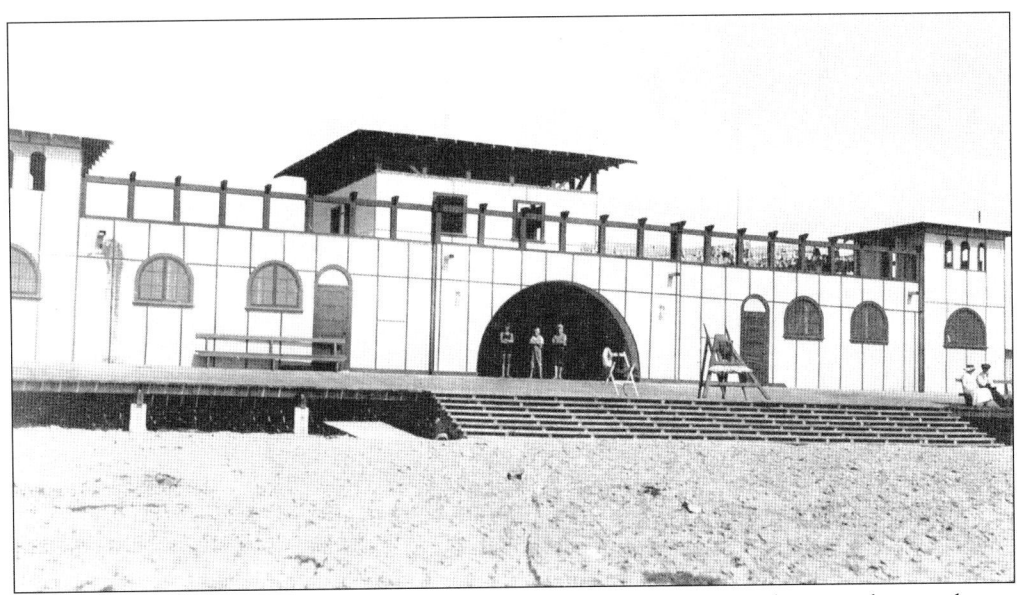

The west side view of the bathhouse shows the wooden boardwalk along the oceanfront and steps down to the beach. The bathhouse was turned into a bowling alley in the mid-1930s. (Courtesy of Pell Mell.)

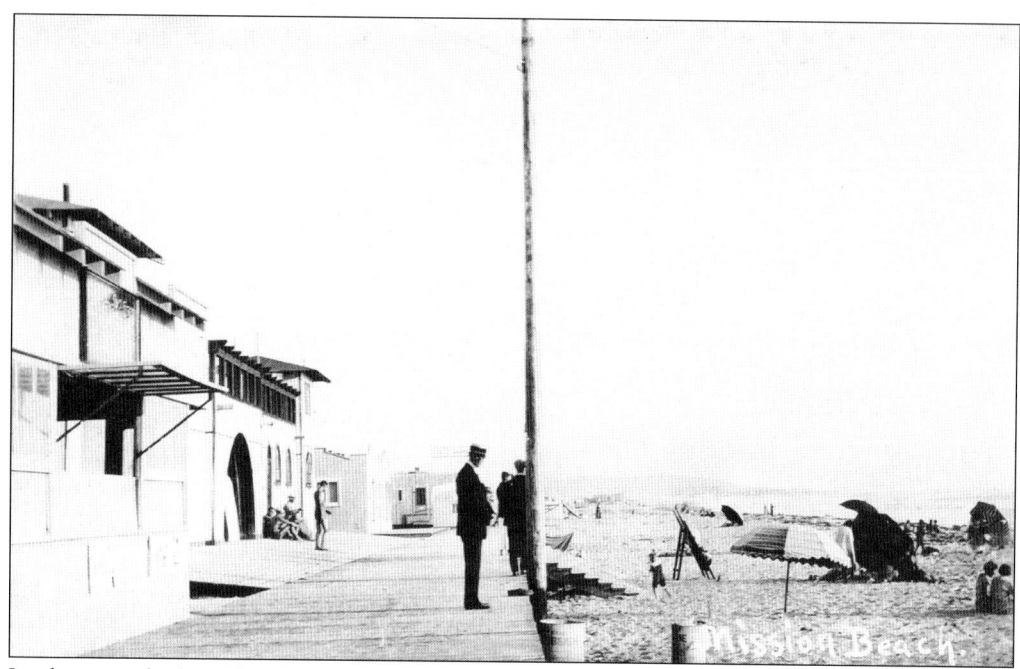

Looking south along the boardwalk in the summer of 1916, Al Harris's bungalows are visible just south of the bathhouse at Queenstown Court. (Courtesy of Marge Harris.)

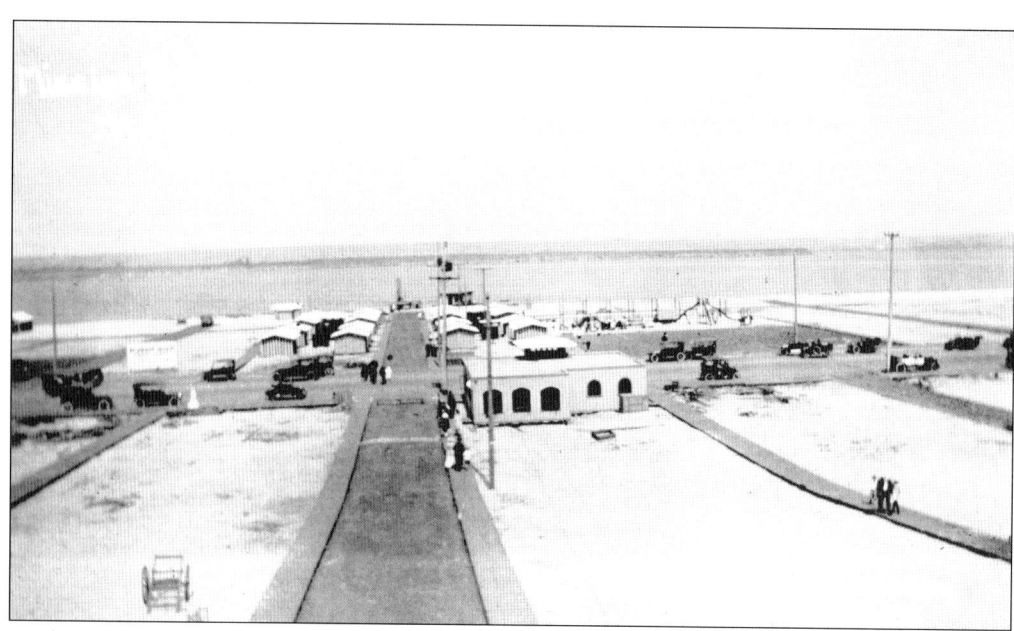

Looking east from the back of the bathhouse to the bay, the building in the foreground is the real estate office, and Asher's tent city and playground are beyond. The walkway on the left is Redondo Court. The people on the right are walking on Queenstown Court. (Courtesy of SDHS.)

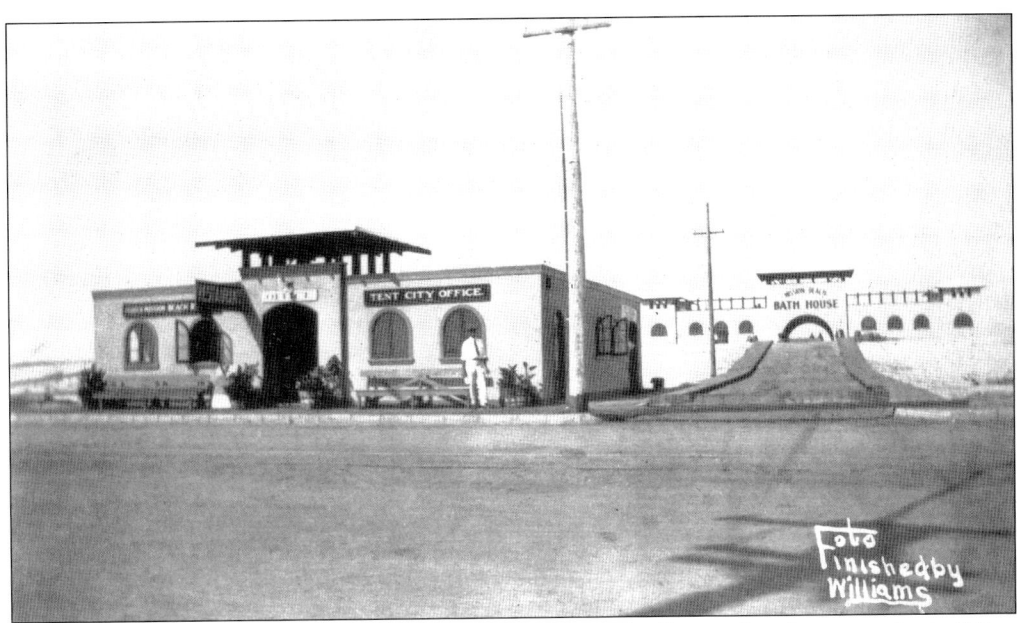

This is a quiet day at the Mission Beach Tent City rental office and real estate sales building as seen from Mission Boulevard c. 1915. Note the new power poles bringing electricity to the community. (Courtesy of SDHS.)

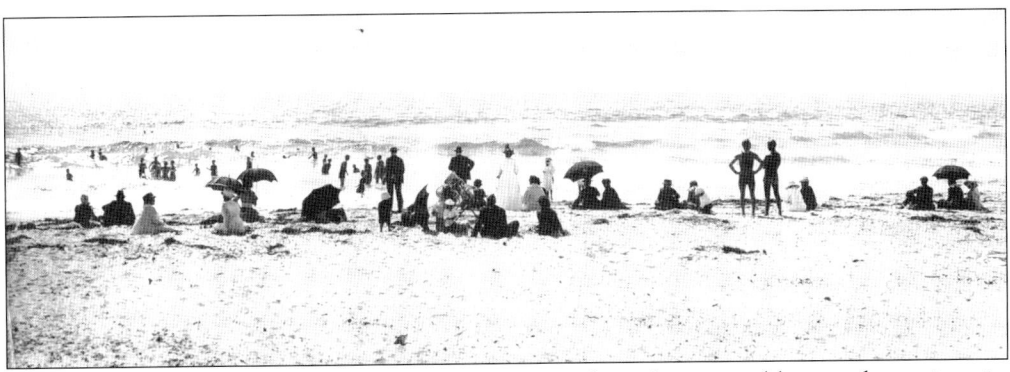

This beach scene from around 1916 shows women in long dresses and hats and men in suits watching the waves and the swimmers. Weekends at the beach were as popular then as they are today; only the beach attire has changed. (Courtesy of Willie Skinner.)

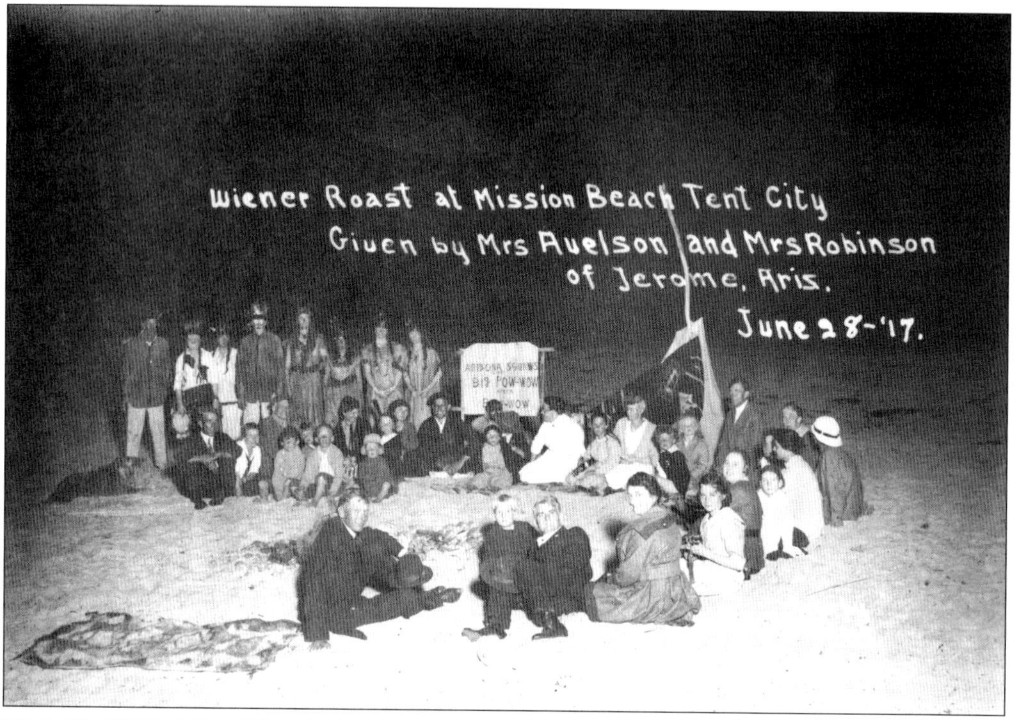

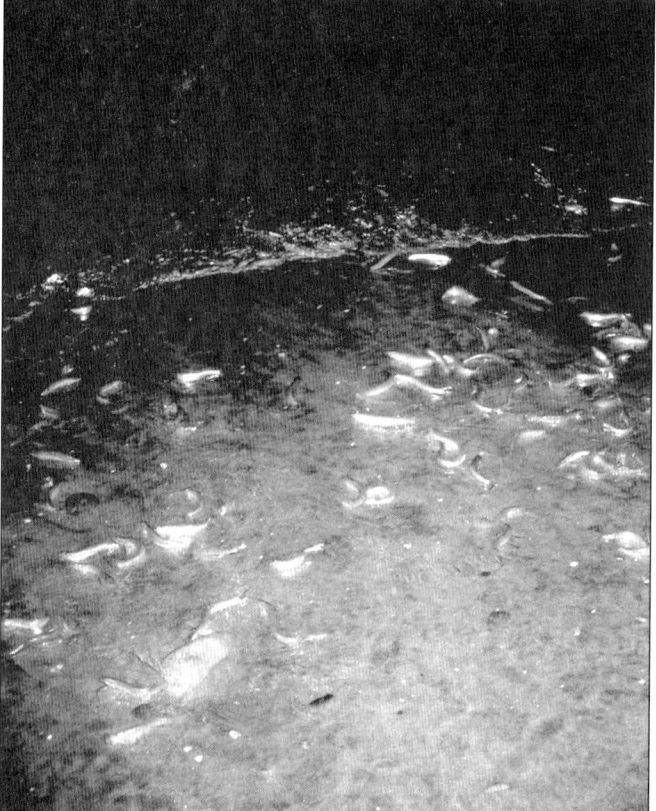

On the evening of June 28, 1917, Mrs. Avenson and Mrs. Robinson hosted a wiener roast on the beach. Nighttime beach parties were a new concept, and beach attire was somewhat formal. The sign in the background says, "Arizona Squaws big Pow-Wow." (Courtesy of SDHS.)

What better way to top off a beach party than to catch a few grunion. These small, silvery fish come ashore at night by the hundreds during the summer months and lay their eggs just after high tide. The eggs lay in the sand until the next full moon. At high tide, water flows over the eggs, hatching the young ones who go back to sea with the waves. (Courtesy of authors.)

Two
THE ROARING TWENTIES

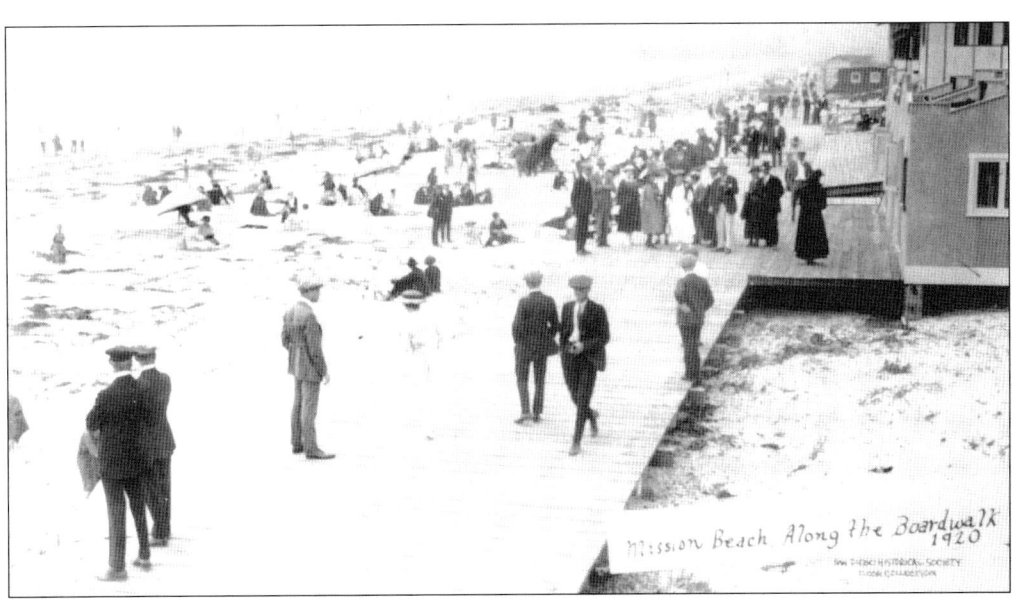

By 1920, Mission Beach had become a popular weekend destination for San Diegans. San Diego's population was just over 74,000. They came by streetcar and by automobile over the new bridge. A few houses had been built along the oceanfront boardwalk, but most visitors were there for the day to enjoy the sunshine. Coats and neckties for the gentlemen and long dresses for the women were the fashion of the day. (Courtesy of SDHS.)

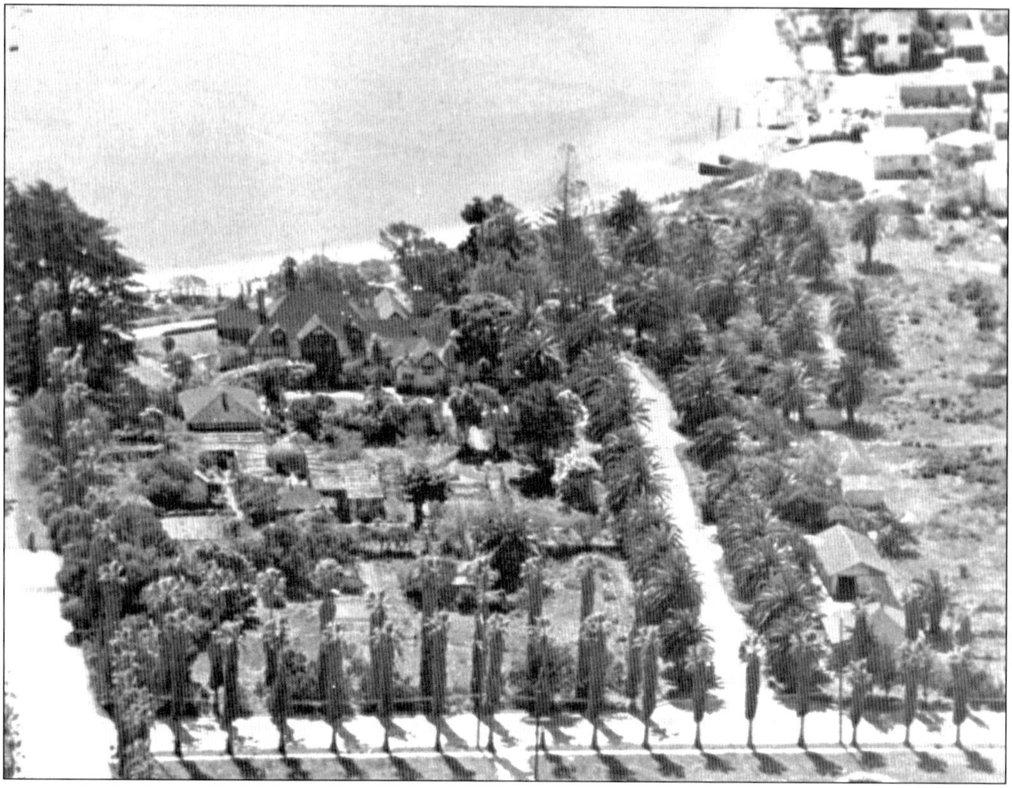

Owned by F. T. Scripps, son of newspaper magnate E. W. Scripps, the family home, Braemar, was located at the north end of Mission Beach. Pacific Beach Drive is in the foreground, and Mission Bay is in the background. This aerial appears to have been taken around the late 1920s. The home was sold and razed in 1958 to build the Catamaran Hotel. (Courtesy of Frank Munson.)

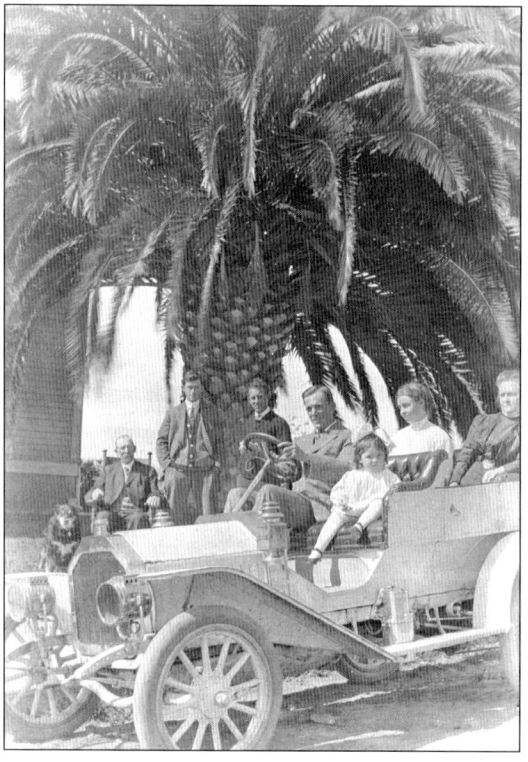

Tom Scripps and his family pose in their new car at Braemar in the early 1920s. Note the wooden spoke wheels and the fine leather upholstery. The Scripps family was well known for their philanthropy, and they made a major impact on San Diego. E. W. Scripps was a main contributor to Scripps Institution of Oceanography, and Tom was an early organizer of the San Diego Yacht Club. (Courtesy of Willie Skinner.)

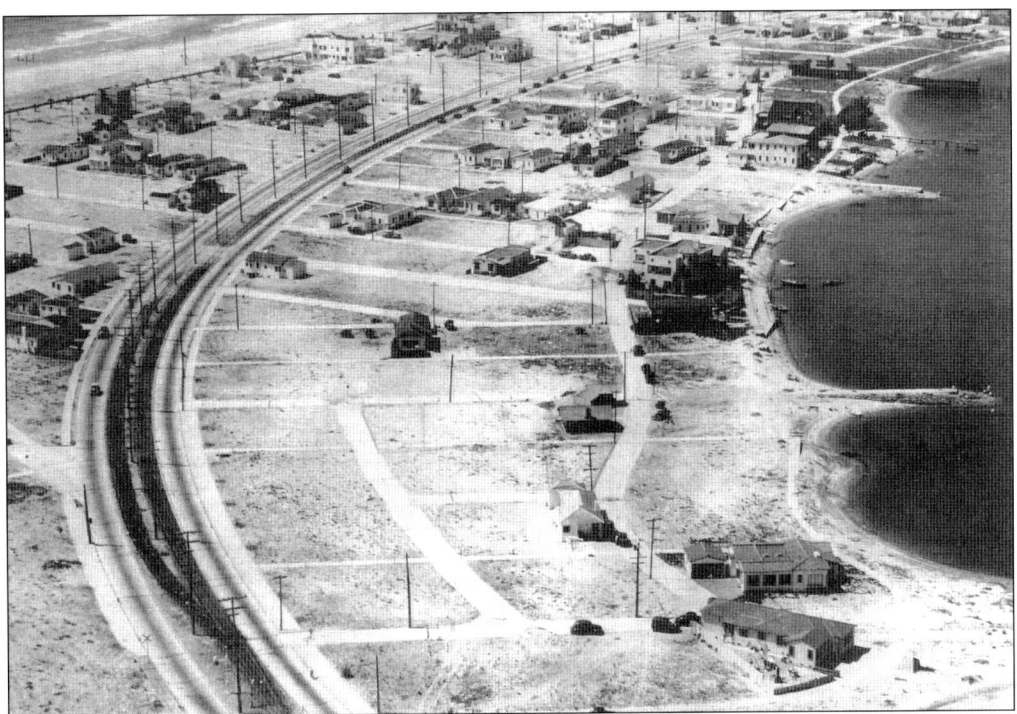

This 1929 aerial shows South Mission Beach looking north from the bay channel entrance. Along the bayfront are piers extending into Mission Bay. The new homes are becoming much more substantial than the beach shacks of the last decade, and permanent residents are moving in. Several of the houses pictured are still standing. (Courtesy of John Chadwick.)

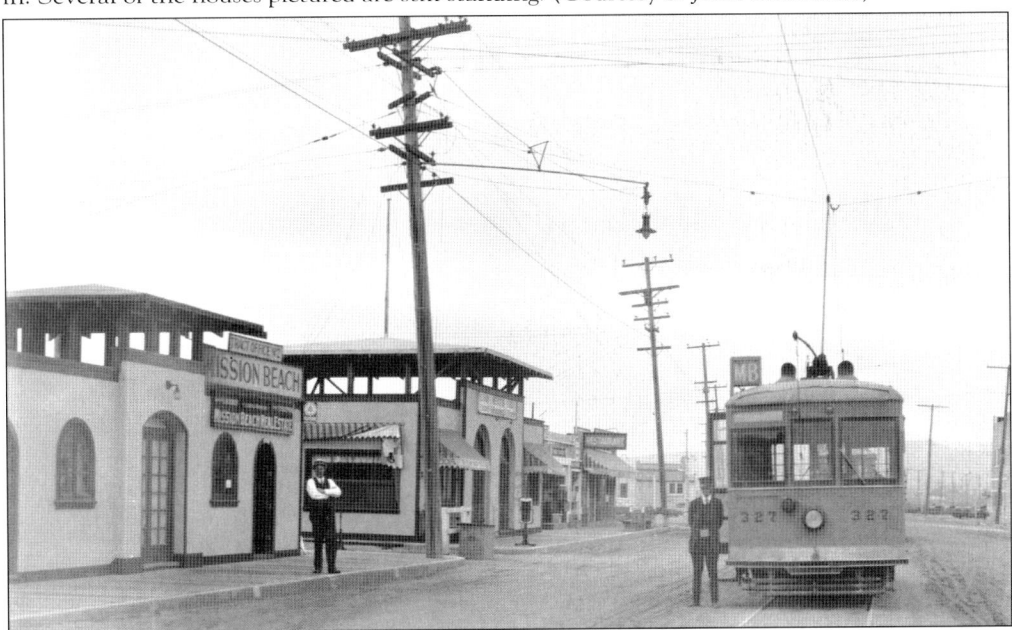

The trolley waits for passengers at the end of the line at Redondo Court in 1924. The rail lines were later extended through Pacific Beach to La Jolla. The second building on the left is the site of Saska's Restaurant today. (Courtesy of SDHS.)

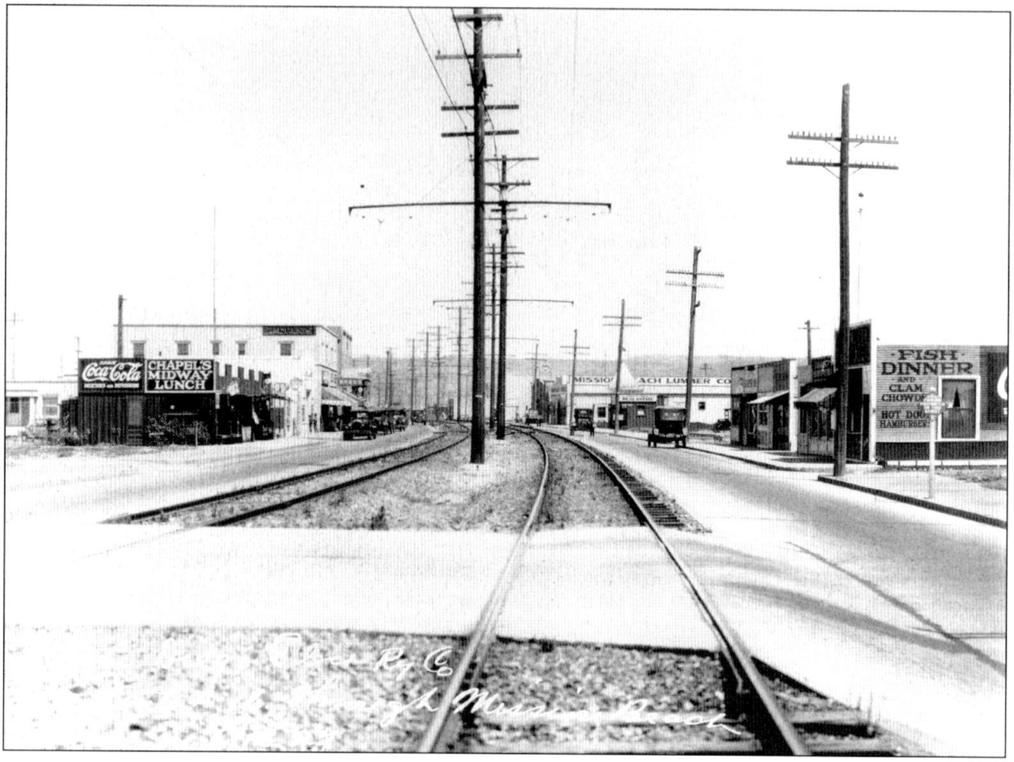

This view of downtown Old Mission Beach looks north from Santa Clara Place on August 13, 1927. Above is Chapel's Midway Lunch that later became Mr. D's Café. The Mission Beach Lumber Company can be seen on the right in the background. Below is the Strand Hotel over the original Safeway grocery store. Safeway later moved next door into larger quarters. The streetcar tracks in 1927 now extend north beyond Mission Beach. (Courtesy of SDHS.)

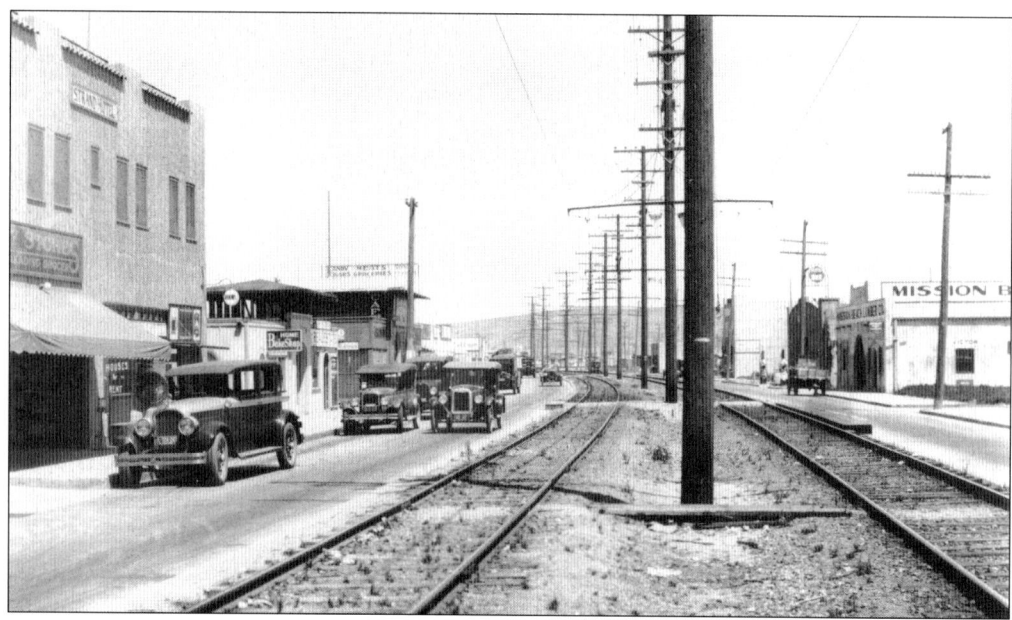

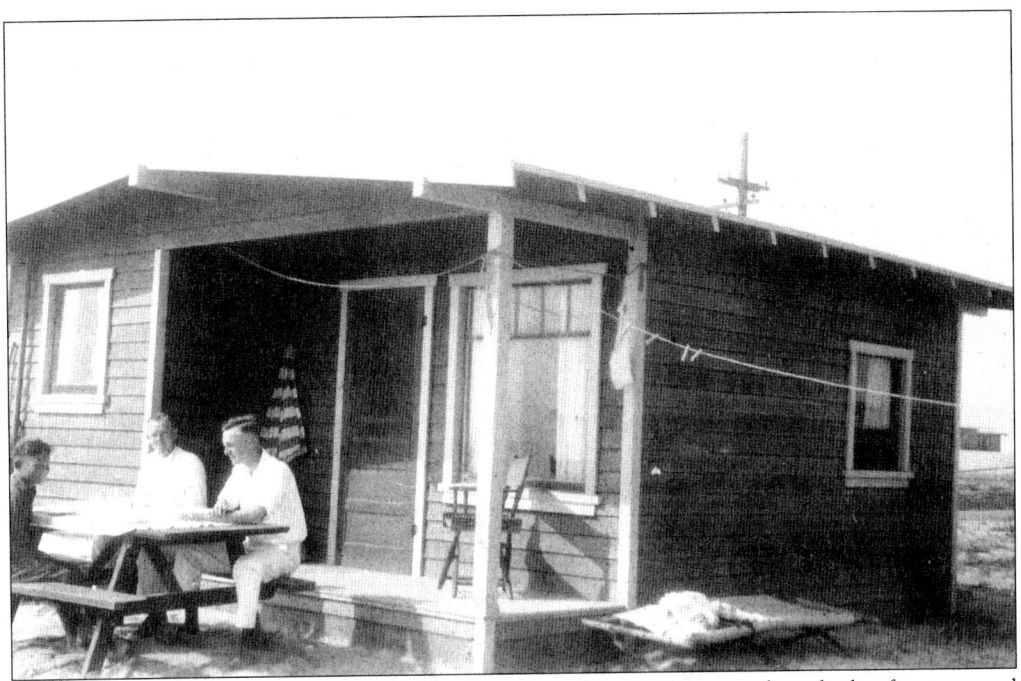

Roger Howe built this summer "shack" (his description) in 1923. Located on the bayfront around San Raphael Place, it was enjoyed by the Howe family until a more permanent home could be constructed near San Jose Place. (Courtesy of Ann Howe Mansfield.)

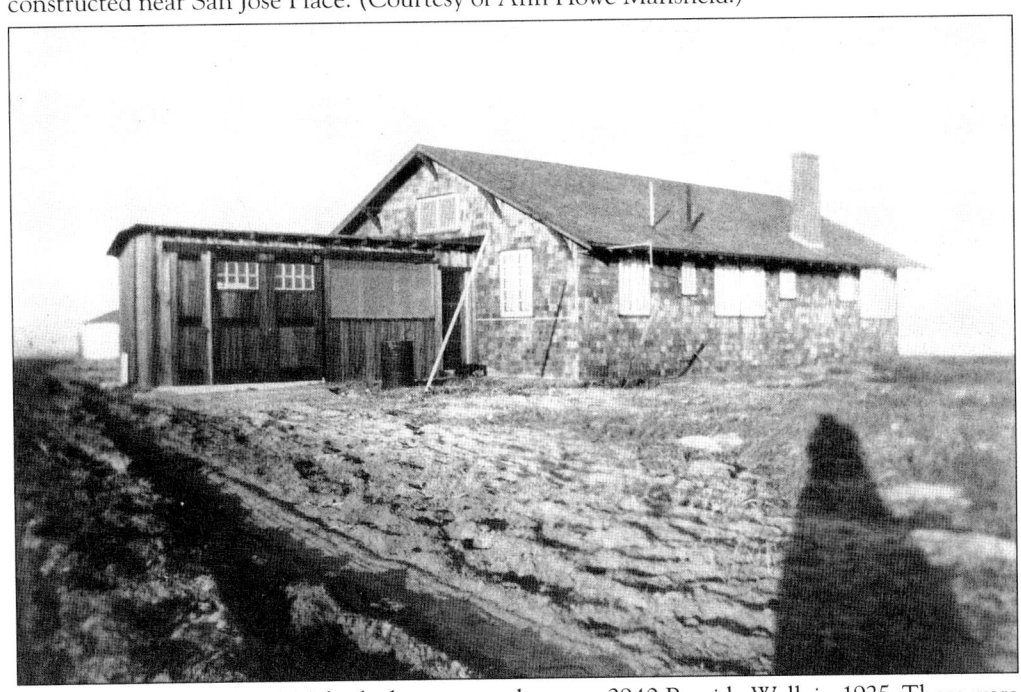

George Marston, 1850–1946, built this summer home at 2940 Bayside Walk in 1925. There were few neighbors when the house was new. This home still stands and looks much as it did in 1925. Marston, the owner of the successful Marston's department store, located in downtown San Diego, promoted city parks, city planning, and social reform. (Courtesy of Richard Clark.)

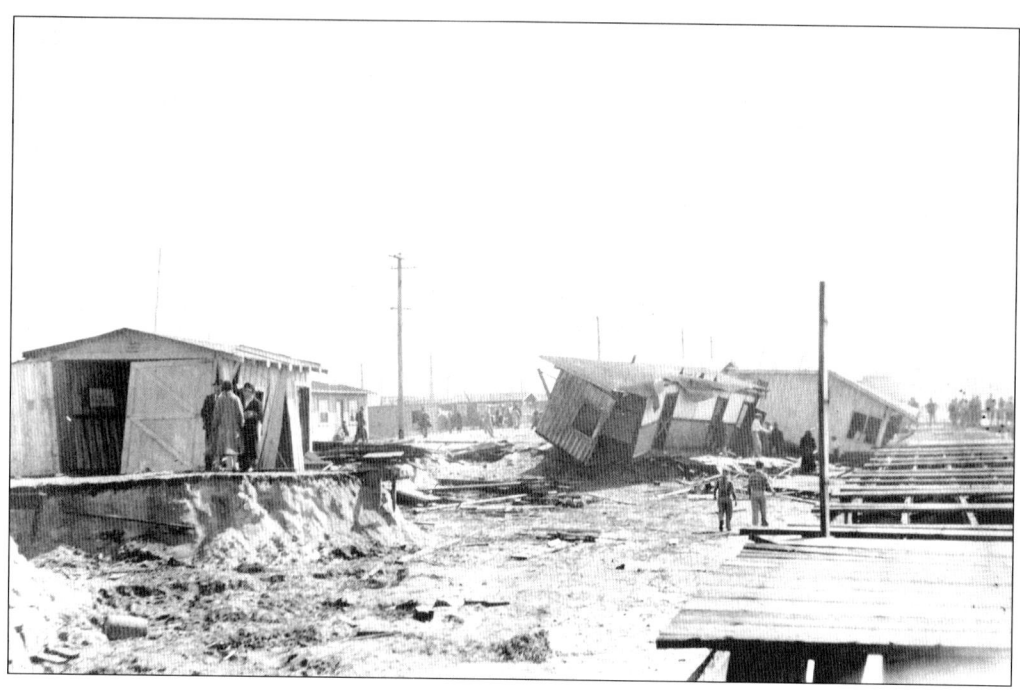

Winter storms wreaked havoc on oceanfront homes in 1922 and 1924. Newspaper accounts estimated that damage amounted to between $100,000 and $250,000 to the 50 or more homes that were destroyed or badly damaged. The Mission Beach Chamber of Commerce began a campaign to plan and install a permanent seawall to protect property. The view above looks south from Portsmouth Court, below looks north. (Courtesy of authors.)

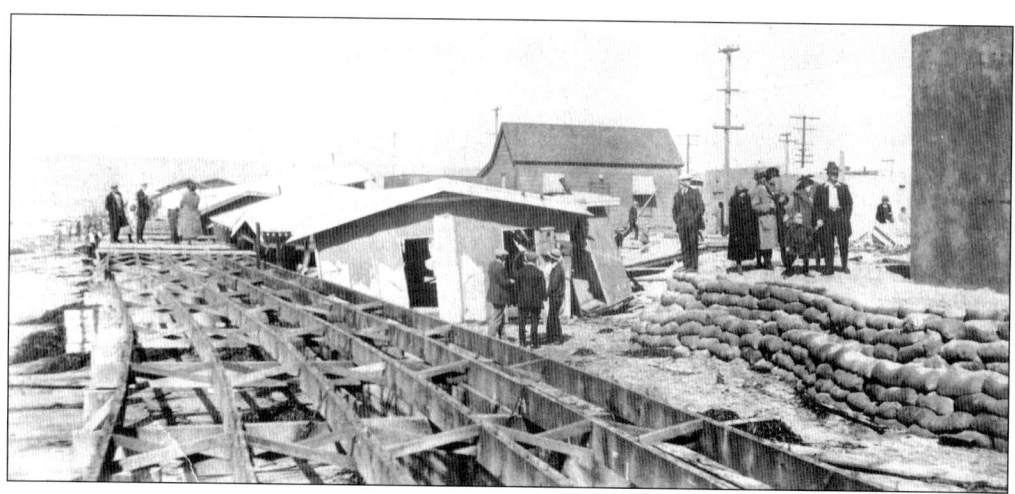

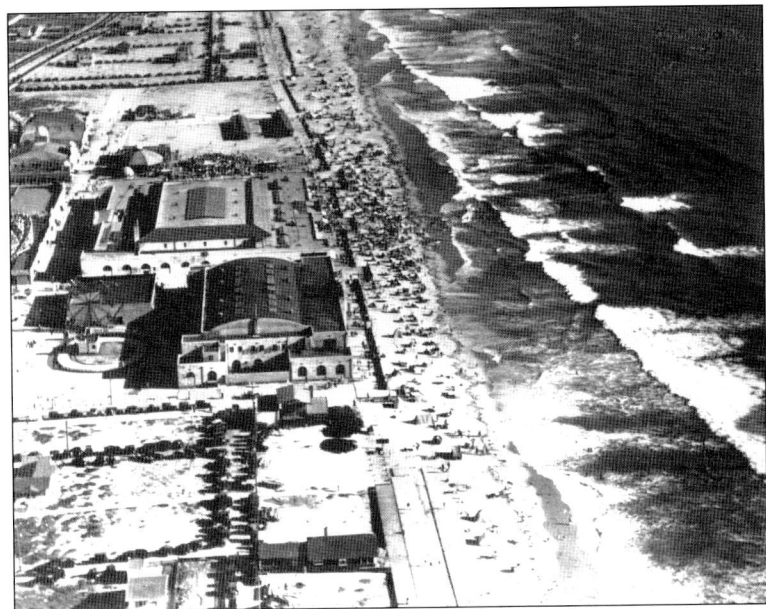

This 1926 aerial view shows Mission Beach Amusement Center (Belmont Park) on a busy day at the beach. In the foreground is the new concrete seawall and walkway just seaward of the old wooden boardwalk. The large building in the foreground is the Mission Beach Ballroom. (Courtesy of John Chadwick.)

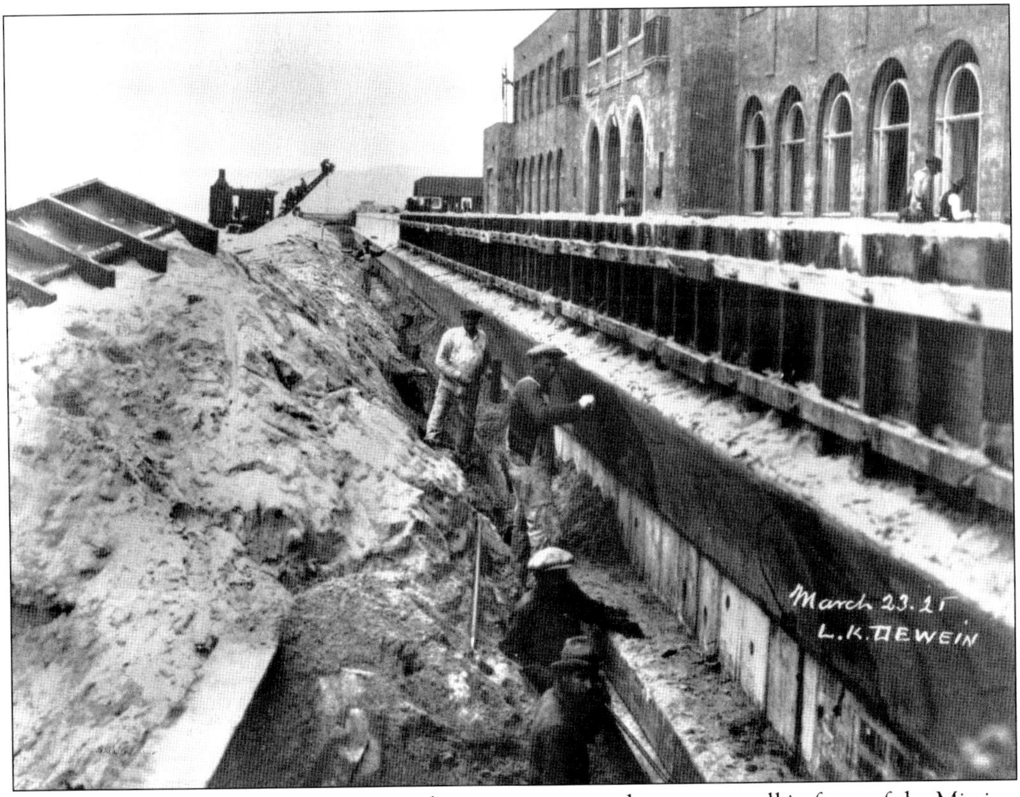

This March 1925 photograph shows workers constructing the new seawall in front of the Mission Beach Ballroom. The concrete pilings went down to bedrock, and the wall has withstood the test of time and weather for over 80 years. Eventually, the wall extended nearly three miles, from the south end of Mission Beach north into Pacific Beach. A wide concrete walkway replaced the boardwalk. (Courtesy of SDHS.)

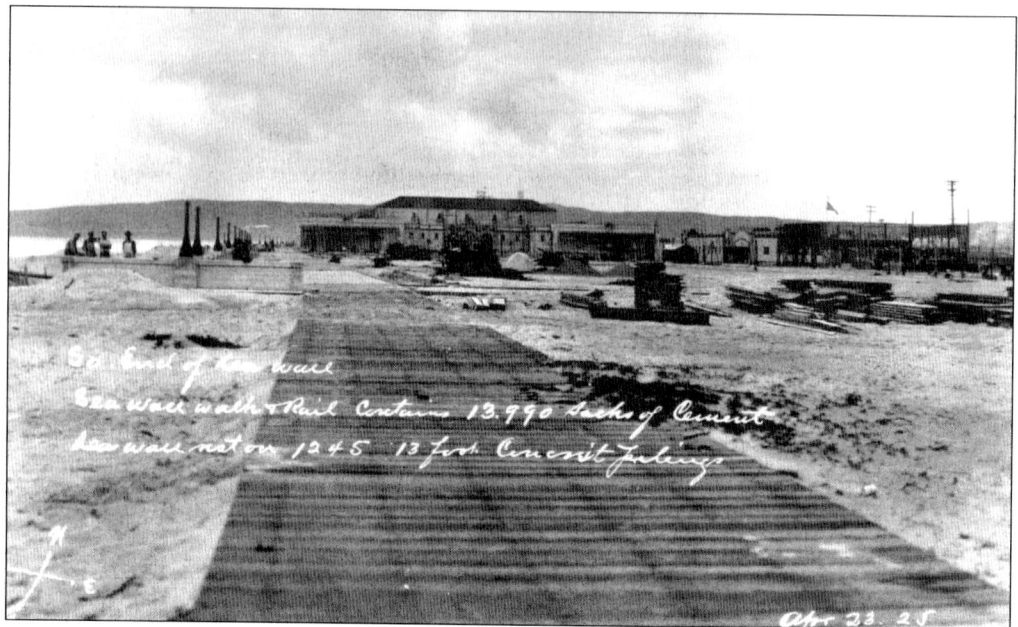

This 1925 scene shows the south end of the seawall at San Fernando Place. The wooden walkway south to Balboa Court was replaced after the north end of Mission Beach was protected. The construction pace was phenomenal considering the concrete was mixed by hand and wheelbarrowed into place. The concrete pilings were poured on site and then driven to bedrock with a steam-driven pile driver. (Courtesy of John Chadwick.)

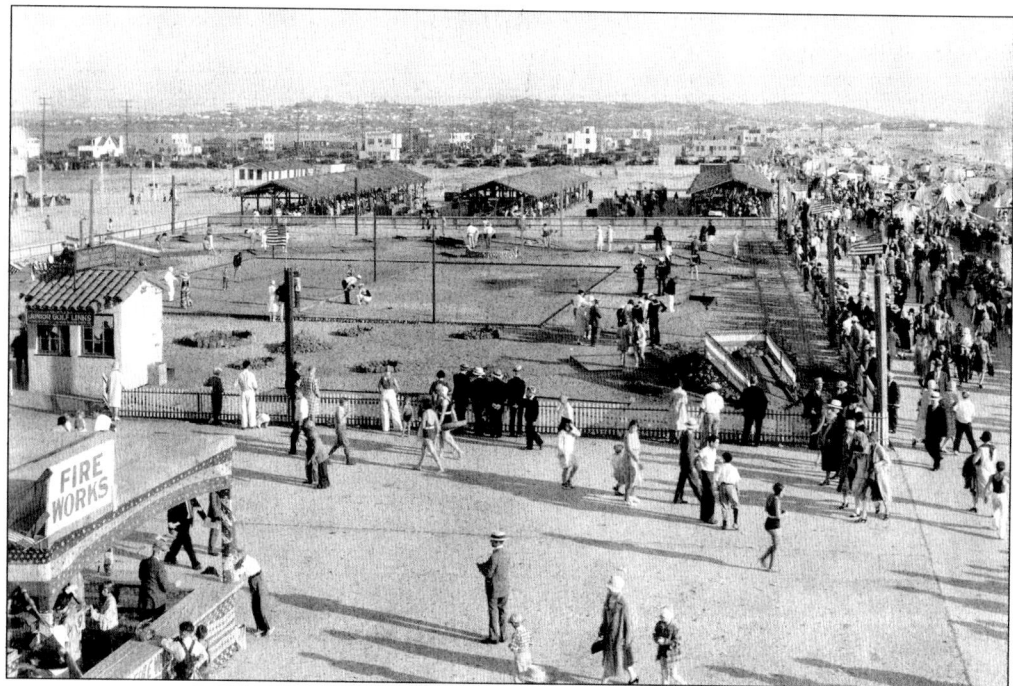

This July 4, 1927, view looks south from the roof of the Mission Beach Plunge building. Fireworks are being sold in the foreground, croquet games are being played, and huge crowds cram the beach and the walkways. (Courtesy of George Stanley.)

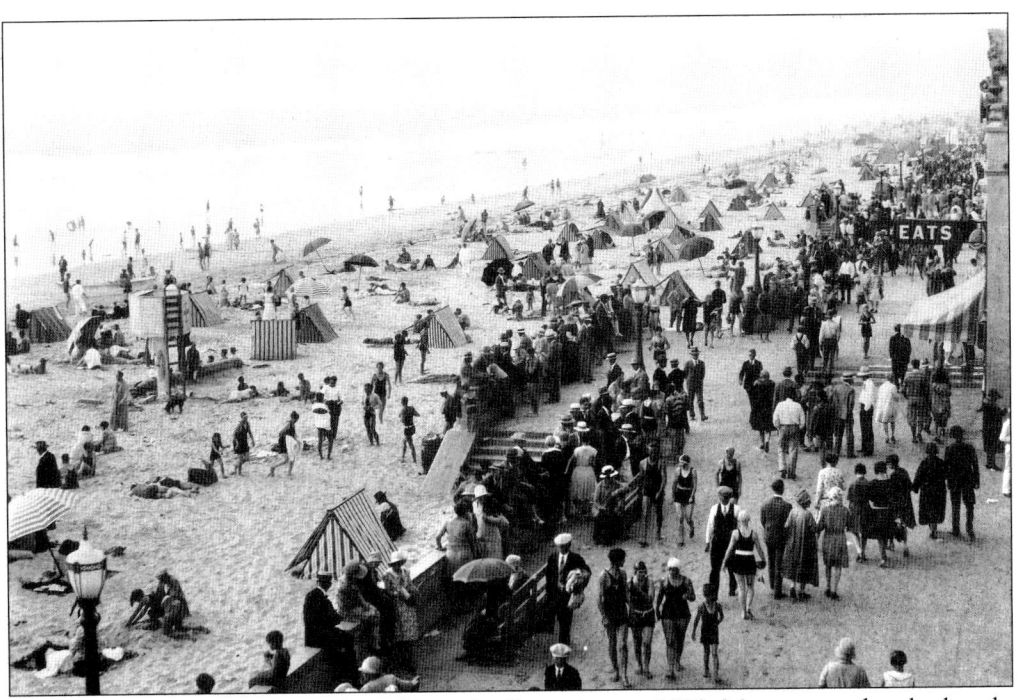

A large crowd enjoys the beach and boardwalk in August 1928. Many tents dot the beach, providing shade and changing rooms. A later ordinance required that at least two sides of a tent be open. They certainly would not have wanted anything racy going on inside those tents, would they? The lifeguard tower on a post is visible on the left side of the photograph. (Courtesy of Chuck Whitmarsh.)

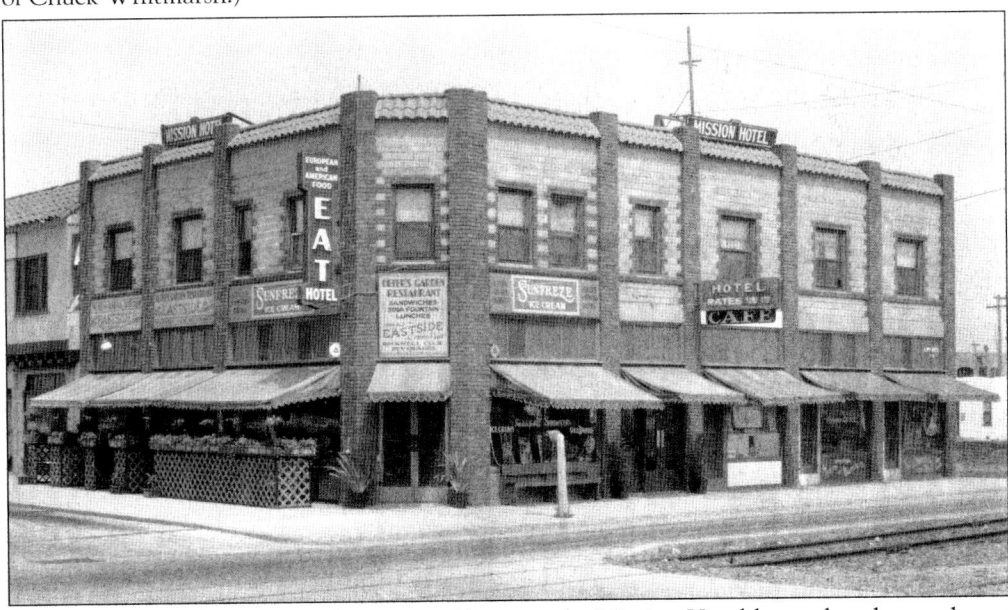

In 1929, for $1 or $1.50 per night, one could stay at the Mission Hotel located at the northwest corner of Ventura Place and Mission Boulevard, just a few steps across the street from the amusement center and the roller coaster. This building still stands and looks much the same today. (Courtesy of SDHS.)

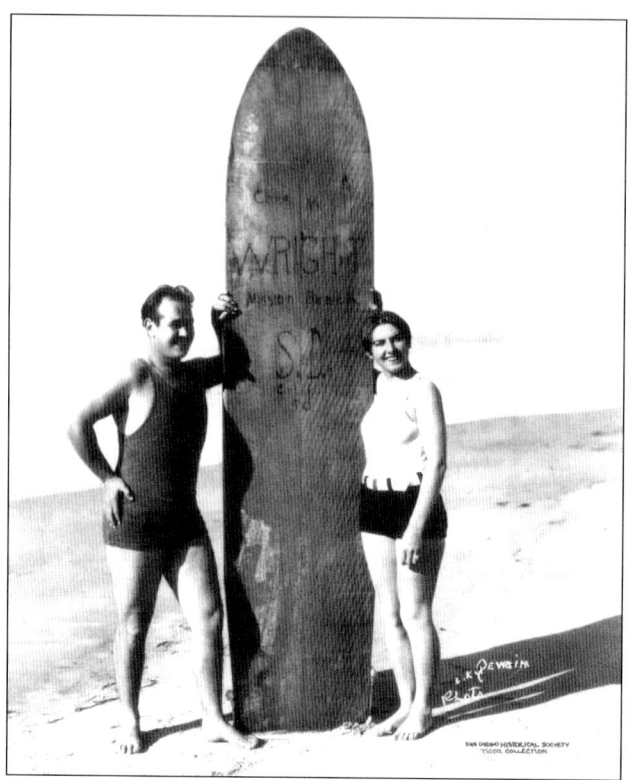

Charles Wright and Faye Baird show off Wright's surfboard c. 1920. The board was fashioned on a Duke Kahanomoku design and made of two large pine planks glued together. Wright was one of the first to take up board surfing in San Diego, and Faye Baird became the first woman to master the sport. Wright won the first California surfing contest in 1925.

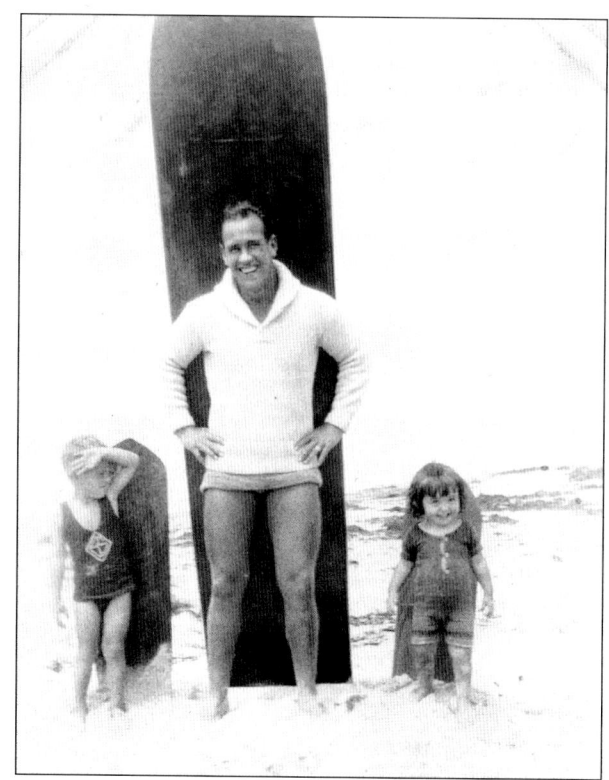

Charles Wright poses with young admirers Billie Schiefer and Marilyn Morse c. 1920. Note the mini-boards for the kids. It appears that no age is too young to learn to surf. (Courtesy of Duncan McFarland.)

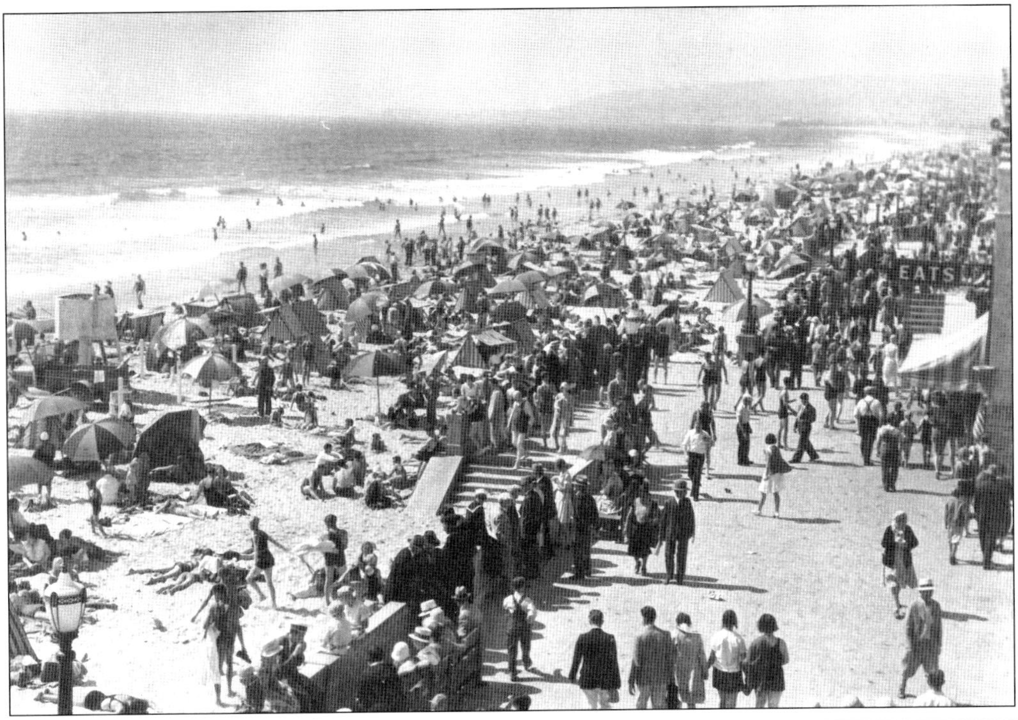

There are lots of beachgoers but few swimmers in this 1927 scene. Most visitors were unaccustomed to ocean swimming and preferred to just enjoy the sand and the sun. (Courtesy of authors.)

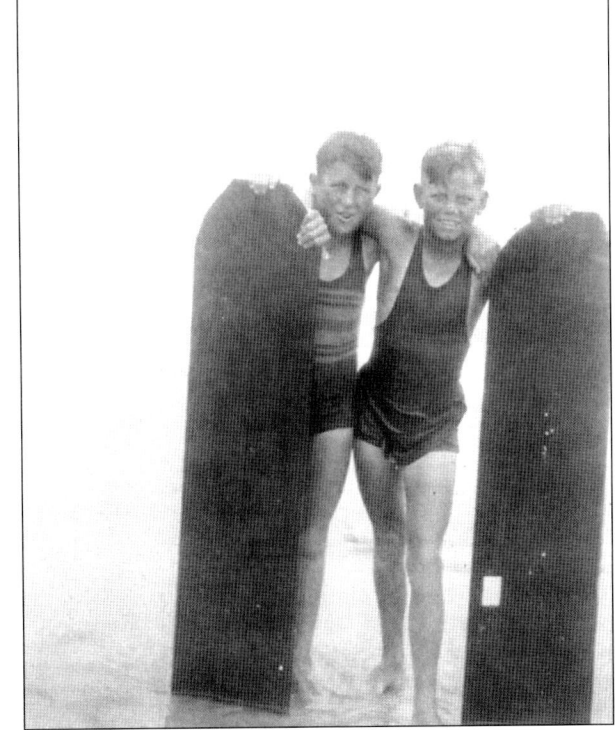

Local kids Webster (left) and Norris Howe pose with their short surfboards on August 16, 1923. These small boards were ridden lying prone, similar to the modern boogie boards. In 1930, Norris Howe became a San Diego City lifeguard. (Courtesy of Anne Howe Mansfield.)

Charles Wright designed and built this rock house on Pismo Court around 1924. He collected the stones on the beach at Bird Rock and hauled them to Mission Beach. Much of the lumber used in the home was salvaged after devastating storms demolished several oceanfront houses. The home is still owned by Wright's daughter Cleo. (Courtesy of authors.)

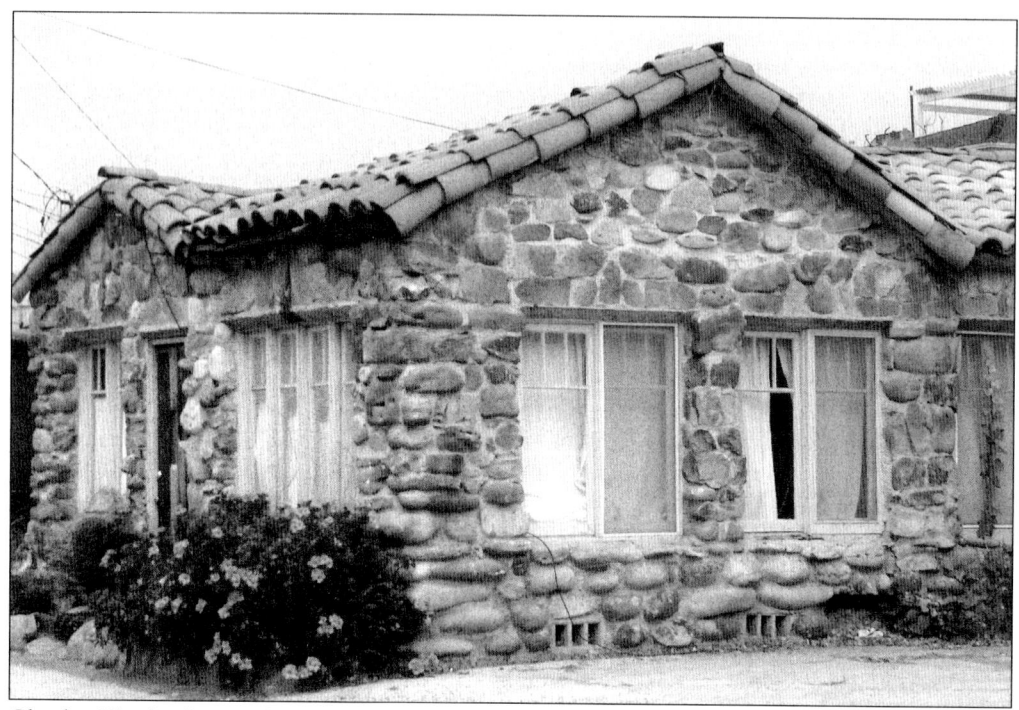

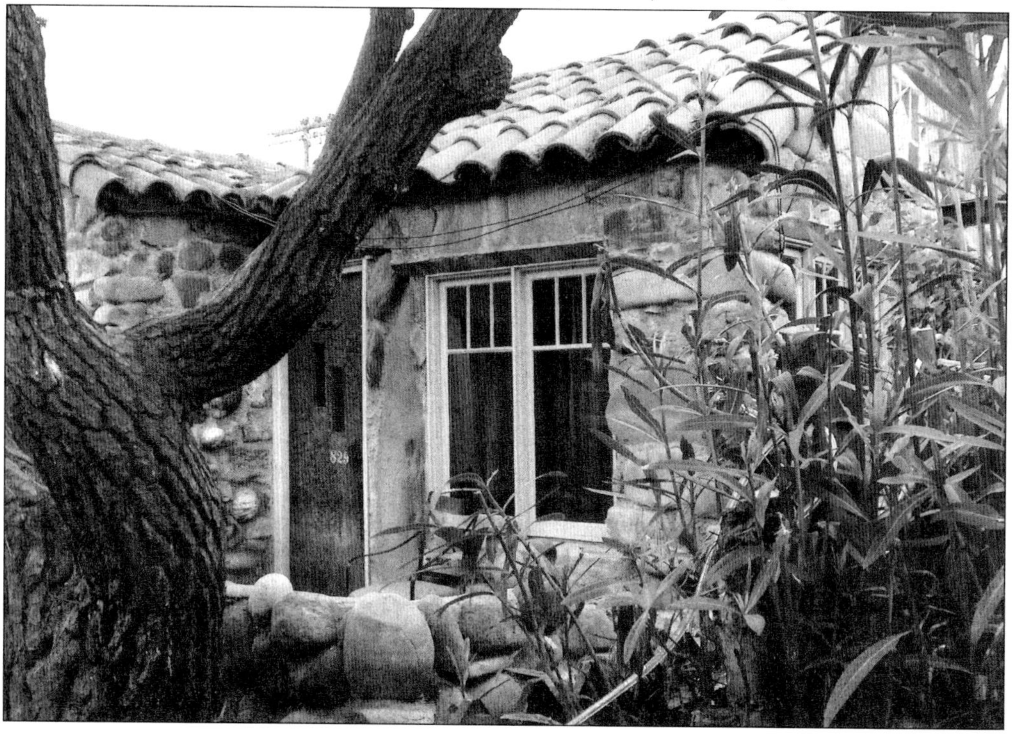

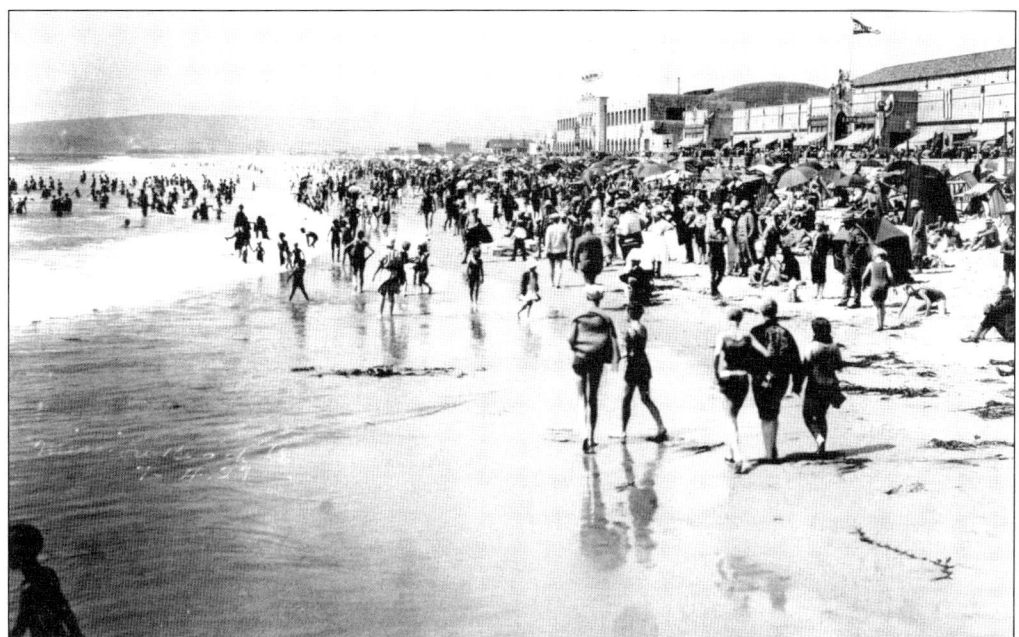

On July 4, 1927, the beach is just as crowded as it is today. The buildings on the right are the plunge and bathhouse, and the building beyond is the Mission Beach Ballroom. The empty hillside of La Jolla is visible in the background. (Courtesy of George Stanley.)

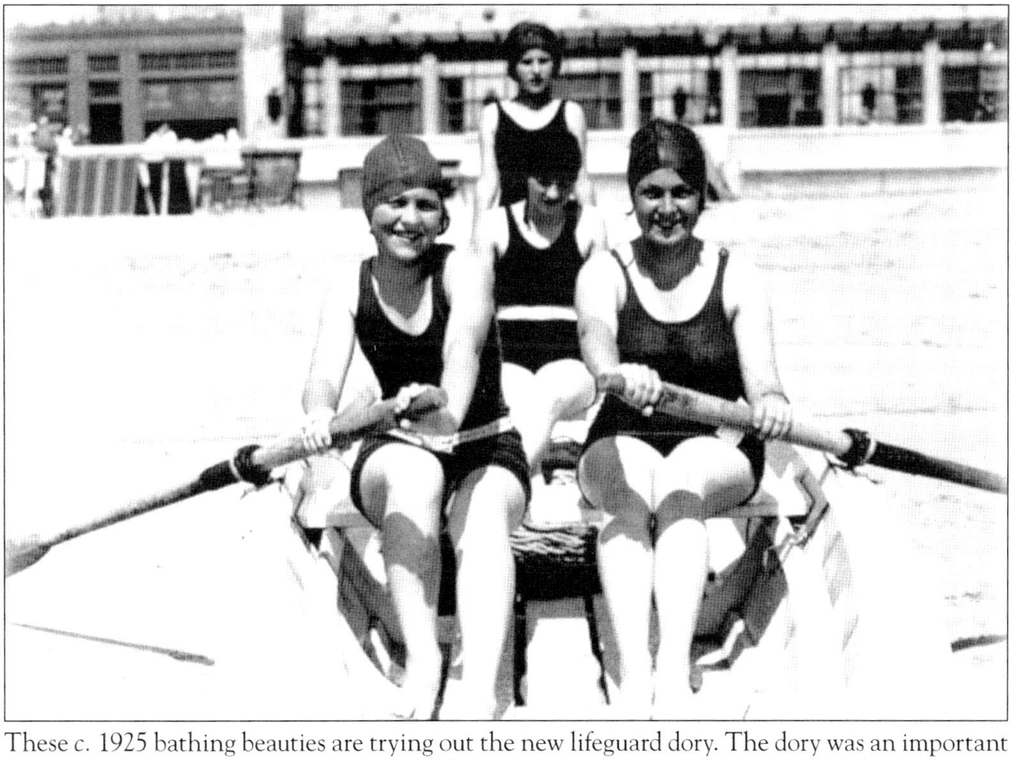

These c. 1925 bathing beauties are trying out the new lifeguard dory. The dory was an important part of lifesaving equipment and used if there were several people in trouble at the same time. (Courtesy of authors.)

Santa arrives by plane and lands on the beach in front of the amusement center in Mission Beach in 1925. A large crowd is on hand, and the ladies are quick to surround Santa. The bathing suits with the knee socks are very stylish. (Courtesy of SDHS and Chuck Whitmarsh.)

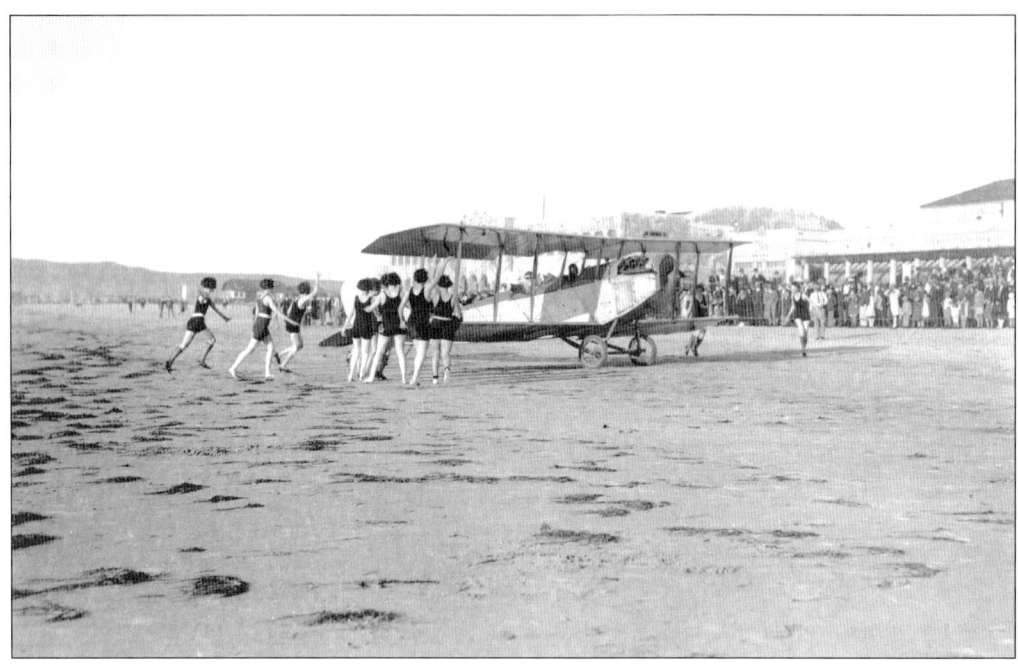

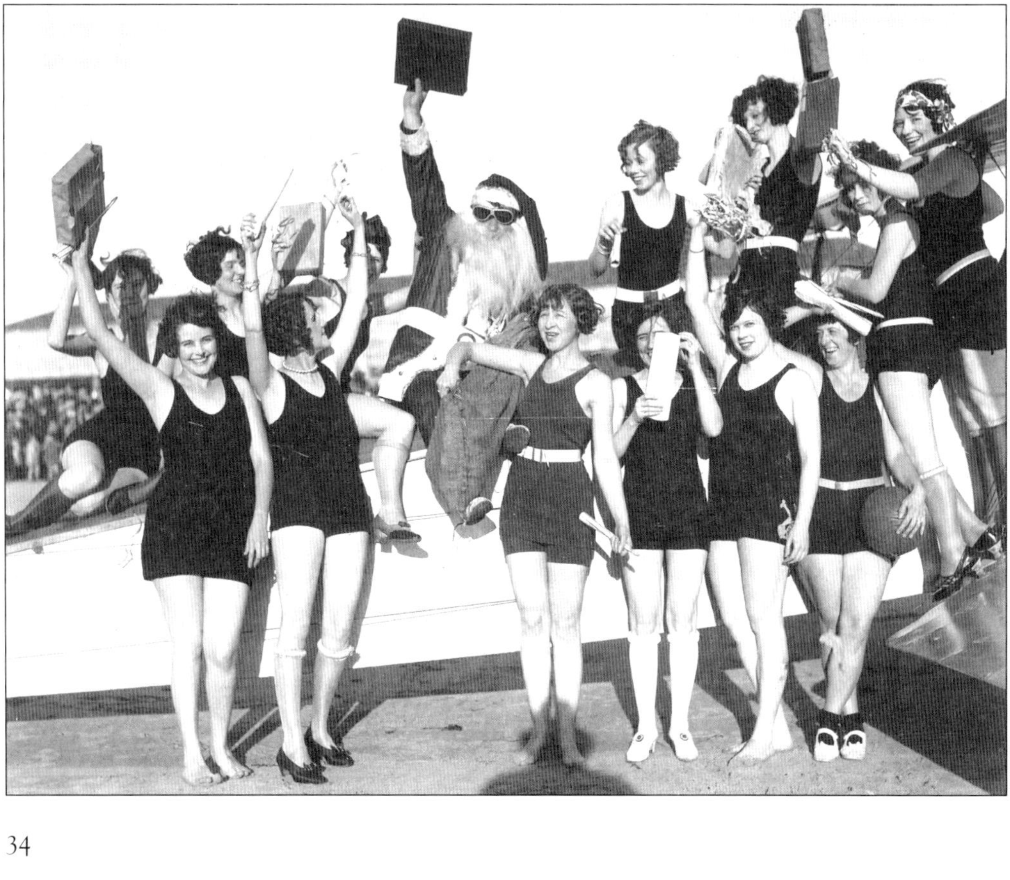

J. A. Harris is giving his best Buster Keaton impersonation on the beach c. 1927. Harris built and operated rental cottages on the oceanfront at Queenstown Court for many years. Harris's daughter Elaine was the first girl to be born in Mission Beach. (Courtesy of Marge Harris.)

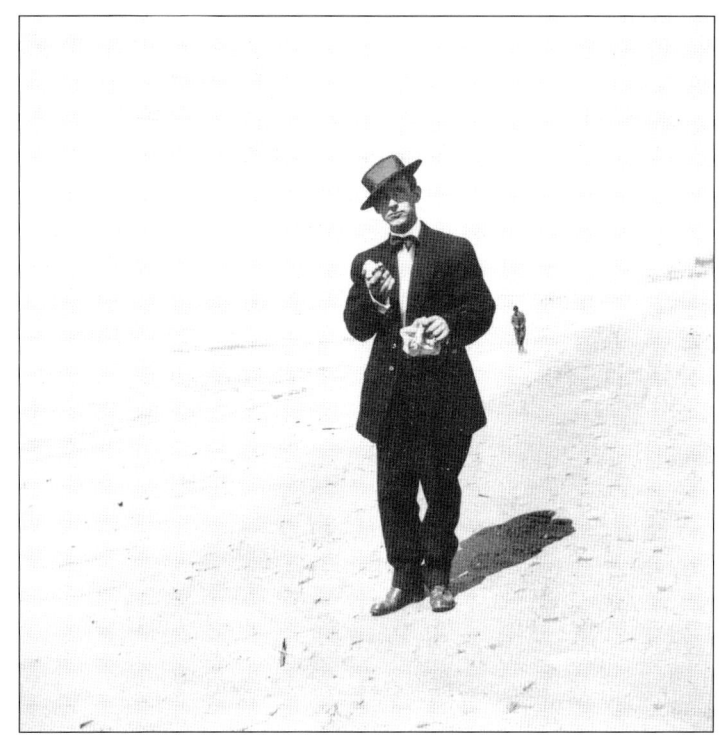

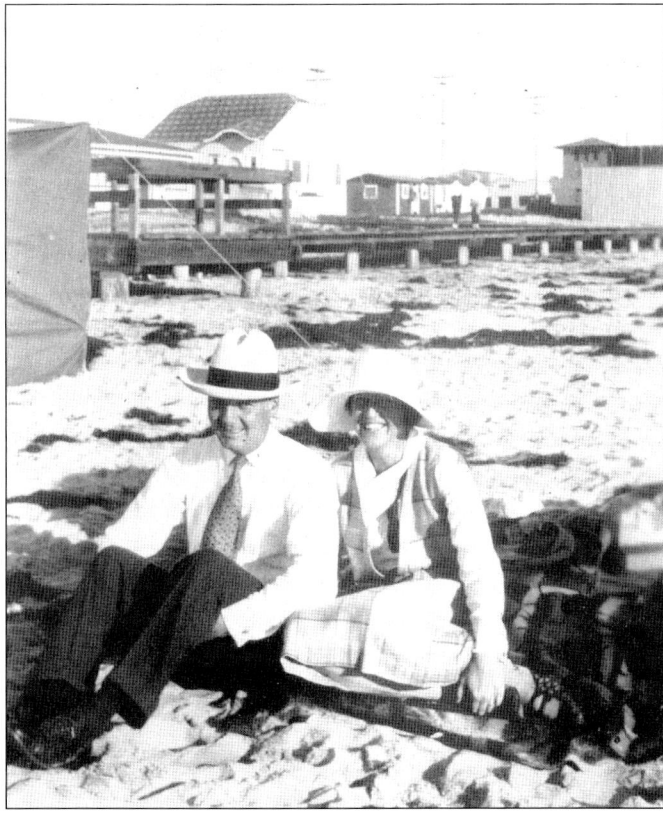

Roger and Coy Howe are pictured in June 1925 at north Mission Beach. The new concrete seawall had not reached this far in June but would soon replace the wooden walkway supported on posts. (Courtesy of Ann Howe Mansfield.)

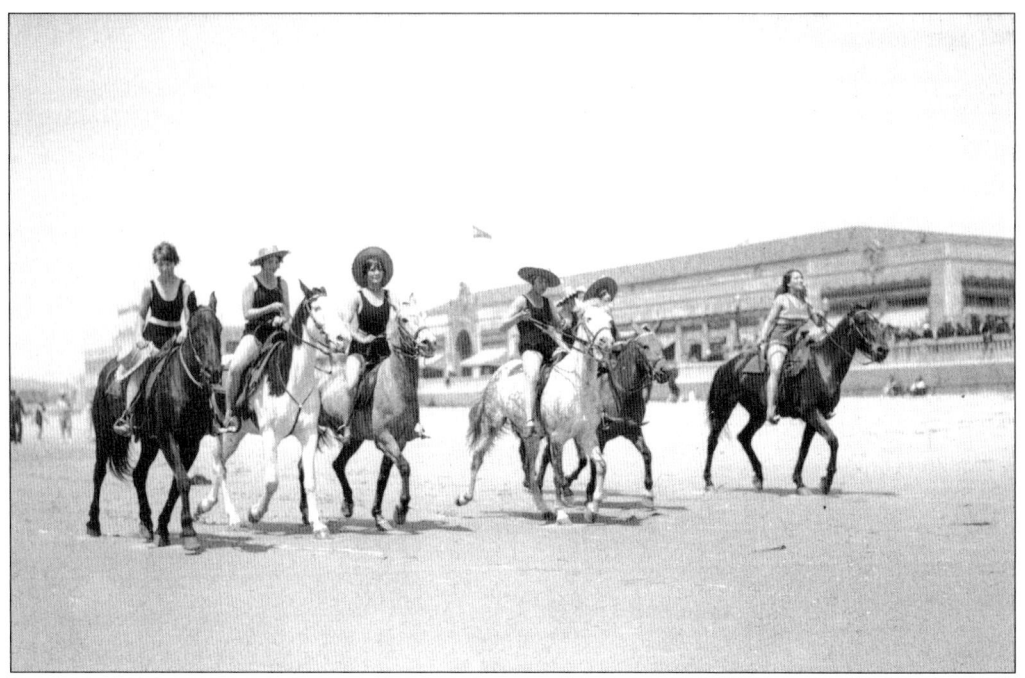

Horseback riding was another popular beach pastime in 1925. This band of roving banditas is having a great time on a not-so-crowded beach. The Mission Beach Plunge is in the background. (Courtesy of SDHS.)

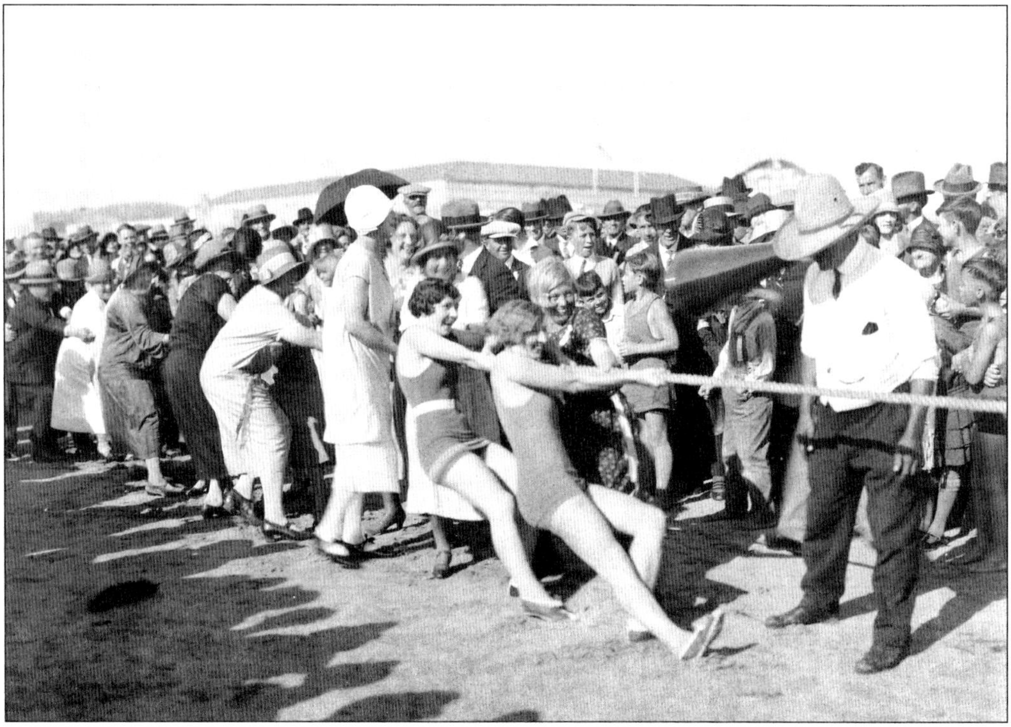

The ladies, young and old, are hard at work in this 1925 tug-of-war game. Everyone appears to be enjoying the contest. (Courtesy of Mike Curren.)

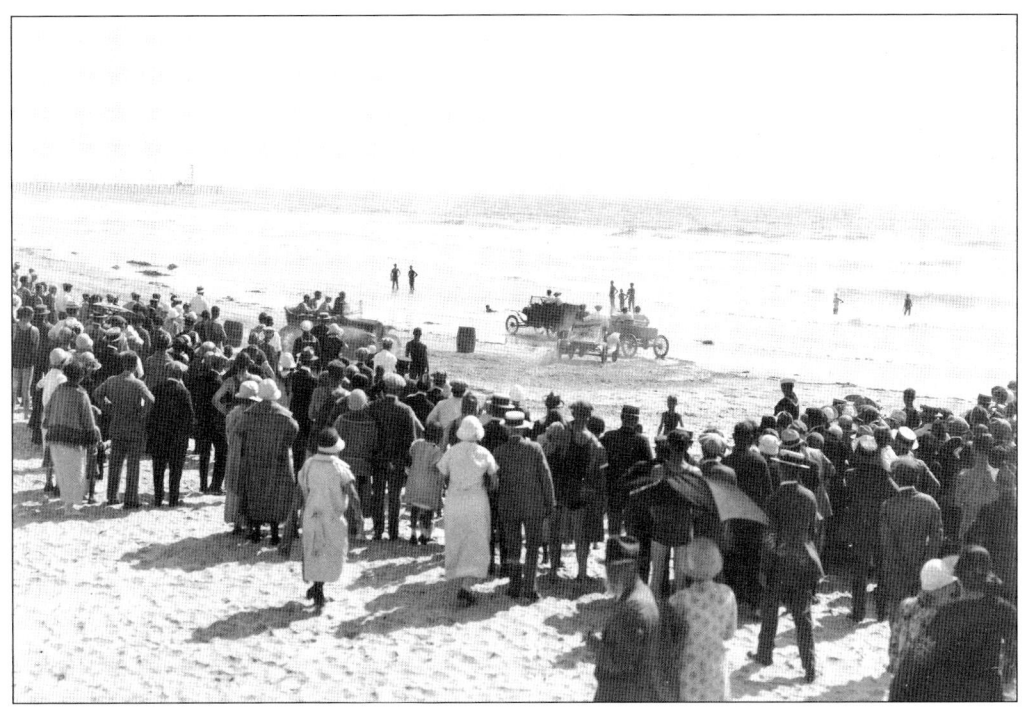

Auto racing on the beach could be counted on to draw large crowds of onlookers in 1925. Above, the racers round a barrel and actually get into the water, while a young swimmer seems to be a little too close to the action. The horses and buggies in the picture below are at a disadvantage to the new horseless carriages. (Above, courtesy of Mike Curren; below, courtesy of SDHS.)

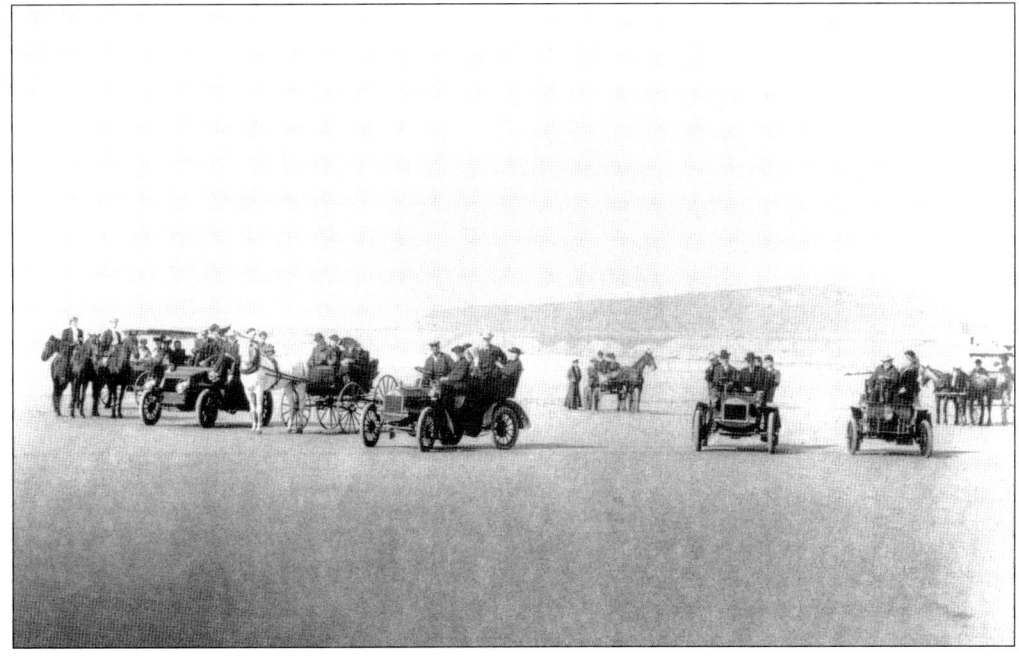

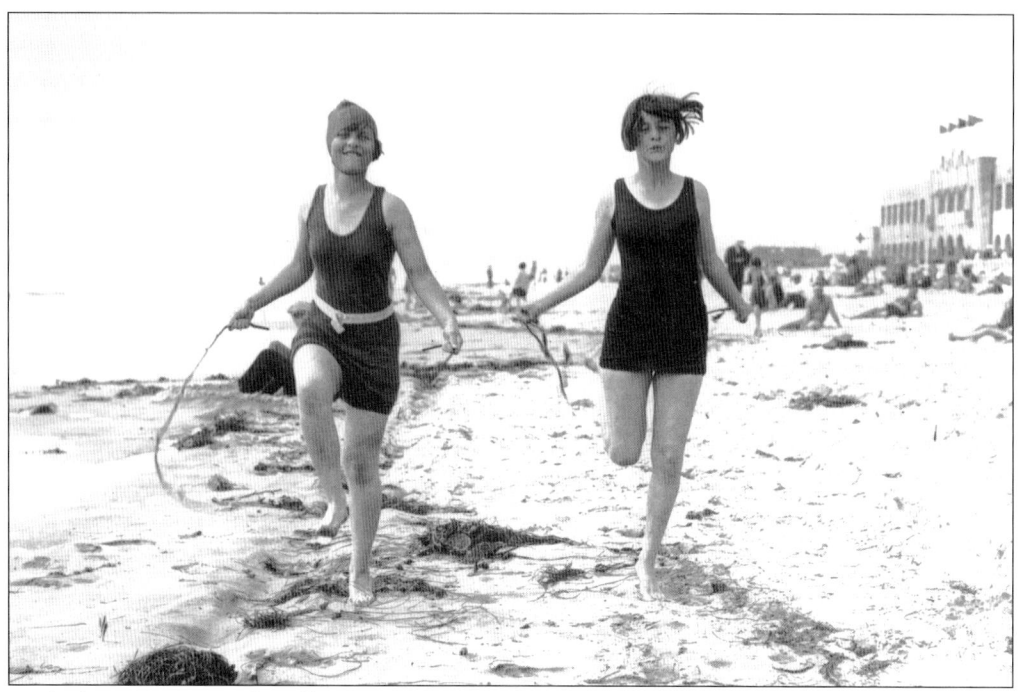
With the Mission Beach Ballroom in the background, these young ladies are enjoying skipping rope using strands of kelp from the beach. In 1925, the City of San Diego did not bother to clean the beaches of kelp on a regular basis as is done today. (Courtesy of SDHS.)

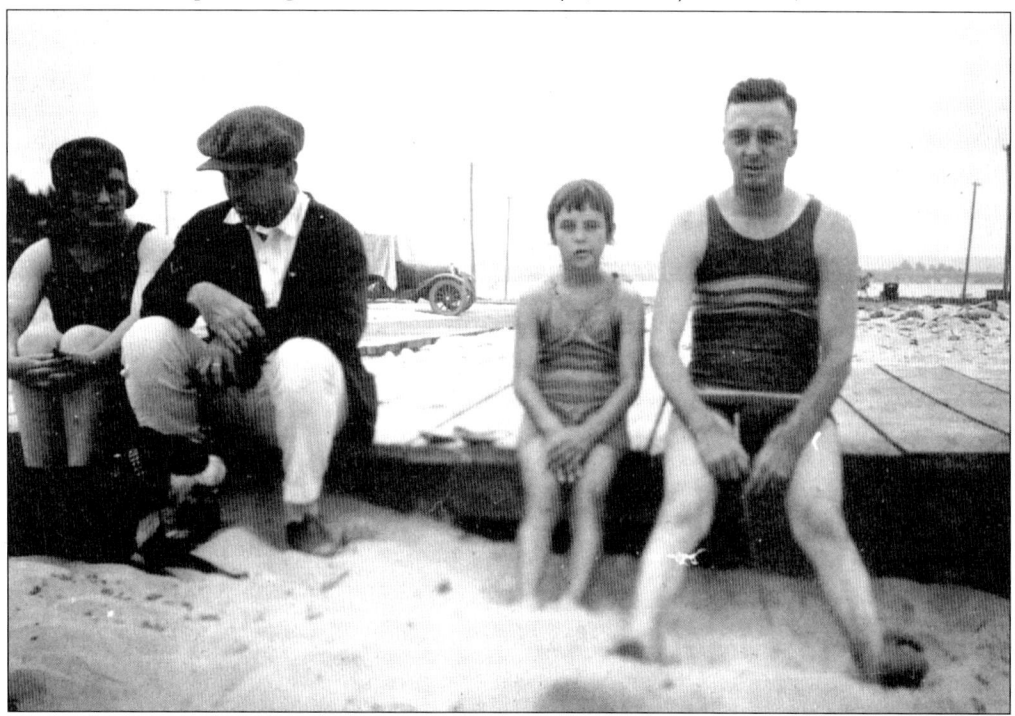
This September 16, 1924, scene, looking east from the oceanfront to Crown Point in the background, shows Mission Beach without a house in sight. (Courtesy of Ann Howe Mansfield.)

Three
THE LIFEGUARDS

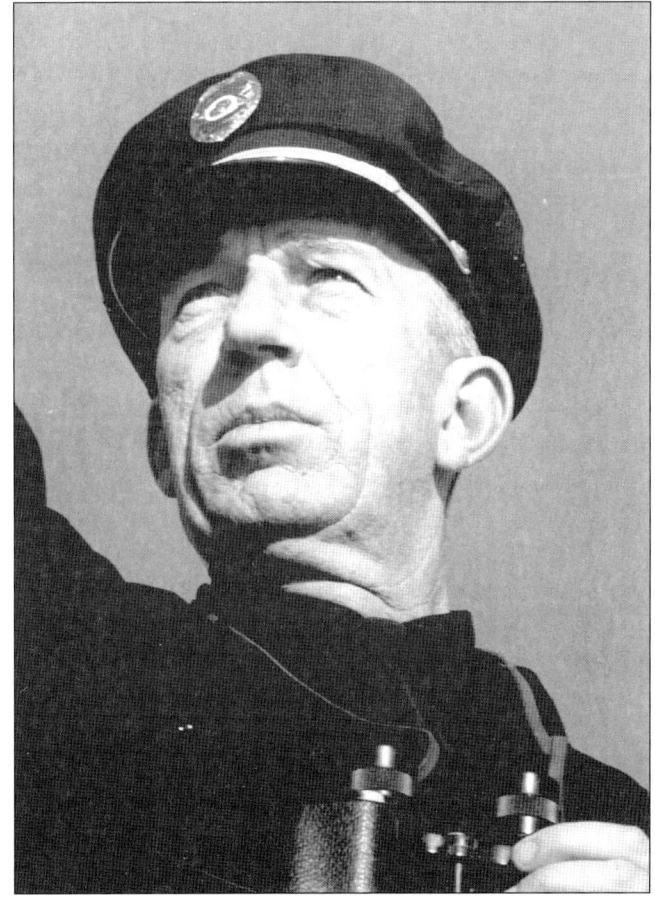

Capt. Charles W. Hardy, born July 12, 1908, was head of the San Diego City Lifeguard Service from 1925 until his death on February 15, 1968. Under his direction, the service developed from a small, undermanned staff using only the most rudimentary equipment to a modern team of professionals with the best tools available. During his tenure, thousands of lives were saved and very few lost. (Courtesy of Burke Royale.)

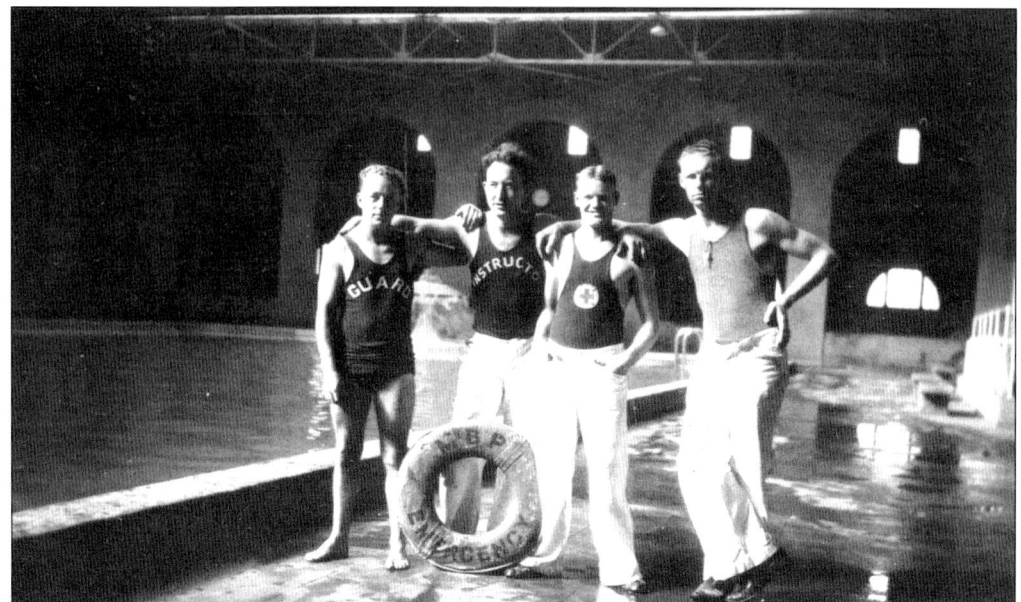

These lifeguards also provided swimming lessons to the public in 1925. Pictured in the Mission Beach Plunge are, from left to right, unidentified, George Freesh, Bill Rumsey, and Chuck Hardy. Bill Rumsey later became captain of the San Diego County Guards, and Hardy was captain of the San Diego City Guards. (Courtesy of Mission Beach Woman's Club.)

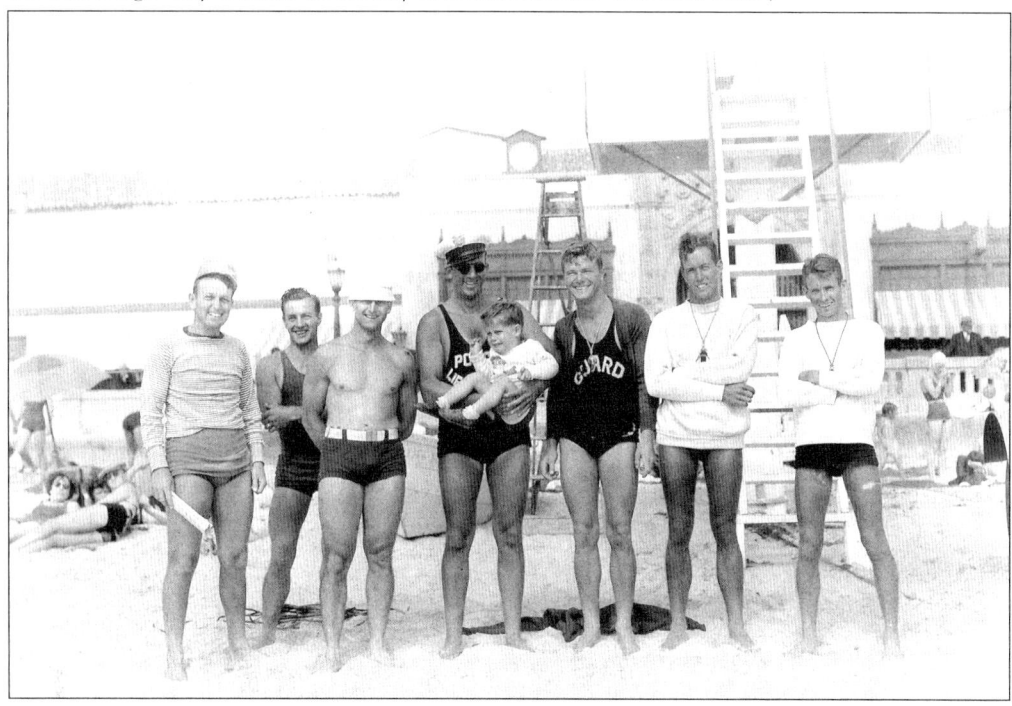

These 1930 lifeguards are, from left to right, Harry Horton, unidentified, Ed Westen, Charles Hardy, unidentified baby, Ernie Seftige, Fred Crowther, and George Stanley. Hardy, Crowther, and Stanley continued their lifeguard careers well into the 1950s. In the background are the lifeguard tower and the Mission Beach Plunge building. (Courtesy of George Stanley.)

George Stanley (left) and Chuck Hardy stand behind this police lifeguard vehicle c. 1930. Narrow tires, two-wheel drive, and soft sand often resulted in the vehicles being mired down. Volunteers were recruited from the beachgoers to help push the trucks in the event of an emergency. (Courtesy of George Stanley.)

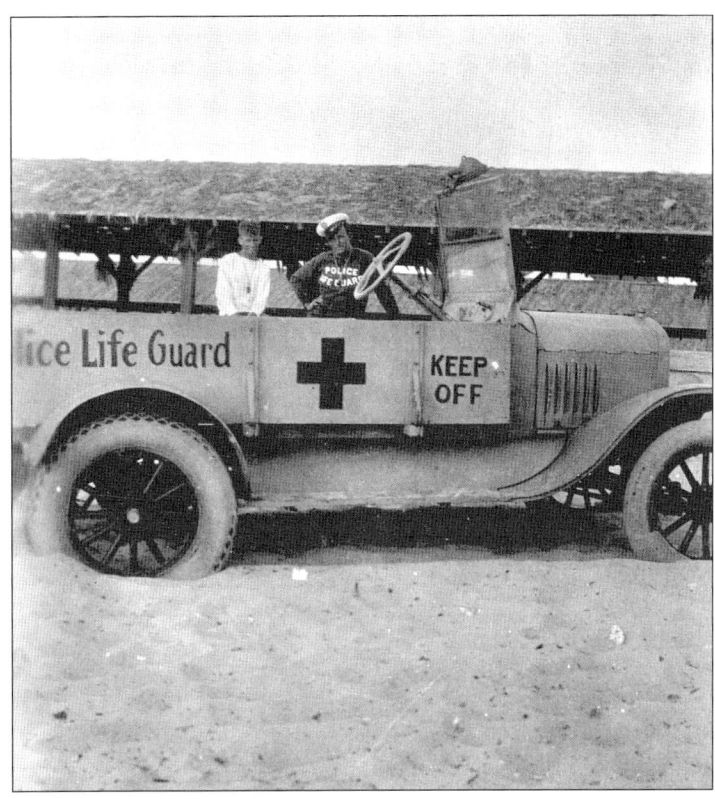

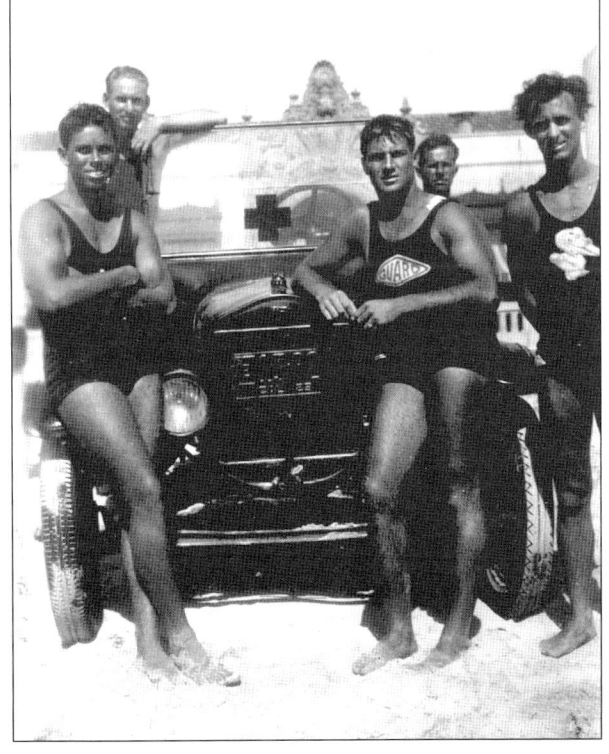

Ed Stotler, left, poses with four of his fellow lifeguards c. 1930. Stotler continued his career with the City of San Diego as a police officer. It was common for the guards to move from the ocean to the fire and police departments since there were few permanent lifeguard positions and little chance for advancement. Today a career as a lifeguard can be very rewarding. (Courtesy of George Stanley.)

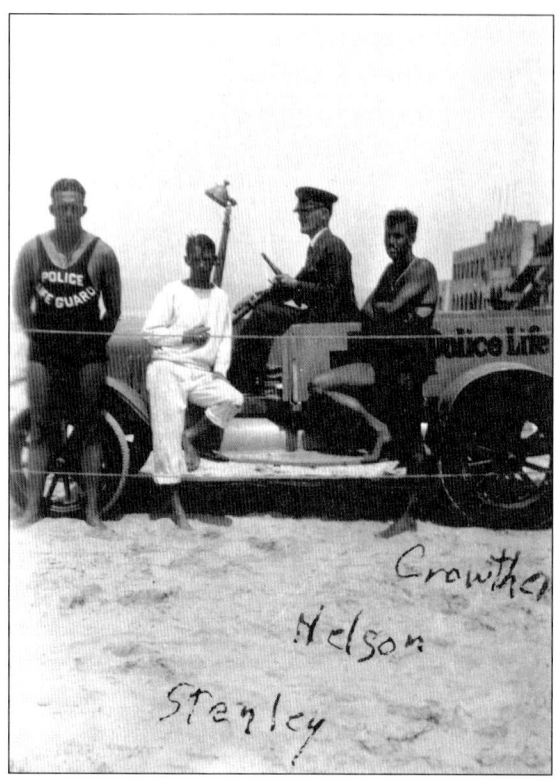

The three full-time guards, Hardy (left), Stanley (center), and Crowther stand beside the truck driven by Robert Nelson, pictured in his police uniform in 1930. (Courtesy of George Stanley.)

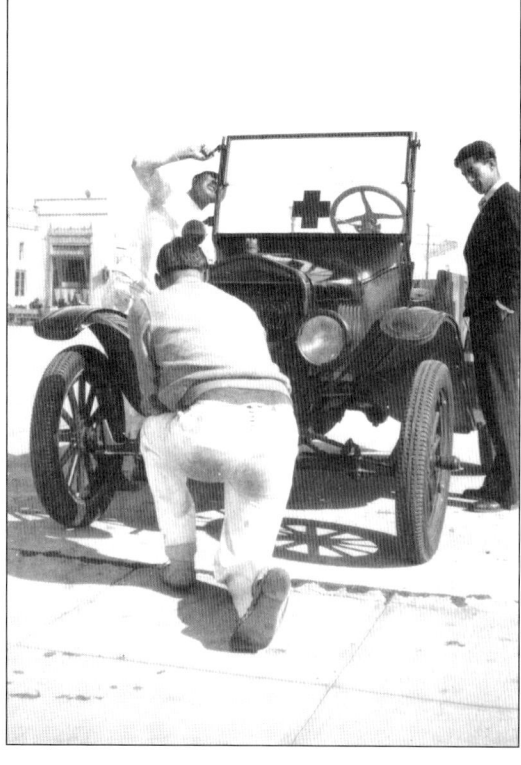

Continuing maintenance was required to prevent corrosion from the saltwater and salty air. This work was done by the on-duty lifeguards. The man on the left is touching up the paint around the windshield, and the well-dressed observer is carefully avoiding the wet paint. (Courtesy of Mission Beach Woman's Club.)

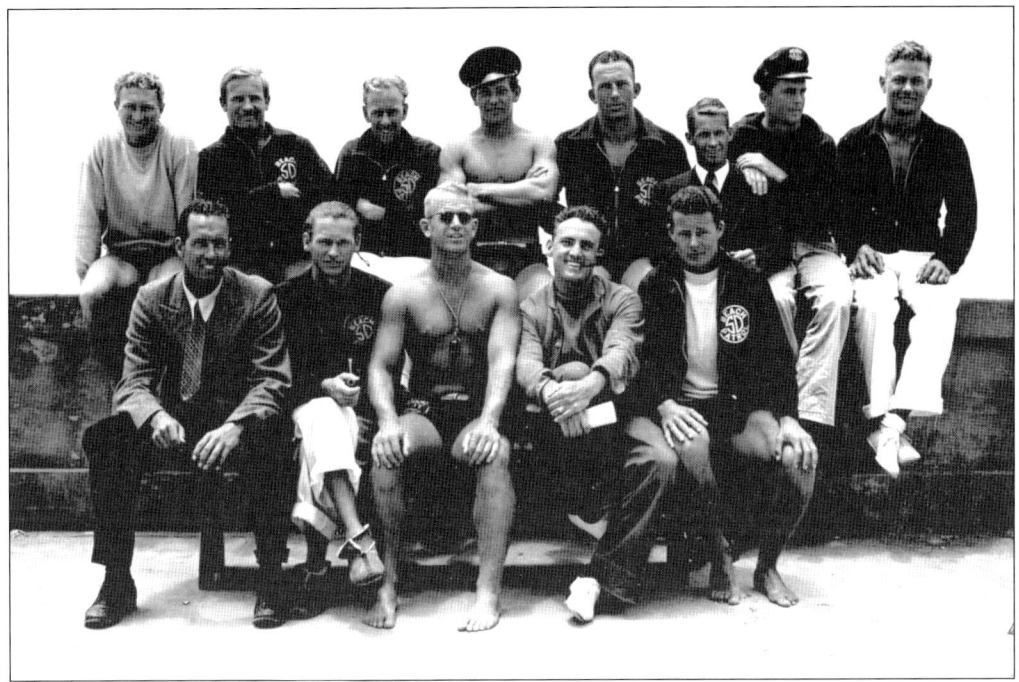

This is the lifeguard team in the summer of 1938. From left to right are (first row) Fred Crowther, unidentified, Bill Rumsey, Riley, and Roy Penwarden; (second row) Walt Schachtebeck, Emil Ziegler, Earl (Goggy) Russell, Dorian Paskowitz, C. W. Hardy, George Stanley, Ed Brennan, and Huntly Gordon. (Courtesy of authors.)

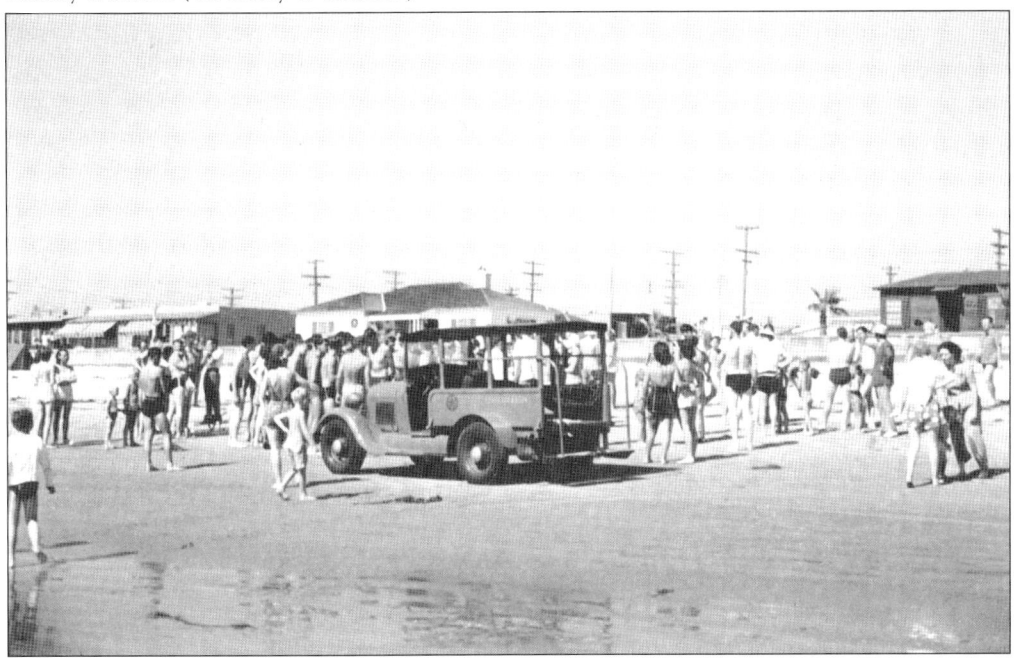

A 1930s-era truck blocks the view of a possible drowning victim. Swimmers were encouraged to swim near the lifeguards, but Mission Beach was 2.5 miles long with only two lifeguard stations, so accidents did happen. (Courtesy of Sterling Suhre.)

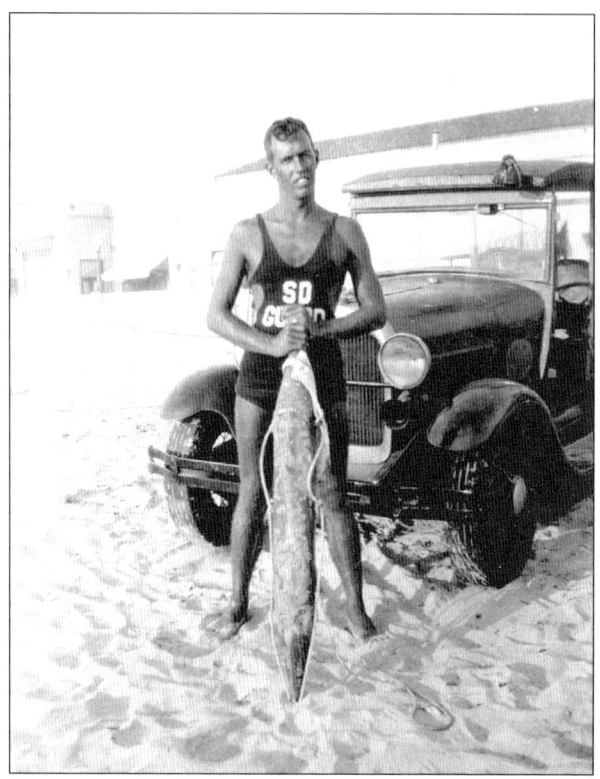

Fred Crowther displays the 1930 model of the life can, a hollow metal float used to support the victim during a rescue operation. Too often, while towing the victim to shore, a wave would separate the victim from the can, and the lifeguard could receive an unexpected knock on the head. Later design improvements lessened the damage. (Courtesy of George Stanley.)

The lifeguards received a brand-new dory in the early 1930s increasing the effectiveness of the organization. The wooden wheel trailer was fine for hard surfaces but was nearly useless in the soft sand of the beach. (Courtesy of George Stanley.)

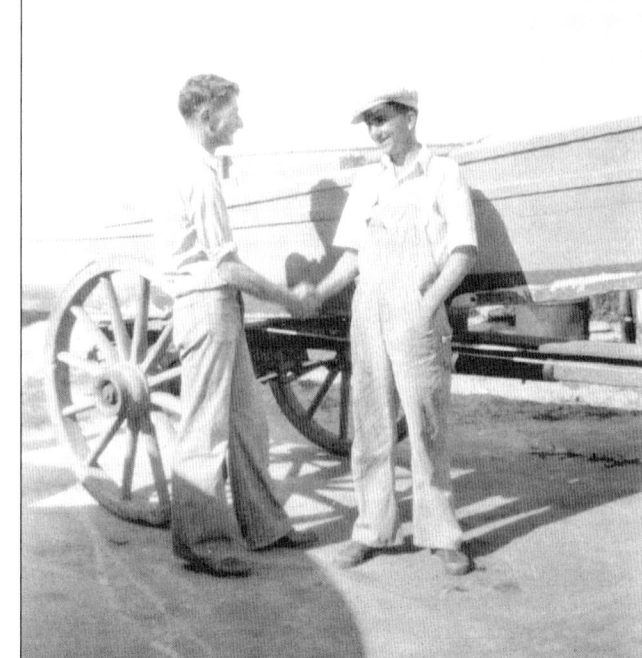

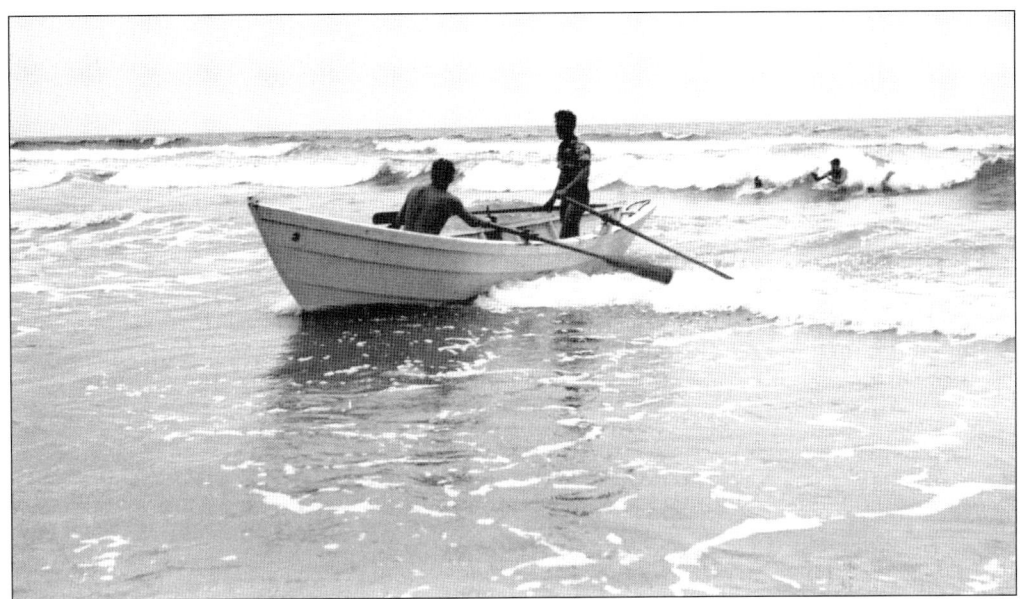

The dory was manned by a bowman seated with his back to the bow and a stern man standing facing the front. It was the stern rower who watched the incoming surf and timed the push through the waves. Large surf created an interesting challenge and required much strong-armed teamwork. The dory was used primarily for multi-victim rescues. (Courtesy of Sterling Suhre.)

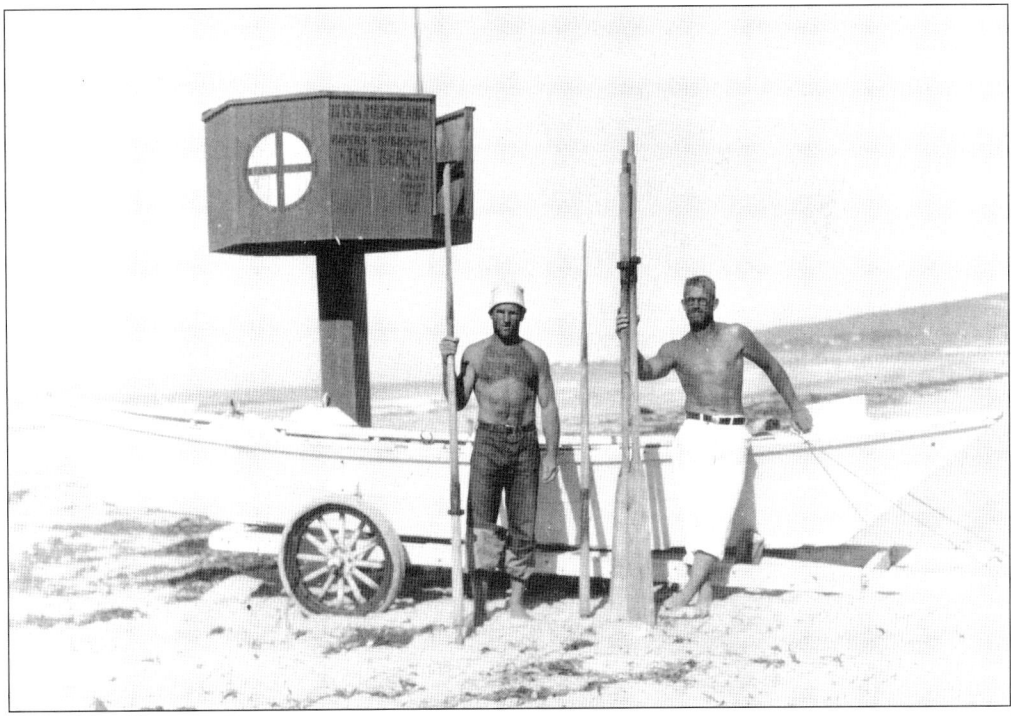

Emil Ziegler, left, and Bill Rumsey rowed this dory to Catalina Island, 24 miles off the coast of Los Angeles, over 100 miles north of San Diego. On day one, they rowed as far as Huntington Beach, where foul weather forced them ashore. They found shelter that night in the jail, out of the rain, and completed the journey the next day. (Courtesy of Norma Griffin.)

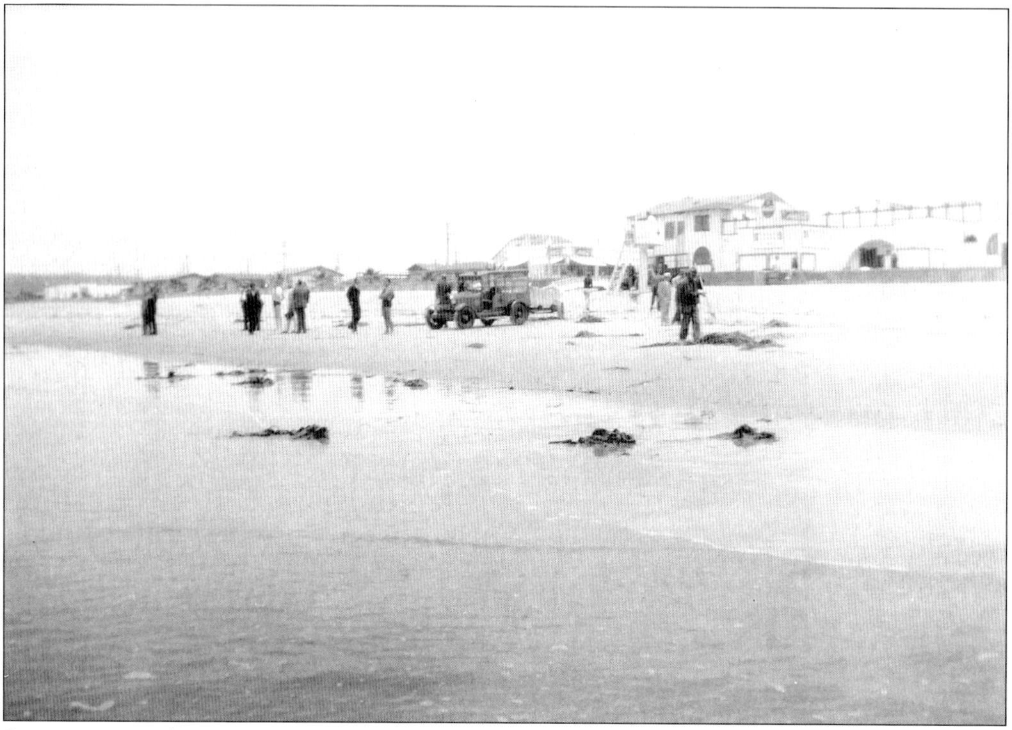

Spectators watch a rescue in progress at Old Mission Beach c. 1933. The dory is hooked to the rear of the lifeguard truck but is not being used in this instance. Usually a guard swimming and towing a life can is able to reach the victim faster. The Old Mission bathhouse is visible in the background. (Courtesy of George Stanley.)

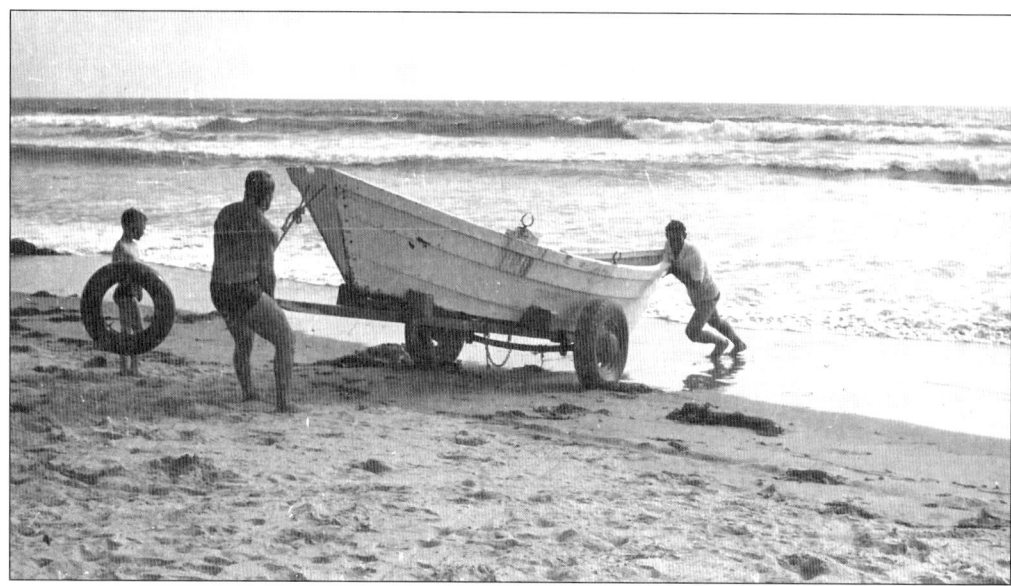

Emil Ziegler (left) and Dorian Paskowitz muscle the dory out of the water in 1941. The dory trailer now has rubber tires and can more easily be towed behind the lifeguard trucks without being bogged down. (Courtesy of Sterling Suhre.)

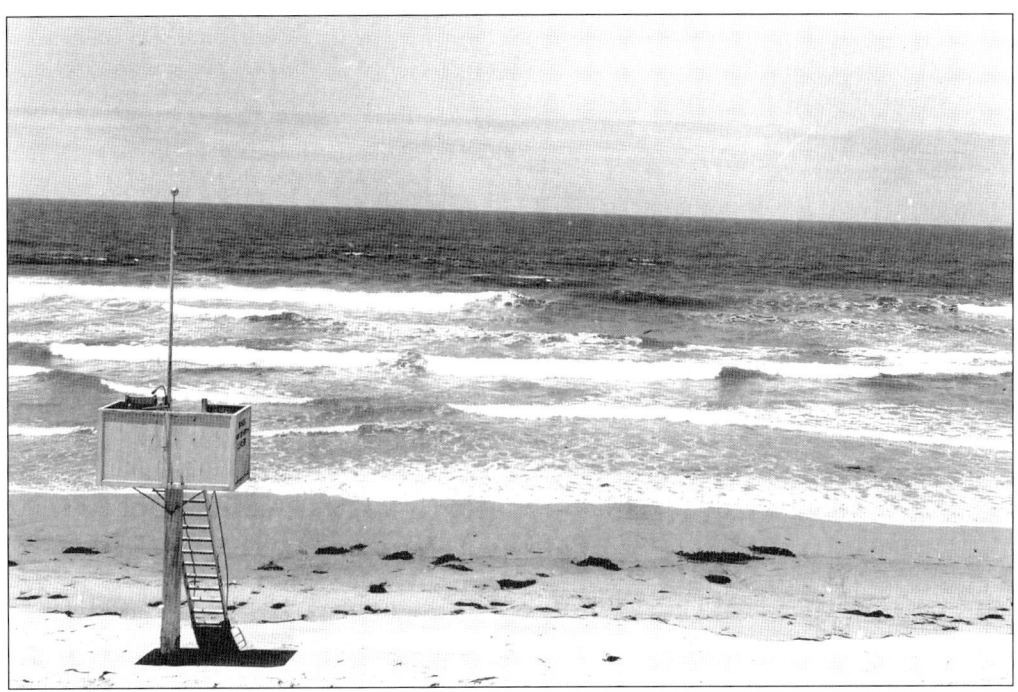

These were cold, lonely beaches. In the early days of the San Diego Lifeguard Service, these boxes on a post were the only observation towers available. They were constantly manned during the busy summer days, but during the winter, cold water and cold winds kept the crowds away. Below, the photograph shows high tide at dusk with the water surrounding the tower. (Courtesy of George Stanley.)

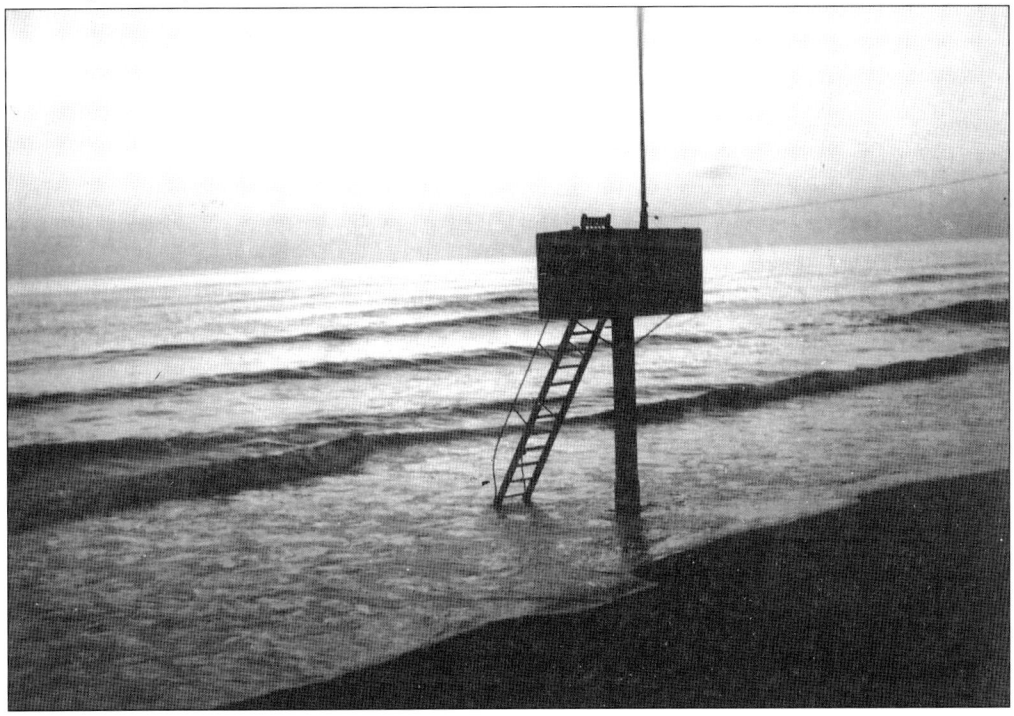

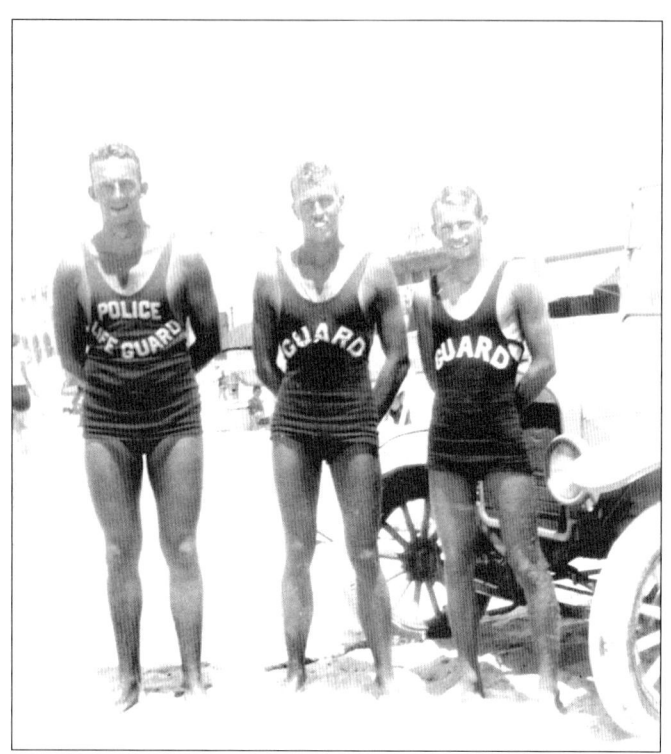

The big three were the heart of the lifeguard service from the 1920s into the 1950s. Pictured c. 1930 are, from left to right, Charles W. Hardy, Fred Crowther, and George Stanley. Hardy was captain, and Crowther and Stanley advanced to positions of lieutenant. (Courtesy of George Stanley.)

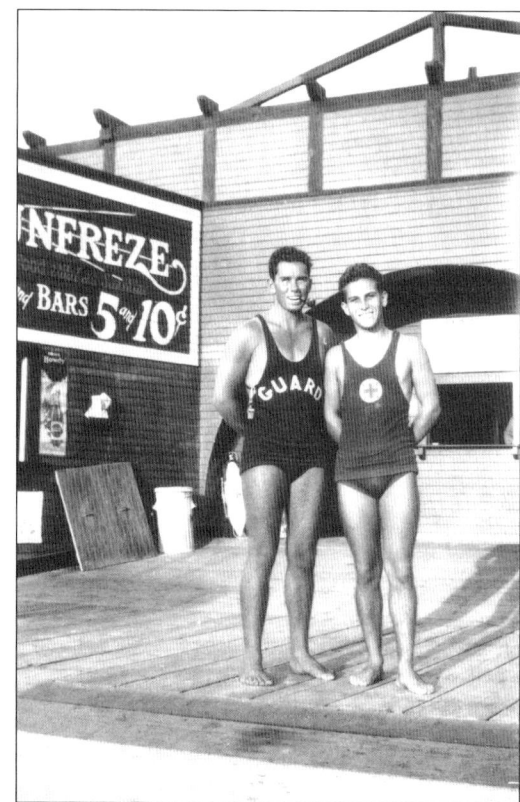

Lifeguard Ed Stotler Sr. and an unidentified Red Cross swim instructor pose in front of J. M. Asher's Old Mission Beach bathhouse around 1930. Ice-cream cones and bars were available for only 5¢ and 10¢. (Courtesy of Mission Beach Woman's Club.)

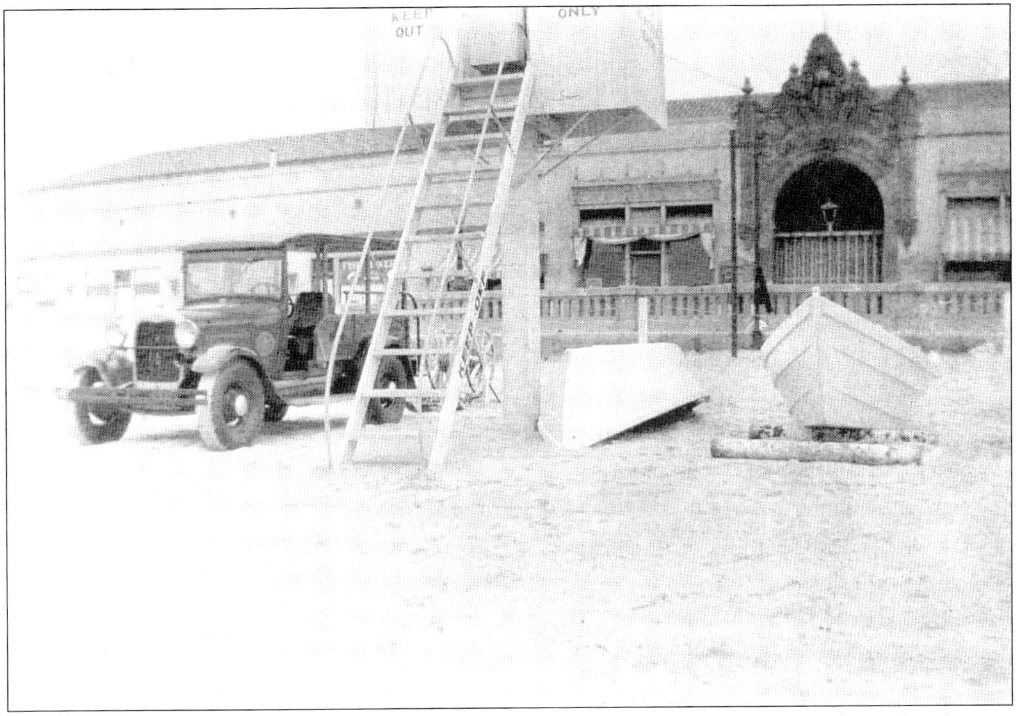

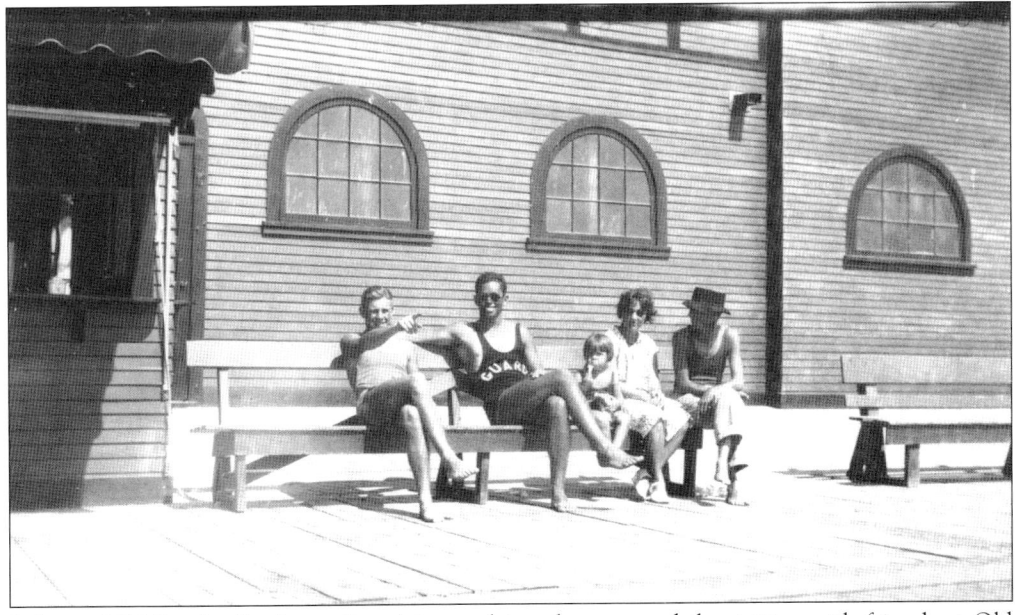

By 1931, usable dory trailers had not yet been purchased, and the guards used wooden logs to roll the heavy boats to the water. Directly behind the truck is a reel of rope, used by the guards to assist in difficult rescues. The line was attached to a swimming guard who, upon reaching the victim, signaled guards on the beach to reel them in. (Courtesy of George Stanley.)

Lifeguard Ed Stotler Sr. (in uniform) is watching the water while visiting with friends at Old Mission Beach c. 1931. (Courtesy of Ed Stotler Jr.)

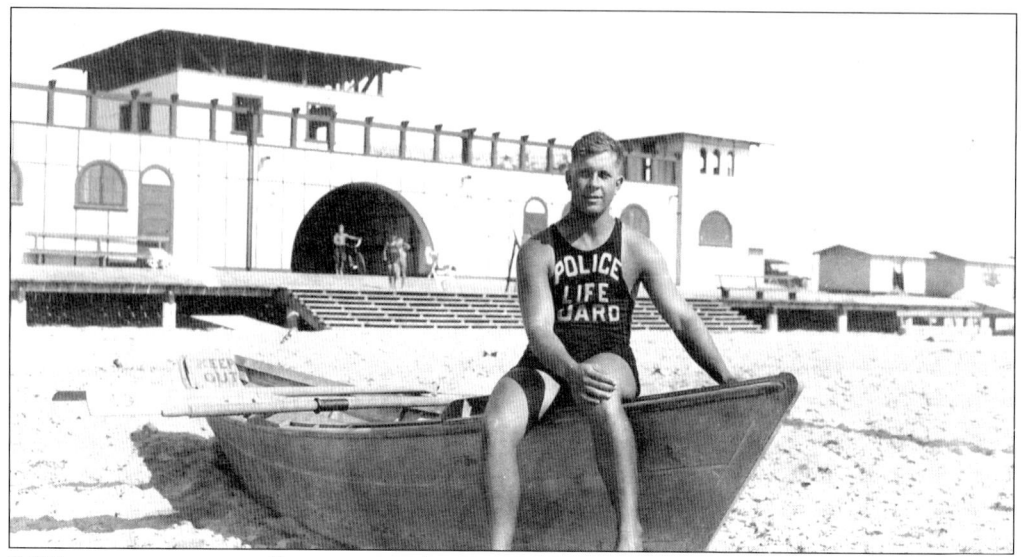

Bill Rumsey sits on a smaller, one-man dory in front of Asher's Bathhouse at Old Mission Beach. Rumsey retired from the San Diego County Lifeguard after many years as captain. He was responsible for developing the county organization from its inception, and his lifeguards covered all San Diego beaches outside of San Diego City limits. (Courtesy of Pell Mell.)

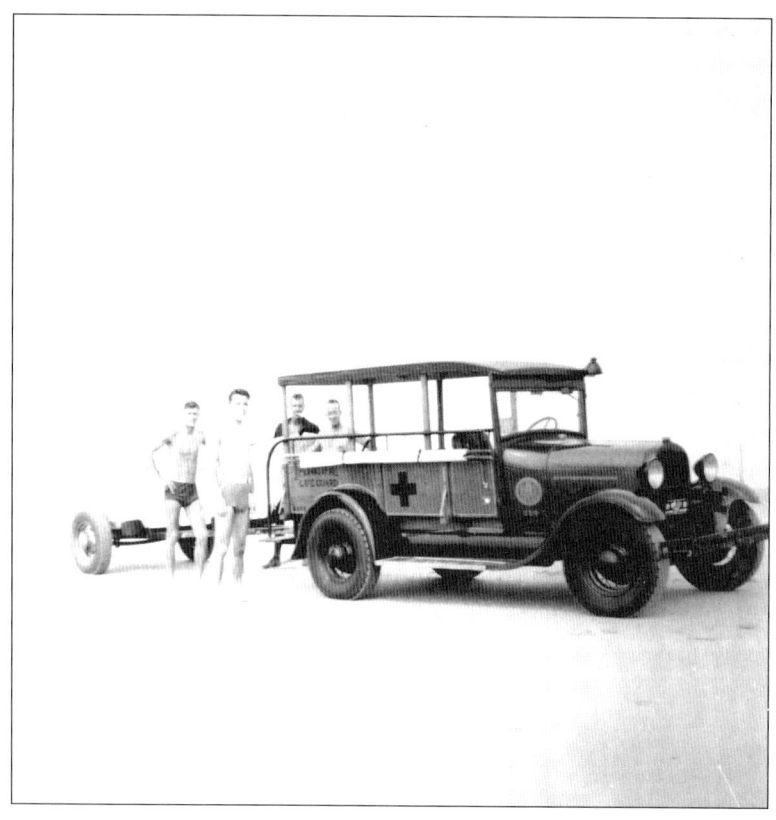

Around 1933, both the truck and the dory trailer are equipped with wider tires, resulting in fewer embarrassing moments when the vehicles had to be dug out of the soft sand. Closer to the waterline, the sand was hard packed and easily driven on. (Courtesy of George Stanley.)

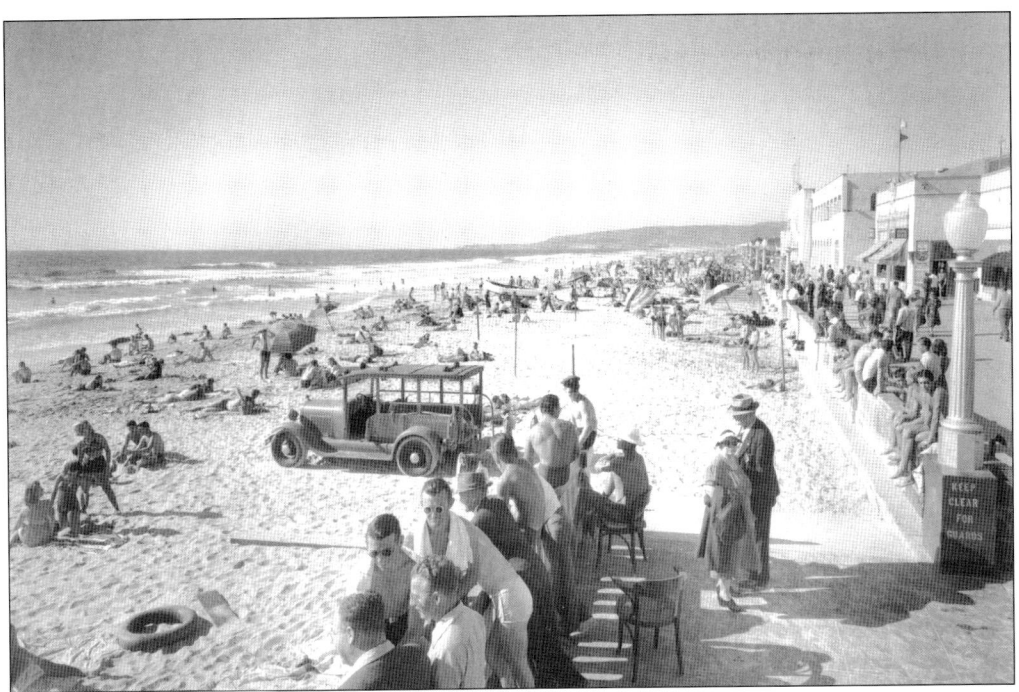

By the 1940s, more lifeguards were hired to cope with the rapidly rising number of beachgoers. This scene is at the Mission Beach Amusement Center (later called Belmont Park). The large building in the right background is the Mission Beach Ballroom. (Courtesy of SDHS.)

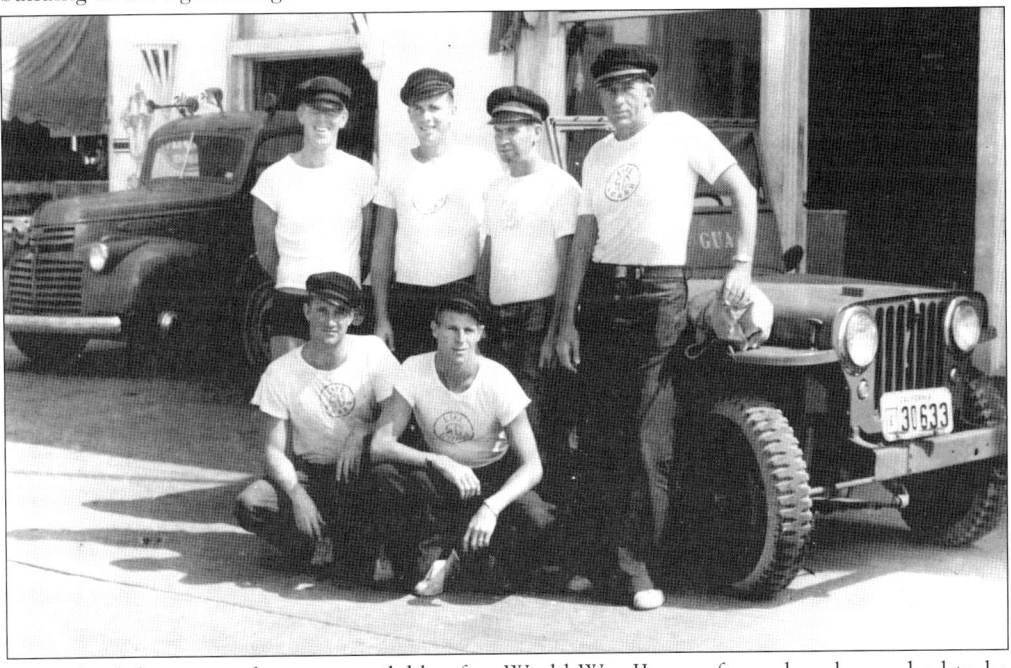

Four-wheel-drive jeeps became available after World War II, so soft sand no longer had to be avoided. Standing from left to right in 1950 are Lieutenants Fran Blankenship, Jim Gilmour, George Stanley, and Capt. Chuck Hardy. Kneeling on the right is Maurice (Sonny) Altheimer with unidentified guard. (Courtesy of authors.)

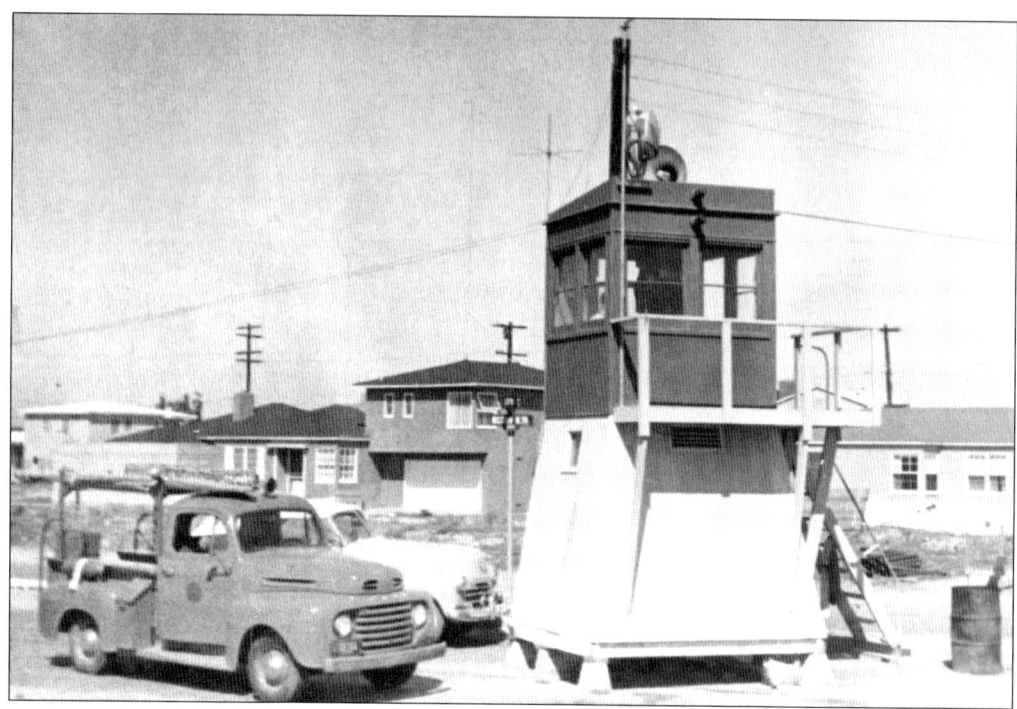

When Mission Bay Channel was opened to boat traffic in 1951, a lifeguard tower was placed at the extreme south end of Mission Boulevard. This February 1953 view shows the tower that was manned 24 hours a day in the event of boating accidents. High surf sometimes closed the channel, and a loudspeaker on the roof was used to warn boaters. (Courtesy of authors.)

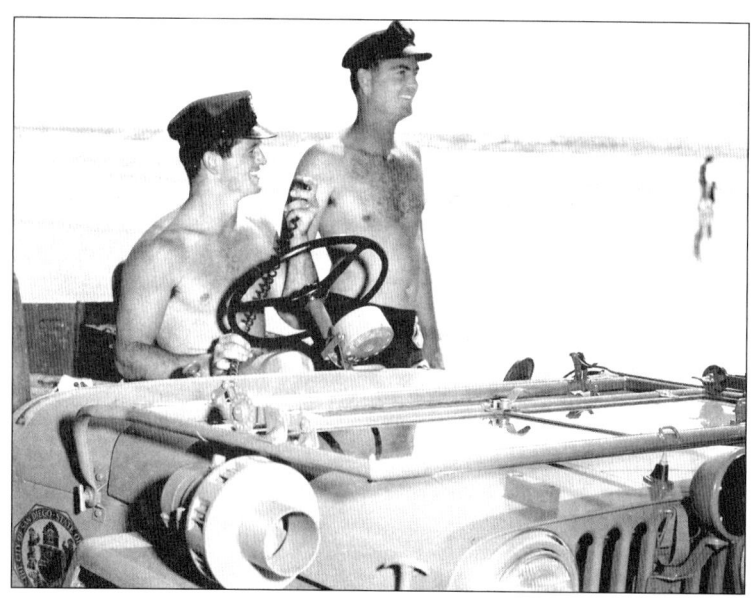

Radio communication between guards in the Jeep and a guard in the tower greatly improved swimmers' safety. Pictured around 1950s, John Largent, seated, is using the radio as Burke Royale stands by. (Courtesy of Burke Royale.)

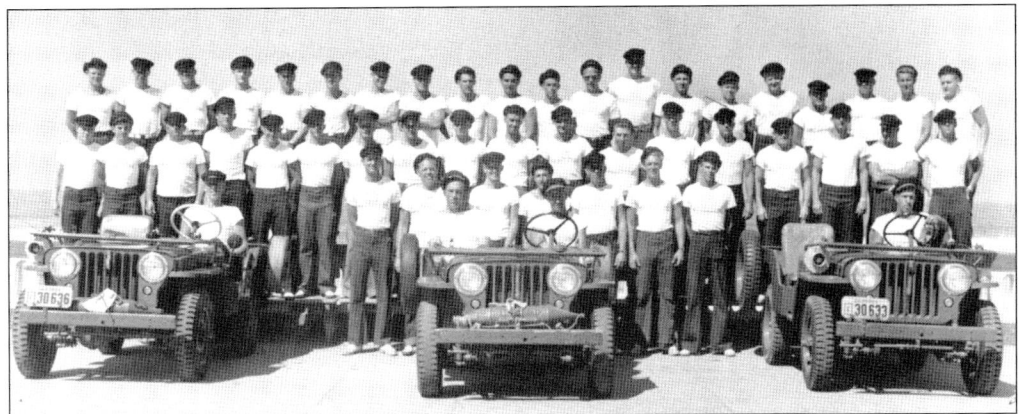

The number of summer lifeguards has grown dramatically, as pictured in this 1947 team photograph. The officers seated in the jeeps are, from left to right, Lt. Fran Blankenship, Capt. Charles Hardy, Lt. George Stanley, and Lt. Fred Crowther. (Courtesy of Burke Royale.)

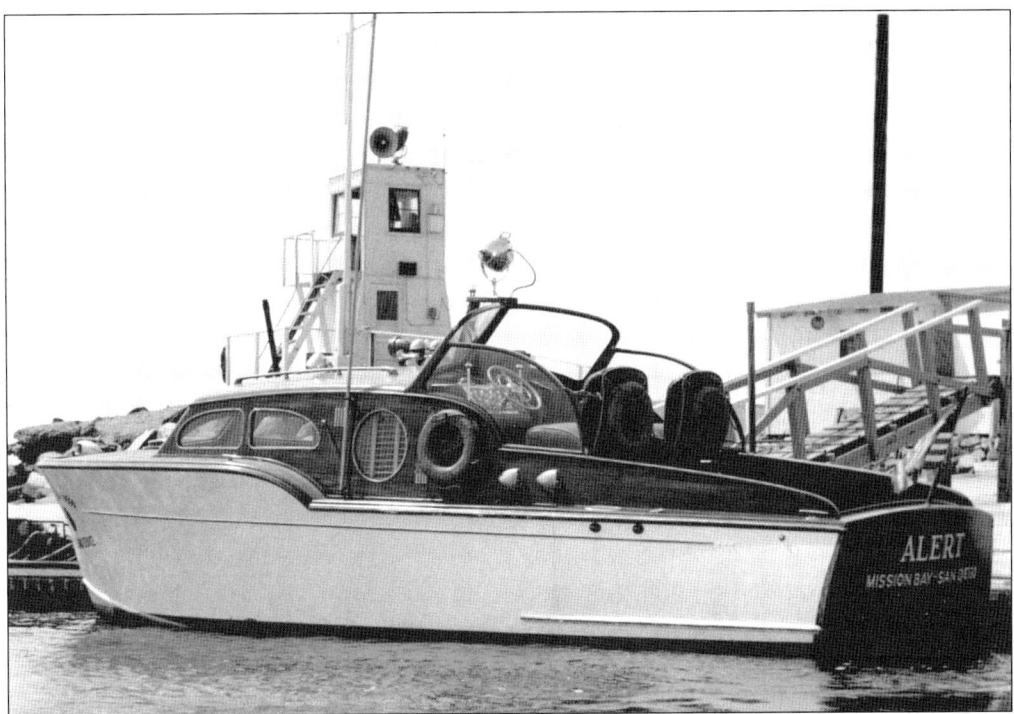

An oceangoing patrol boat, the *Alert* was a much needed addition to the lifeguard service in the early 1950s. With boat traffic getting heavier in the channel and the newly dredged Mission Bay, there were the inevitable accidents. The boat crews were very busy, and many lives were saved. (Courtesy of Burke Royale.)

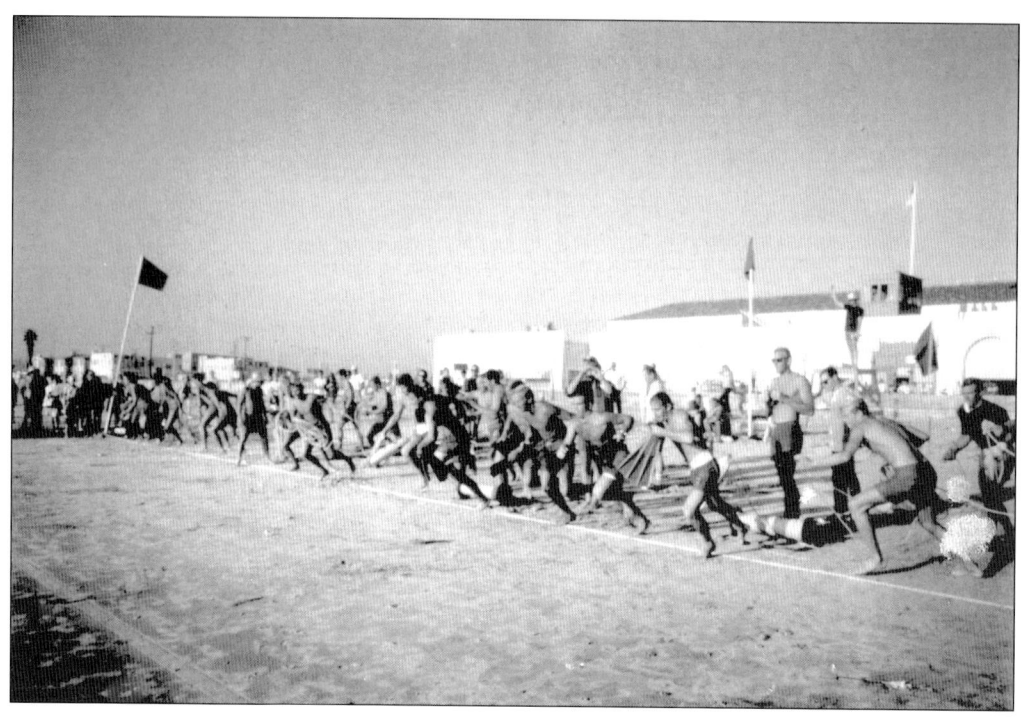

As the number of lifeguards continued to grow, competition between teams of guards became an annual event. The winning team could claim bragging rights as the best lifeguards for at least one year. Let the games begin in 1969. (Courtesy of Donny Hines.)

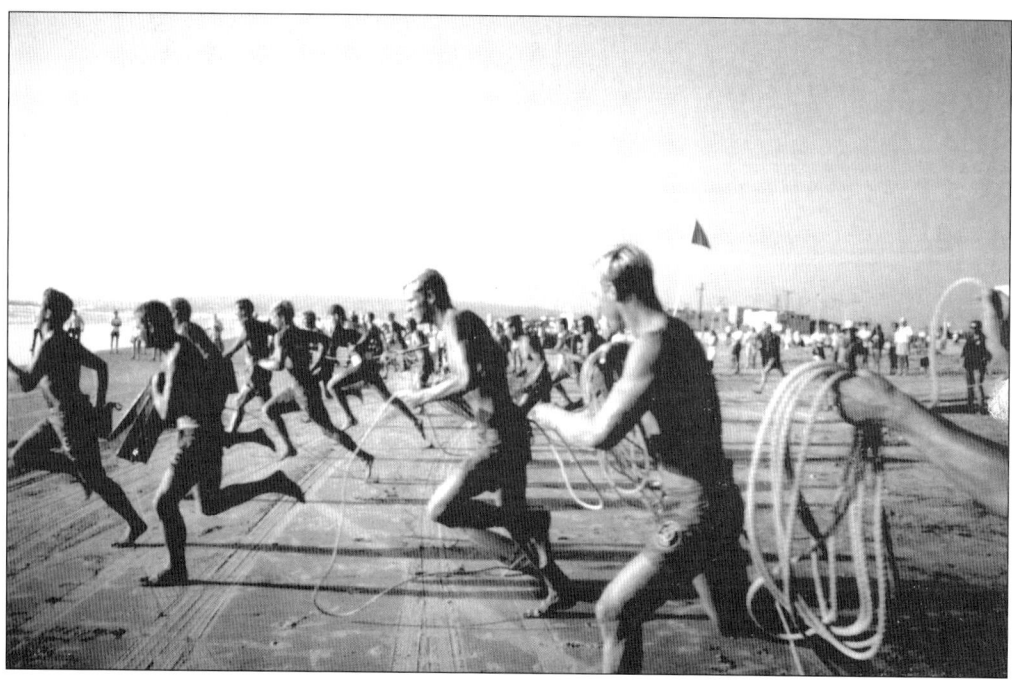

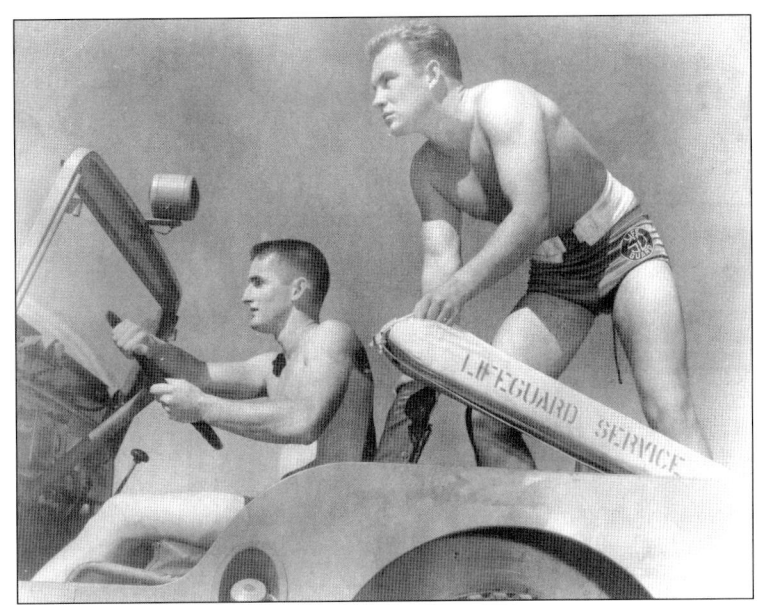

Coauthor Terry Curren, driving, and Gary Duncan respond to a swimmer in trouble in 1956. The canvas-covered lifesaving buoy was an experimental model that should never have left the drawing board. The canvas did not repel the water and instead of being a float, it became an anchor. Needless to say, the guards rejected it. (Courtesy of authors.)

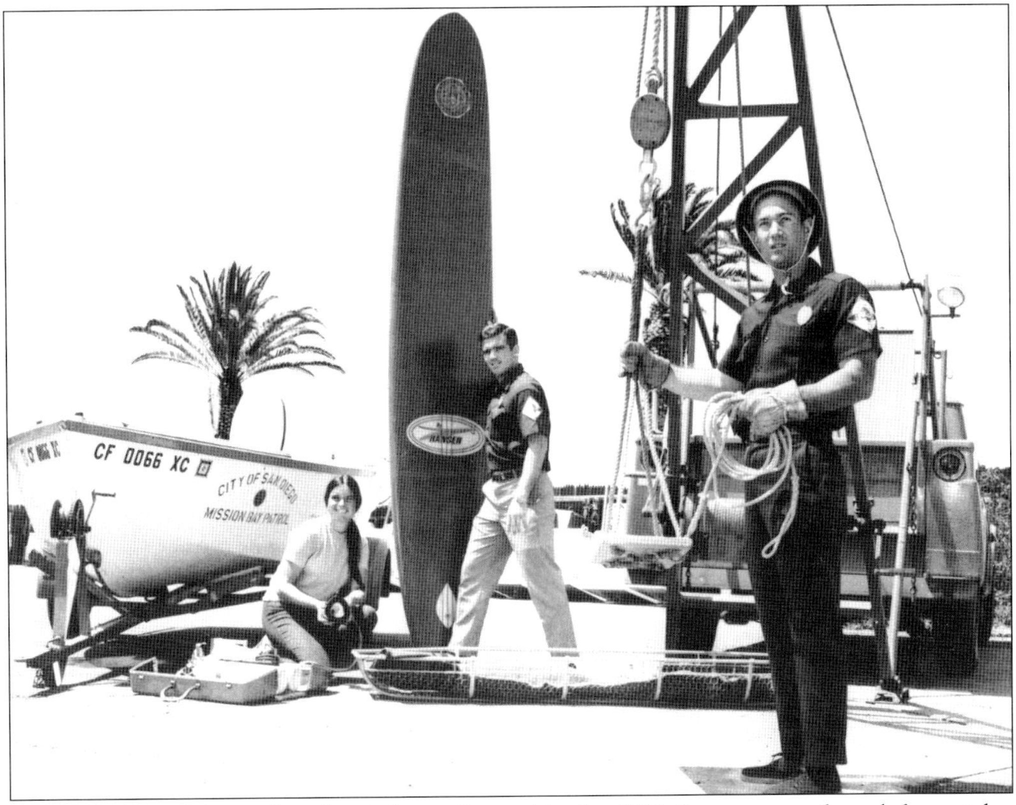

Demonstrating lifeguard tools of the trade in this April 1969 scene are, from left to right, Maureen O'Connor, Pat O'Connor, and Frank Day. Maureen O'Connor was elected to the San Diego City Council in 1971 and served through 1979. She was a port commissioner from 1980 to 1985 and was elected mayor of San Diego in 1985 where she served until 1992. (Courtesy of S. D. Lifeguard Service.)

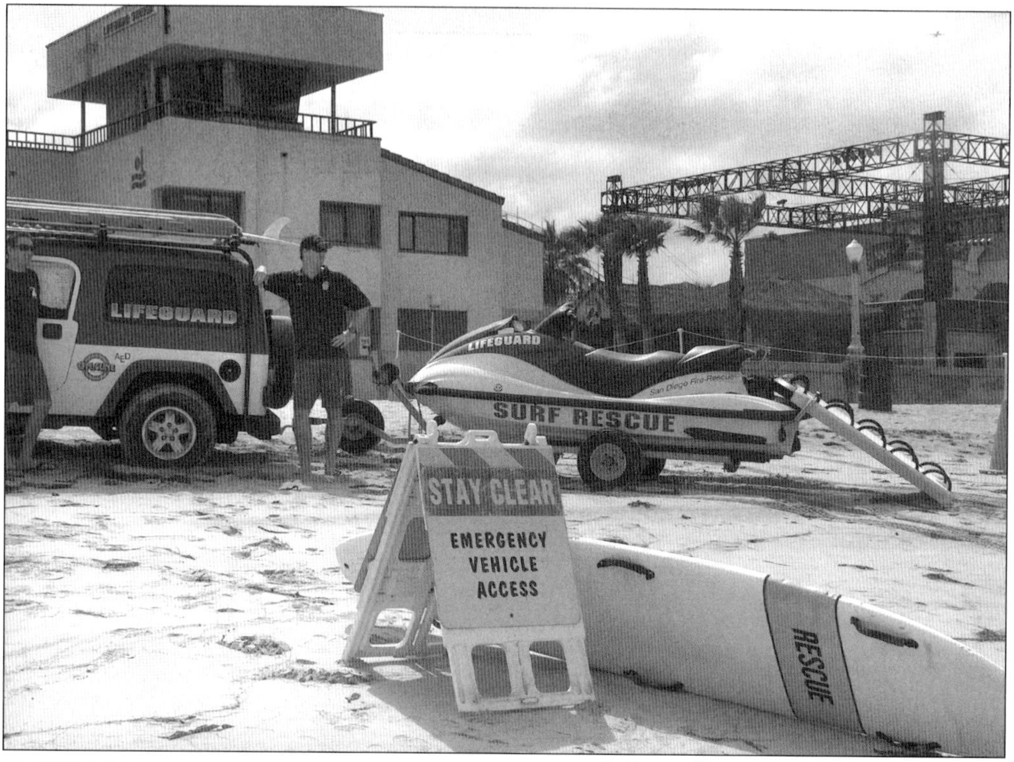

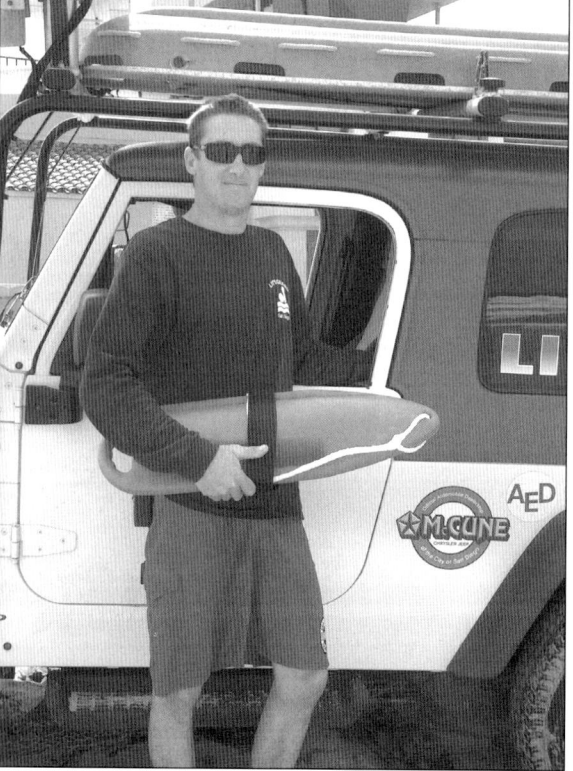

Lifeguard I Erick Winter (left) and Lifeguard II Rob Brown demonstrate modern equipment in front of Mission Beach Lifeguard Station No. 1 in 2007. Personal watercraft has proven to be very effective in lifesaving situations. A skilled handler can move in and out through the surf to reach swimmers in trouble. The rescue board has been designed specifically for lifesaving operations. (Courtesy of authors.)

Lifeguard I Erick Winter holds a modern plastic rescue buoy on May 4, 2007. San Diego Lifeguard Service has come a long way since its inception in 1925. Authors Prather and Curren fondly remember their days as lifeguards, some of the best days of their lives. Phil Prather was a guard in the 1940s, and Terry Curren served in the 1950s. (Courtesy of authors.)

Four
BELMONT PARK

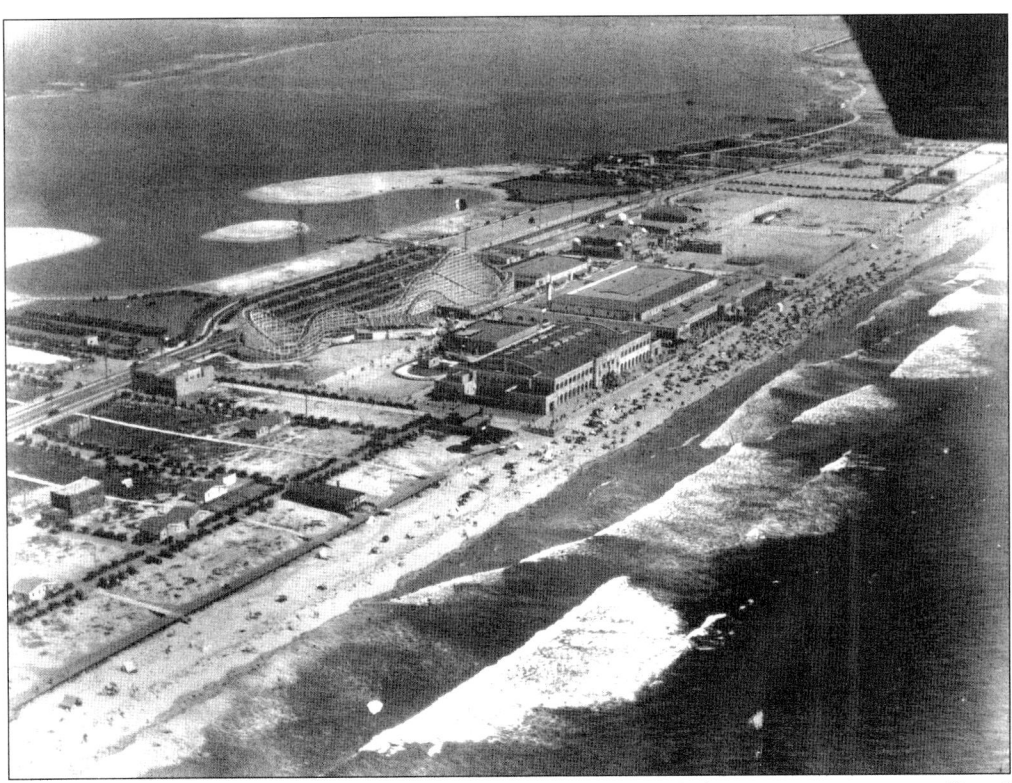

Around 1925, the amusement center was up and running, and the new concrete seawall and sidewalk had been completed along the ocean in front of the park. Wooden walkways were still in place to the north and south. Bonita Cove and island can be seen in the background. (Courtesy of John Chadwick.)

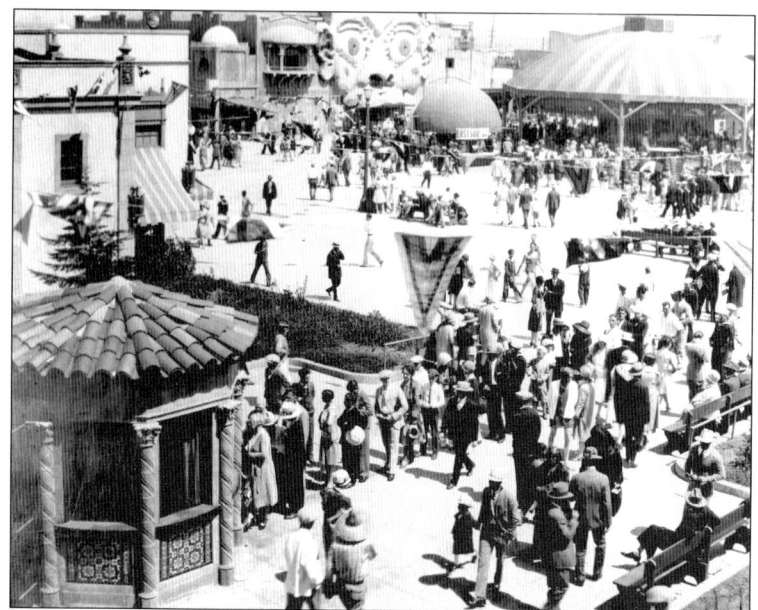

The midway is busy in this 1926 scene. The striped top, round building is the merry-go-round, and the small, domed building next to it sells Eastside beer for 10¢. To the left of the beer concession is the fun house. The original merry-go-round was dismantled and sold when the park closed in 1976. A new merry-go-round was erected when the park reopened. (Courtesy of authors.)

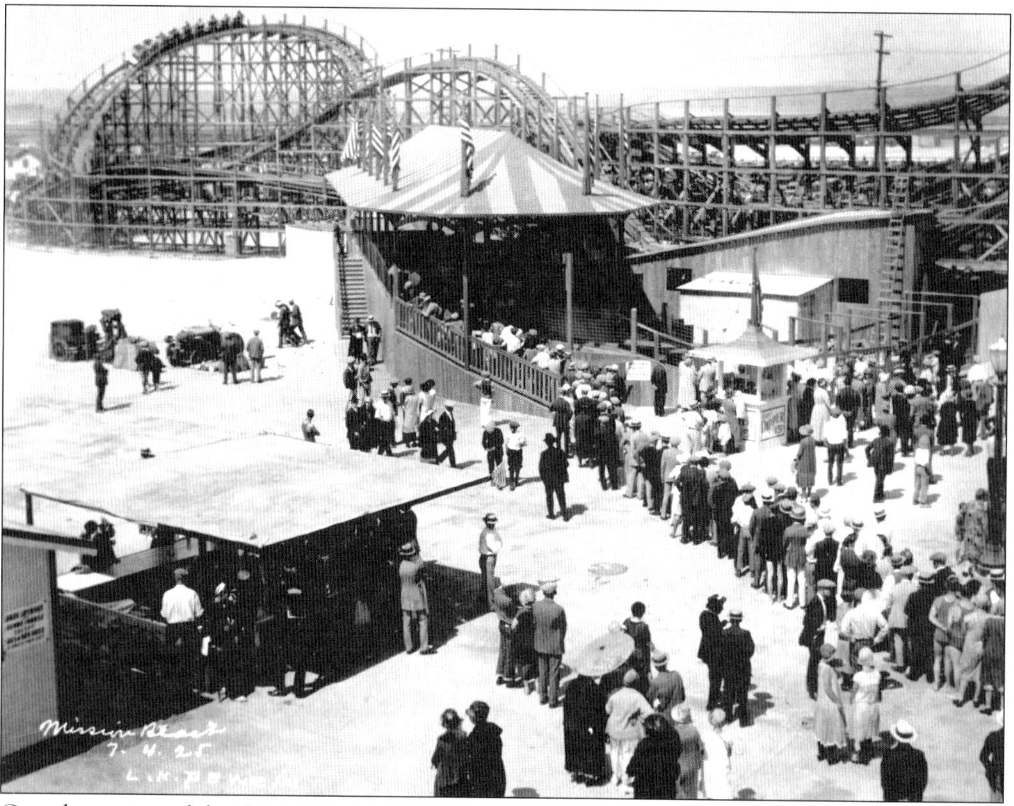

Grand opening of the Giant Dipper roller coaster on July 4, 1925, draws a large crowd lined up to try the new thrill ride, only 15¢. Designed and built by roller coaster specialists Frank Prior and Fred Church, the Giant Dipper remains the largest wooden roller coaster structure on the West Coast. (Courtesy of authors.)

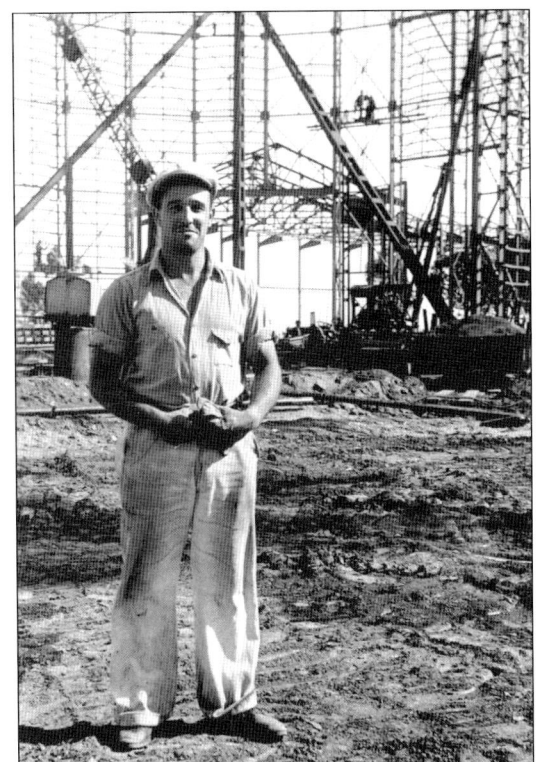

An unidentified construction worker pauses for a photo opportunity in the partially built plunge building c. 1924. The lower scene shows more of the massive steel framework of the side dressing rooms. When the plunge opened in 1925, it was the largest indoor saltwater pool in the world. The plunge measured 175 feet by 60 feet. Later it was converted to fresh water. (Courtesy of George Stanley.)

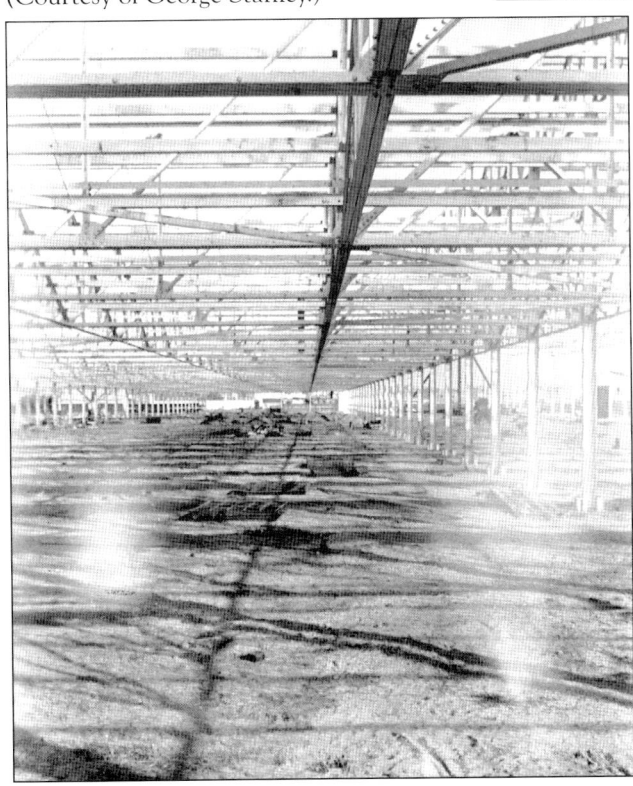

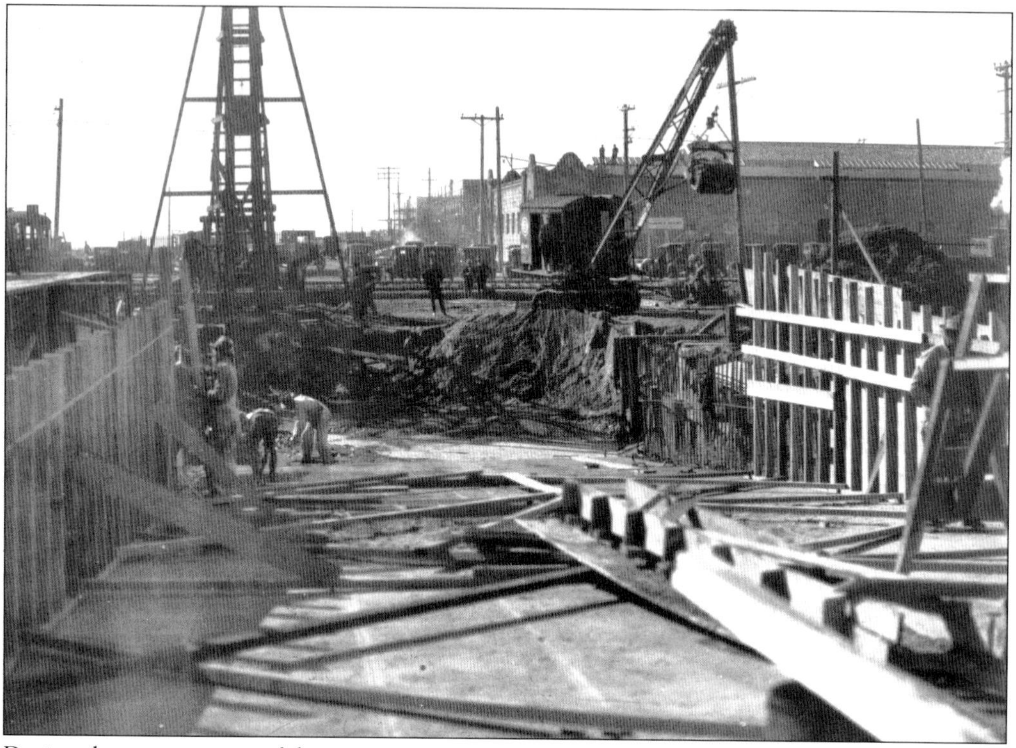

During the construction of the amusement center, an underpass was built to allow pedestrians to safely walk to the bayfront at Bonita Cove. The tunnel passed under Mission Boulevard and the streetcar tracks and was utilized until the late 1950s when it was filled in. (Courtesy of SDHS.)

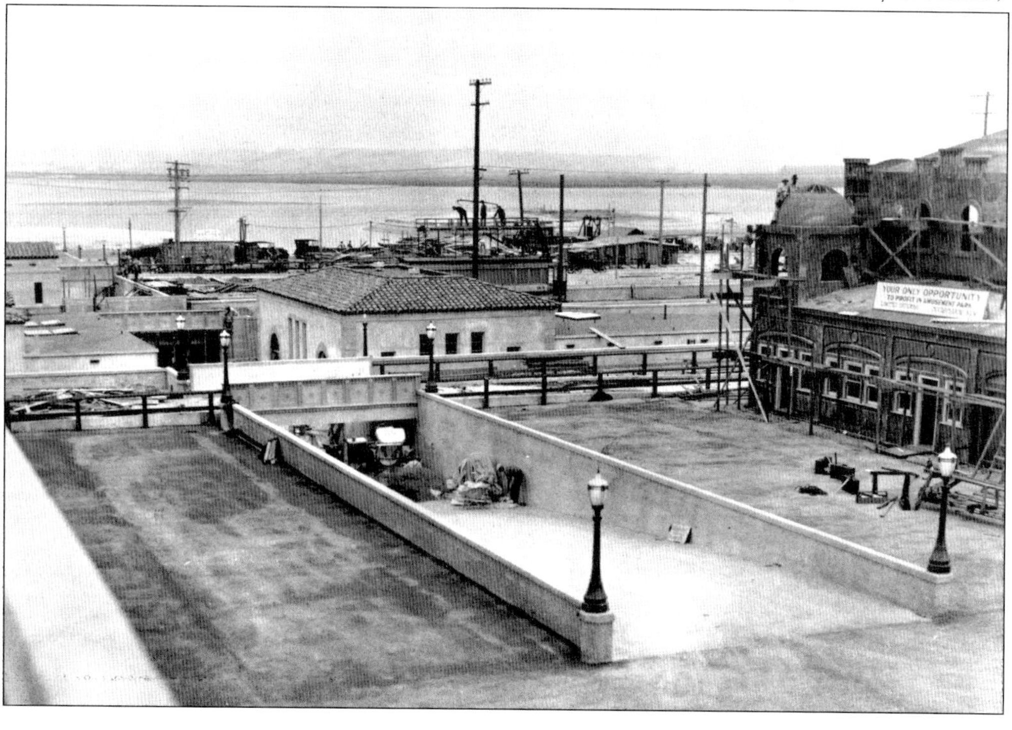

Warmly dressed visitors walk along the oceanfront, beside the colonnade on the west side of the plunge and bathhouse building in 1926. A visit to the beach was a new experience for numerous San Diegans, since many had moved west from their hometowns all across America. (Courtesy of Chuck Whitmarsh.)

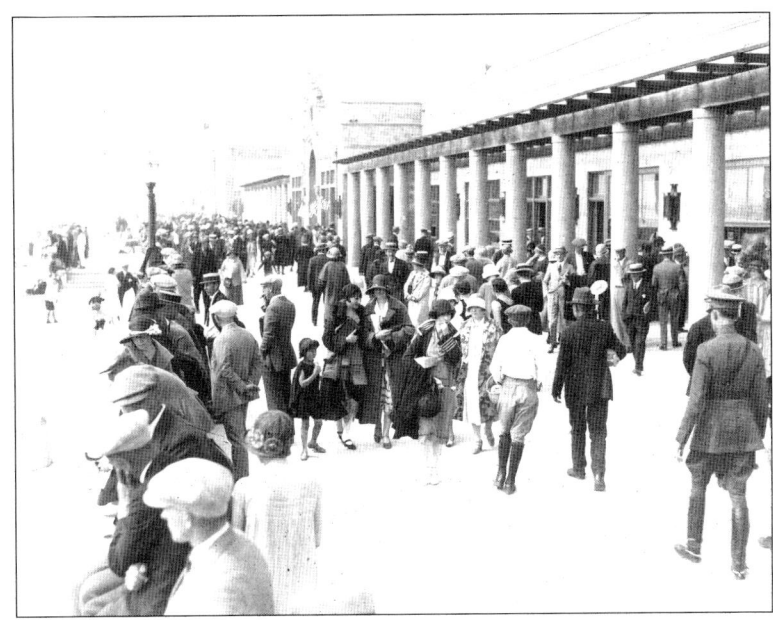

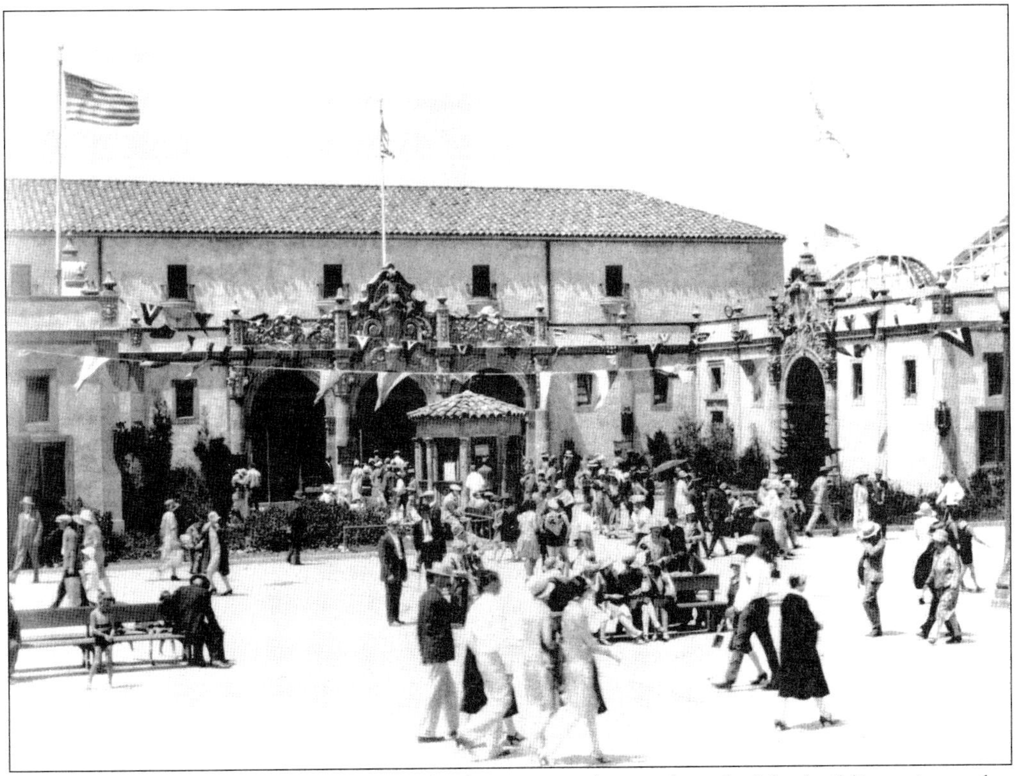

The main entrance to the Mission Beach Plunge is on the south end of the building, pictured c. 1925. Bathing attire could be rented for the day, and the bathers could pass freely back and forth between the pool and the ocean. (Courtesy of authors.)

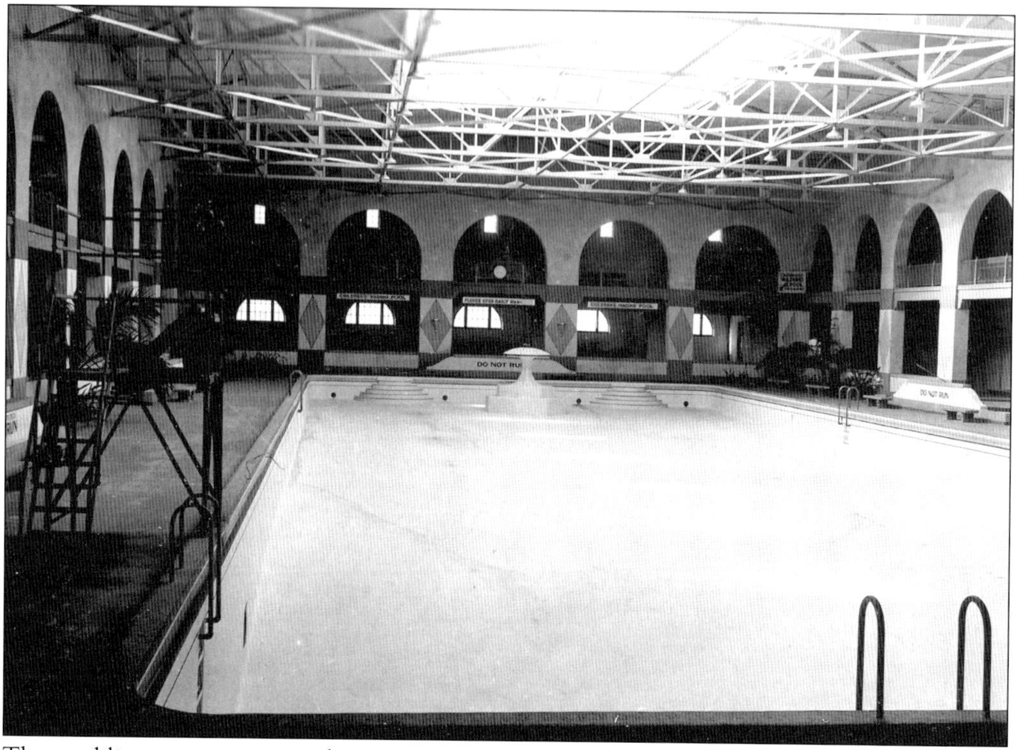

The sparkling new swimming plunge is pictured upon completion in 1925, as well as the fountain that sat in the middle of the shallow end. The pool has not yet been filled with water. The deepest part of the pool was 9 feet deep, and the shallow end was about 2.5 feet. An additional wading pool was available for the small children. (Courtesy of George Stanley.)

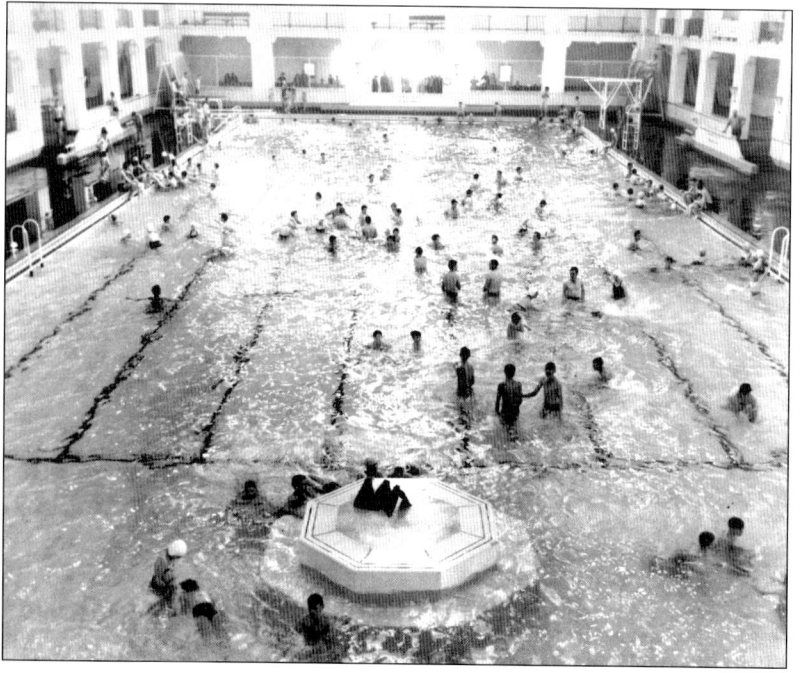

The pool was an immediate success. While open to the public most of the time, it was a venue for many swimming and diving competitions. The Plunge was also used as a training facility for the navy during World War II, where the young recruits would learn the basics of survival in the event of ship sinking. (Courtesy of authors.)

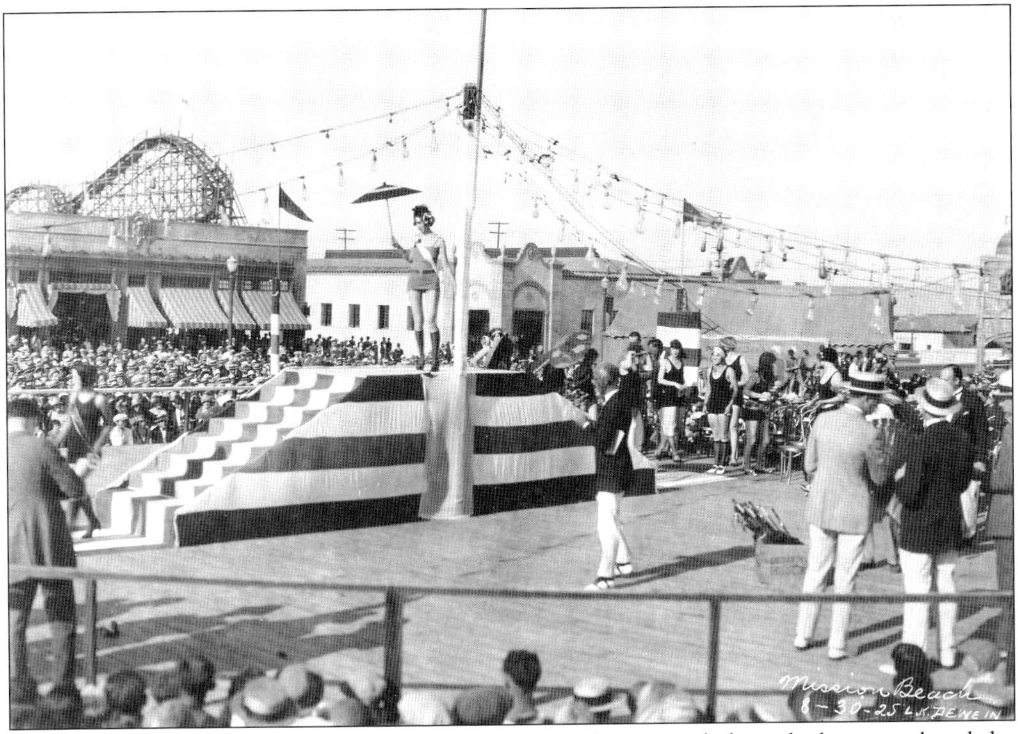

Beauty contests were another crowd pleaser in 1925. This young lady with the parasol and the knee socks must be the winner. The girls on the right are carefully checking out their completion. (Courtesy of Mike Curren.)

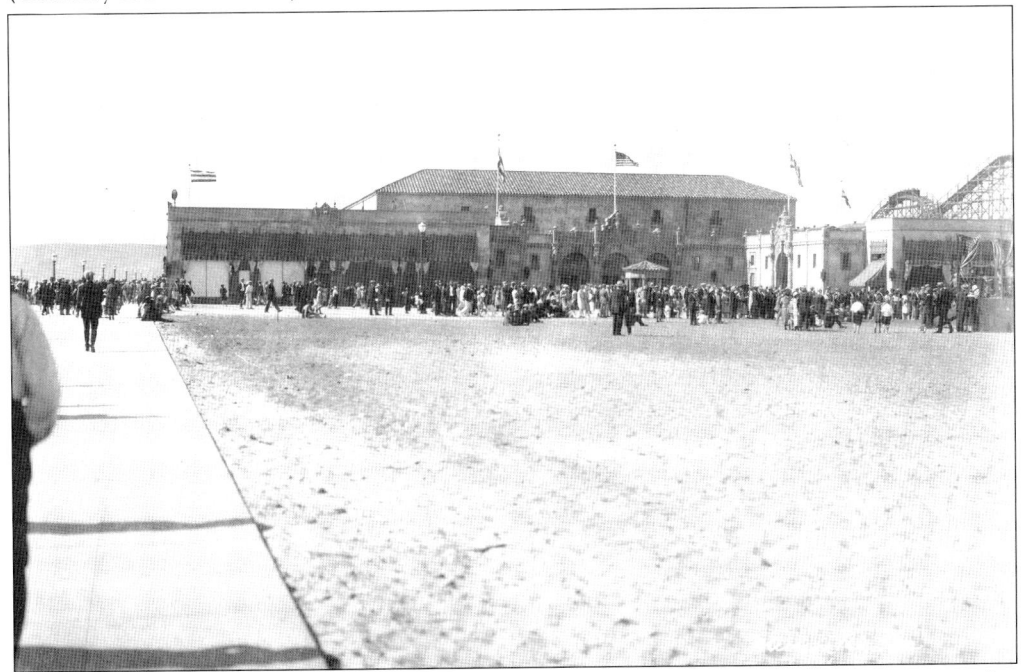

More of the opening day crowd is seen near the entrance to the Mission Beach Plunge. The roller coaster car sits on the summit in the background. (Courtesy of Mike Curren.)

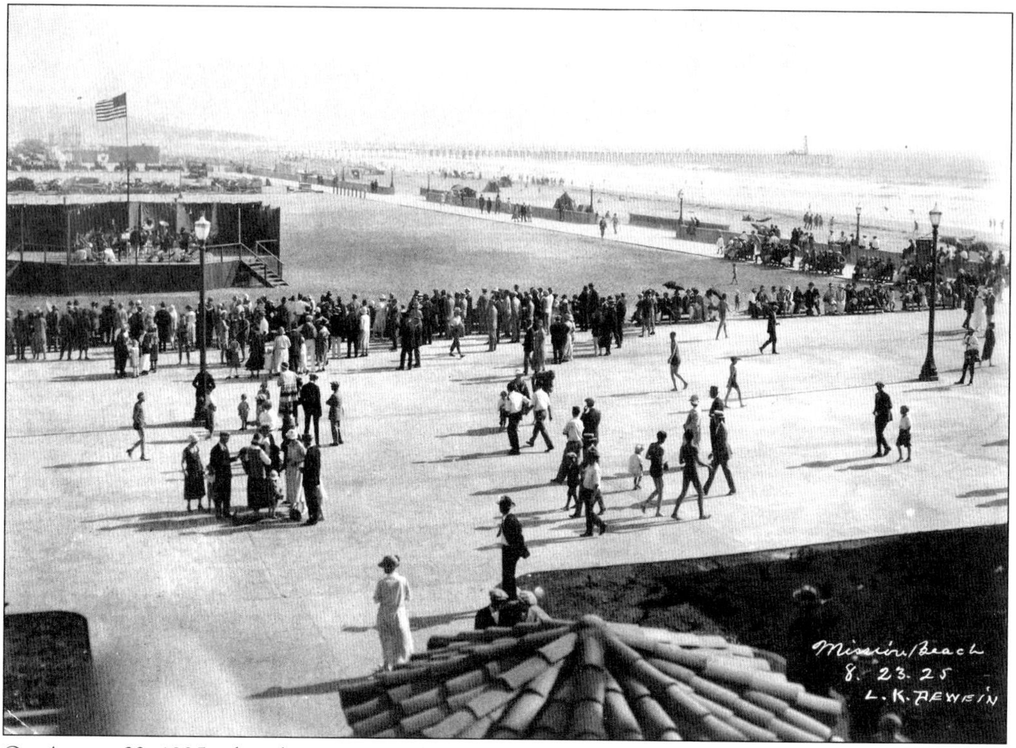

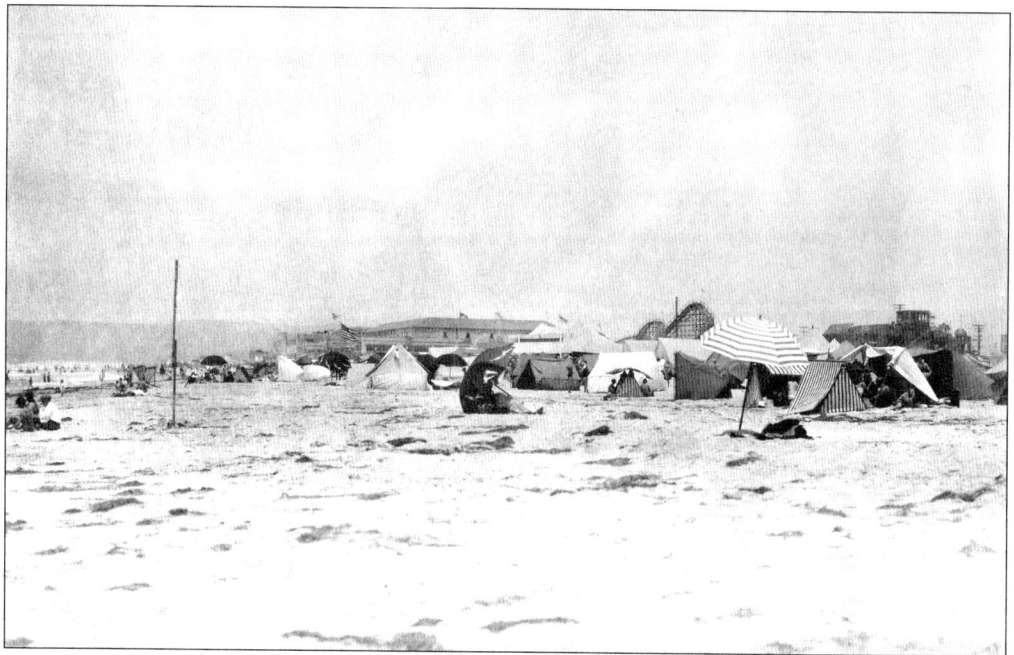

On August 22, 1925, a band concert was held just south of the plunge building. In the background is a pier structure extending seaward, which supported a drainpipe that emptied storm water into the ocean at Brighton Court. (Courtesy of Mike Curren.)

Tents and umbrellas cover the beach in this 1925 scene. The Giant Dipper roller coaster and Mission Beach Amusement Center are in the background. (Courtesy of Mike Curren.)

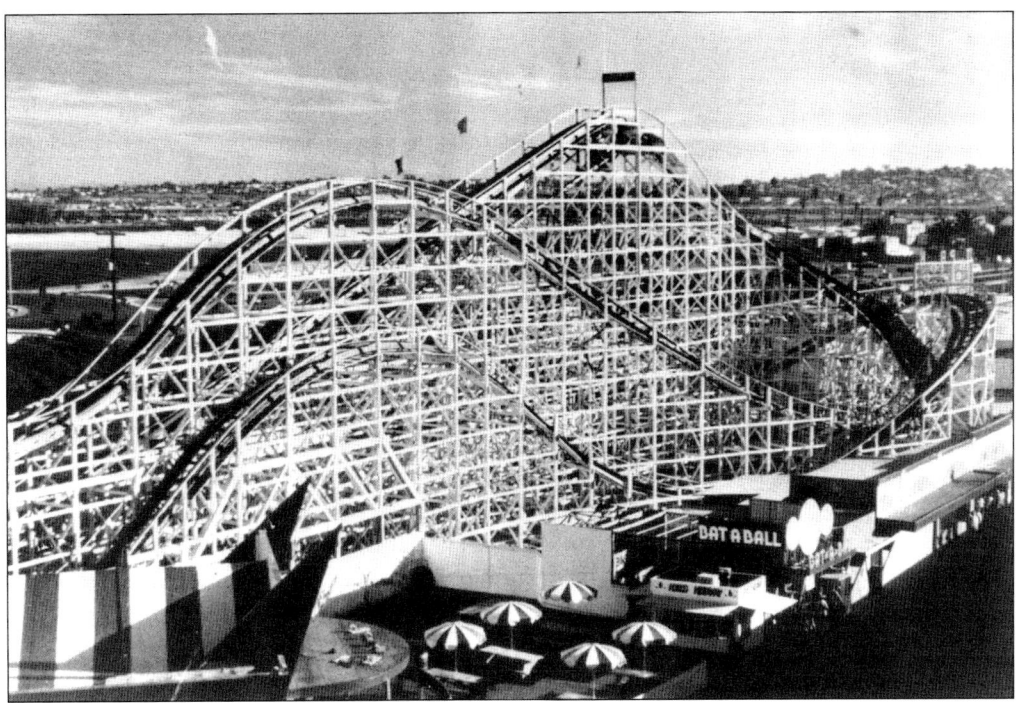

The Giant Dipper, pictured as it looked in 1948, was the major attraction at Belmont Park. This large, wooden structure was the brainchild of John D. Spreckles, the sugar czar, and was designed and built by the team of Prior and Church. A construction crew of 150 men began in May 1925 and completed the job in time for the July 4 opening. (Courtesy of Chuck Whitmarsh.)

Swimming and diving competitions were very popular at the Plunge in the late 1940s and into the 1950s. Clown divers were a well-received, lighthearted diversion to the seriousness of the competition. Here the Dilly Dallys are perfecting a routine to try out on the crowds at the next meet. From left to right are unidentified, Frank Munson, Jim Kennedy, Gordon Jones, Sunny Altheimer, and unidentified. (Courtesy of Burke Royale.)

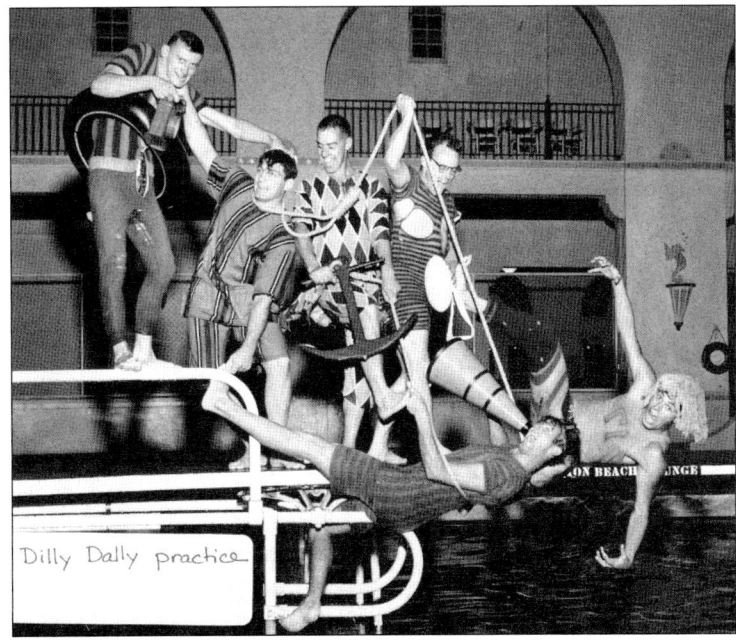

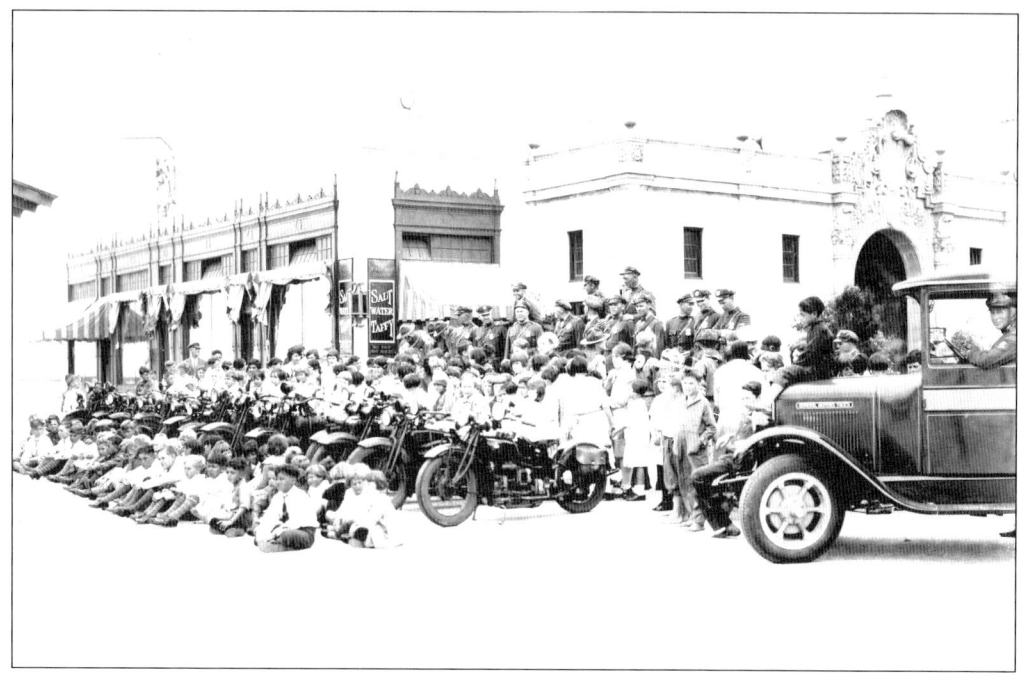

Kids and police pose for a group photograph at the amusement center c. 1927. The school kids of today still have class outings at Mission Beach. (Courtesy of George Stanley.)

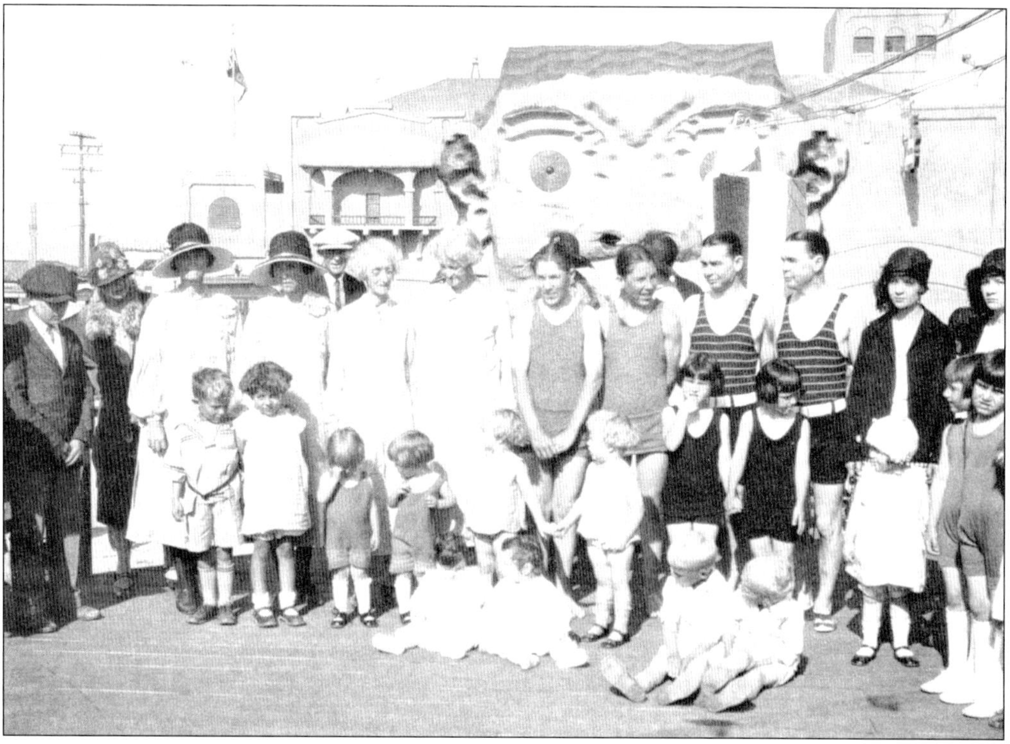

Twins, from the very young to the very old, have entered the twins' competition in 1926. (Courtesy of Dee Lang.)

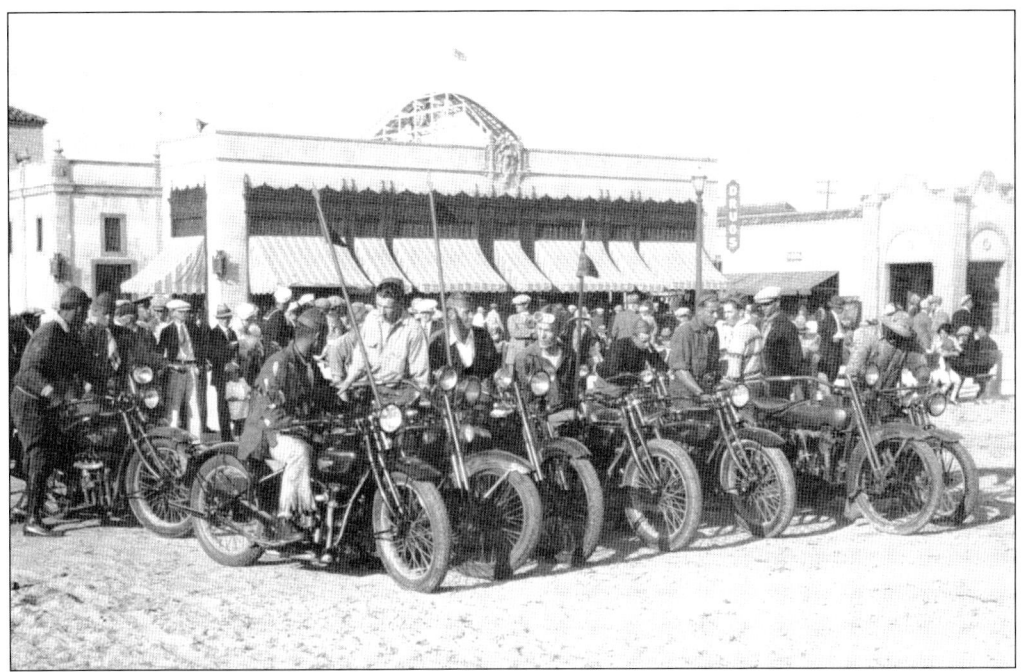

Motorcycle racers get ready for the main event in this c. 1927 scene. The drugstore behind the riders only lasted at this location for a very short time. A new drugstore opened at the corner of Ventura Place and Mission Boulevard. (Courtesy of Dee Lang.)

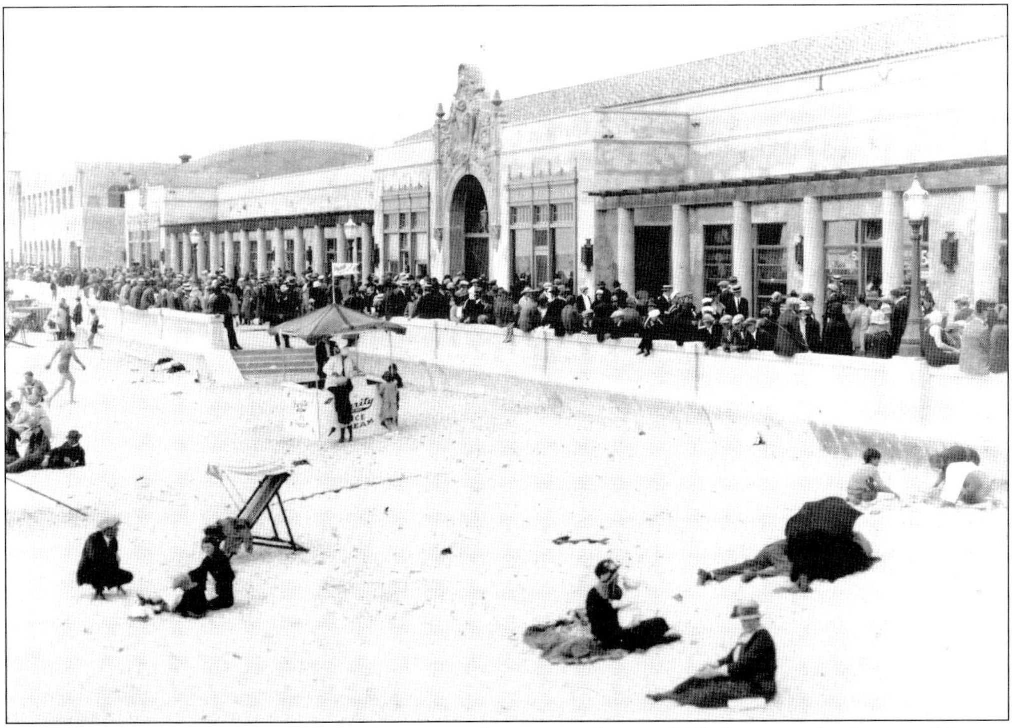

It looks like Henry Ford was the fashion coordinator in this c. 1925 photograph. One could wear any color they liked, as long as it was black. (Courtesy of authors.)

Sailors on leave seem to be having a great time on the Giant Dipper c. 1950, maybe because they have the pretty girl all to themselves. (Courtesy of authors.)

A shuttle bus provided passenger service to South Mission Beach up until the mid-1960s, going back and forth along the one-mile route. This view is looking south from atop the roller coaster. (Courtesy of authors.)

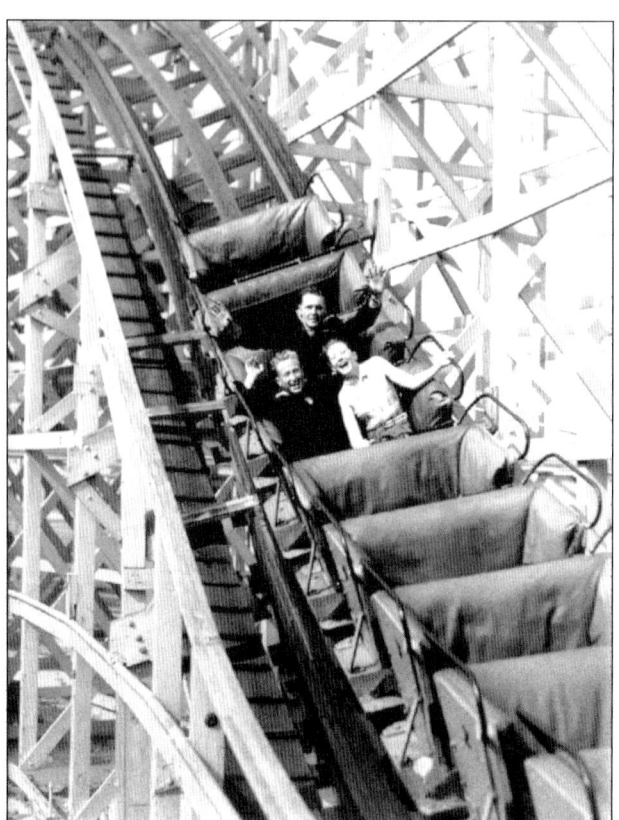

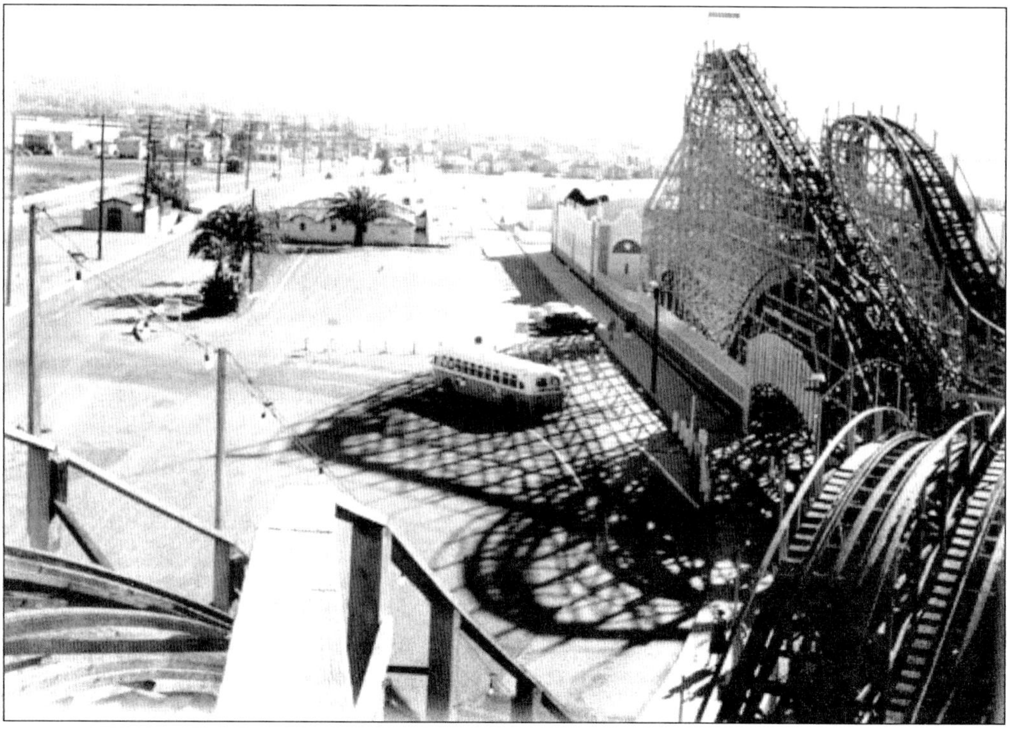

Five
THE 1930S AND 1940S

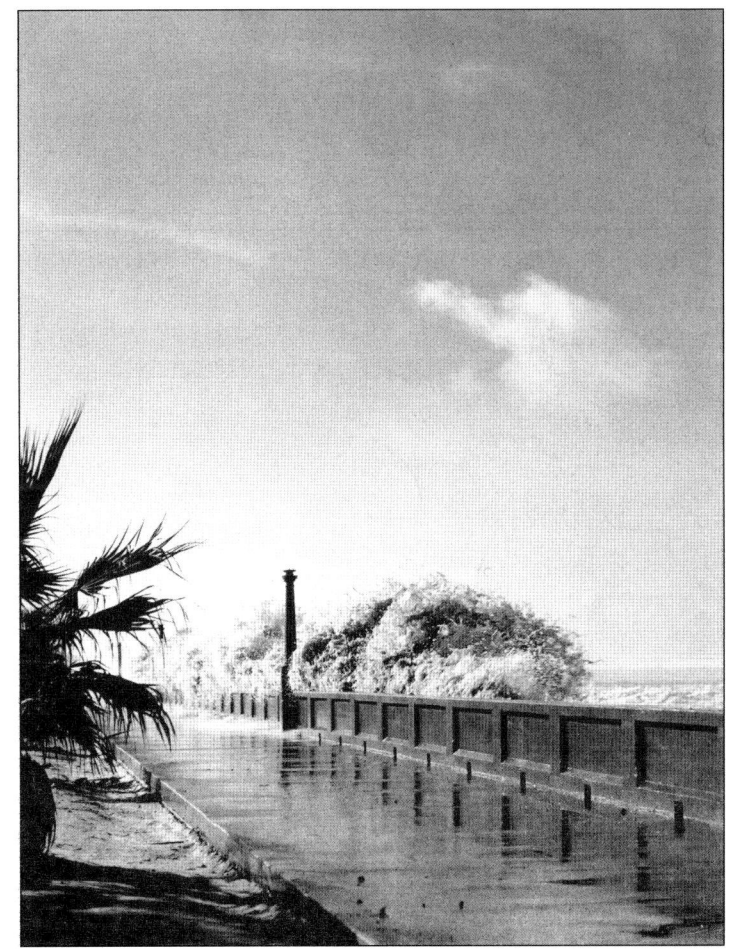

Huge storm surf crashes over the seawall in this January 1939 scene. The new wall held up well and kept property damage to a minimum, unlike the extensive damage caused by storms prior to the wall construction in 1925. (Courtesy of Don Crie.)

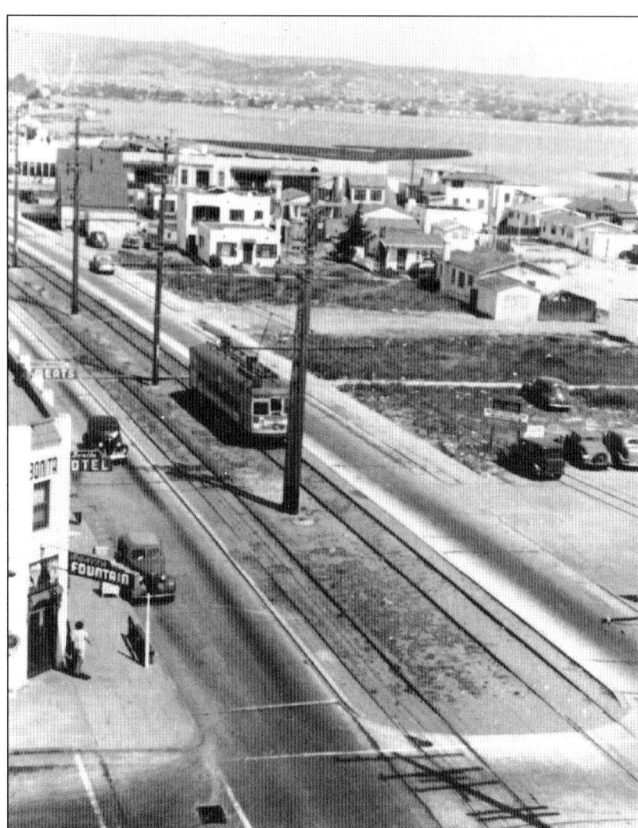

Looking north from atop the roller coaster c. 1936, one can see the No. 16 streetcar heading toward La Jolla. There are still plenty of vacant lots in Mission Beach, and there are just a few houses on the hills of Pacific Beach in the background. The mudflats of Mission Bay are also visible. (Courtesy of authors.)

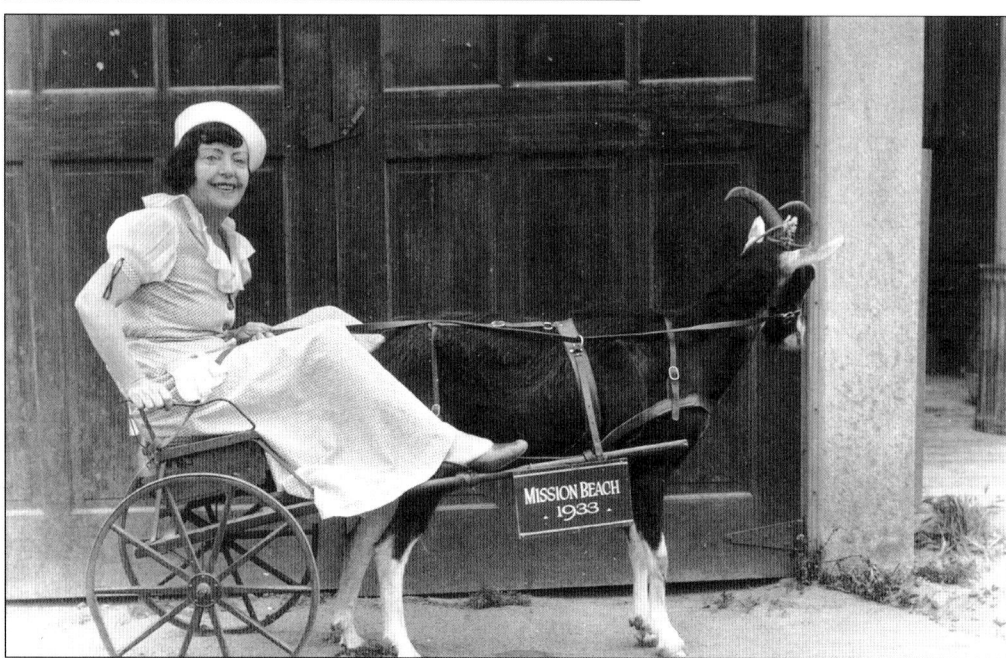

This example of rapid transit by "goatmobile" was unusual, even by Mission Beach standards in 1933. Irene Barrett controls the throttle and brakes. (Courtesy of Ed Stotler Jr.)

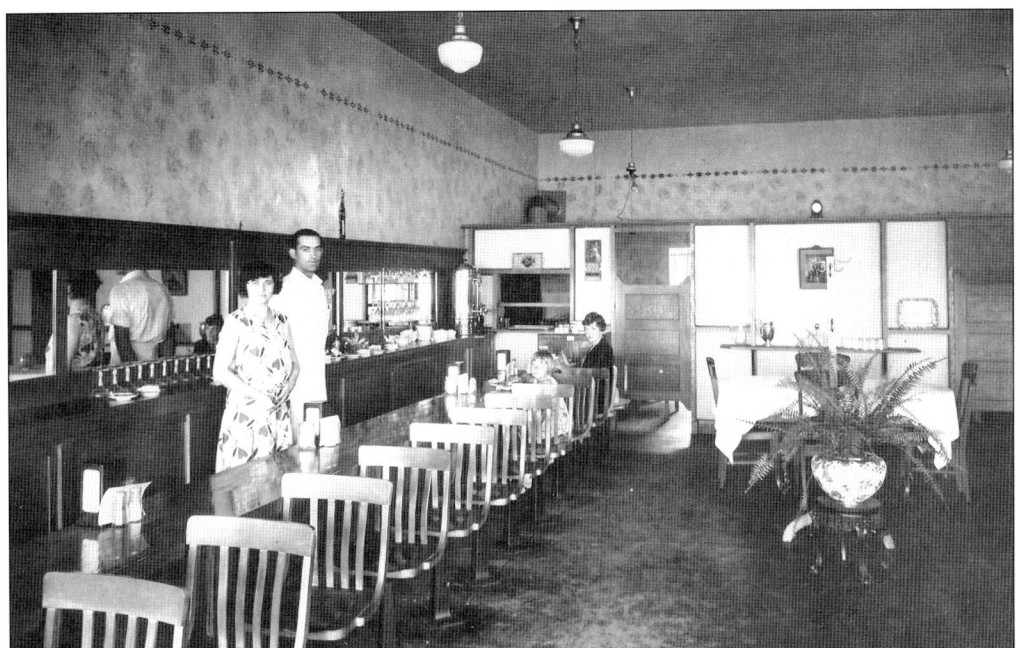

This is the interior of Ben's Café c. 1938. Located in downtown Old Mission Beach, it was usually much busier than in this scene. The selection of public eating places was somewhat limited to a few neighborhood favorites. Ben's later became Eckles' Steak House and Card Room. (Courtesy of Marge Harris.)

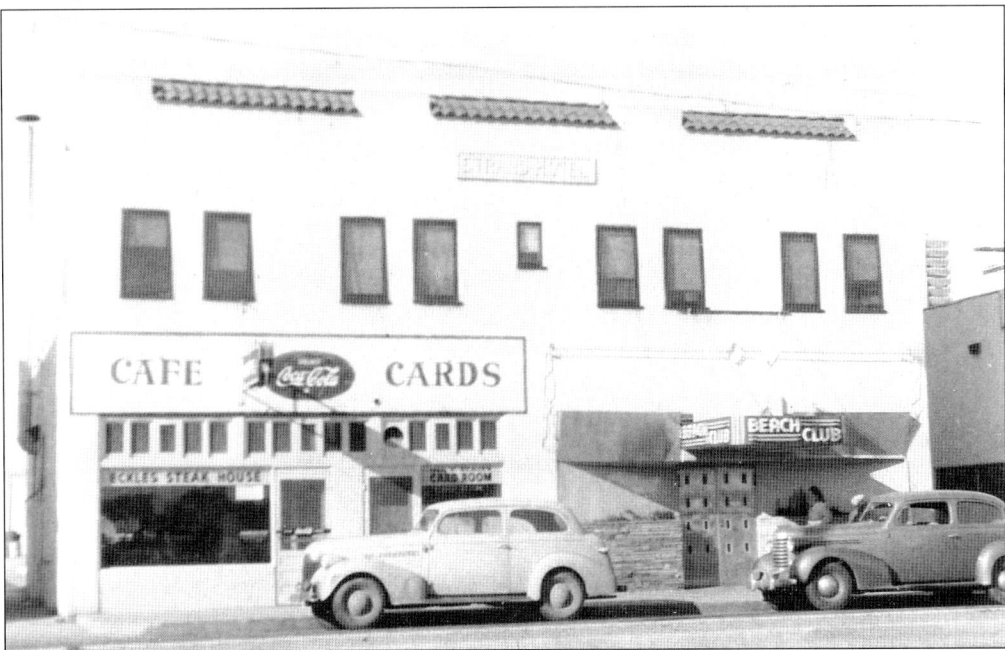

The Strand Hotel occupied the floor above Eckles' Steak House and Card Room and the Beach Club bar in this c. 1940 scene. The building sits on the corner of Mission Boulevard and Queenstown Court. Queenstown is just to the right of the Beach Club sign, behind the darker sedan. (Courtesy of Marge Harris.)

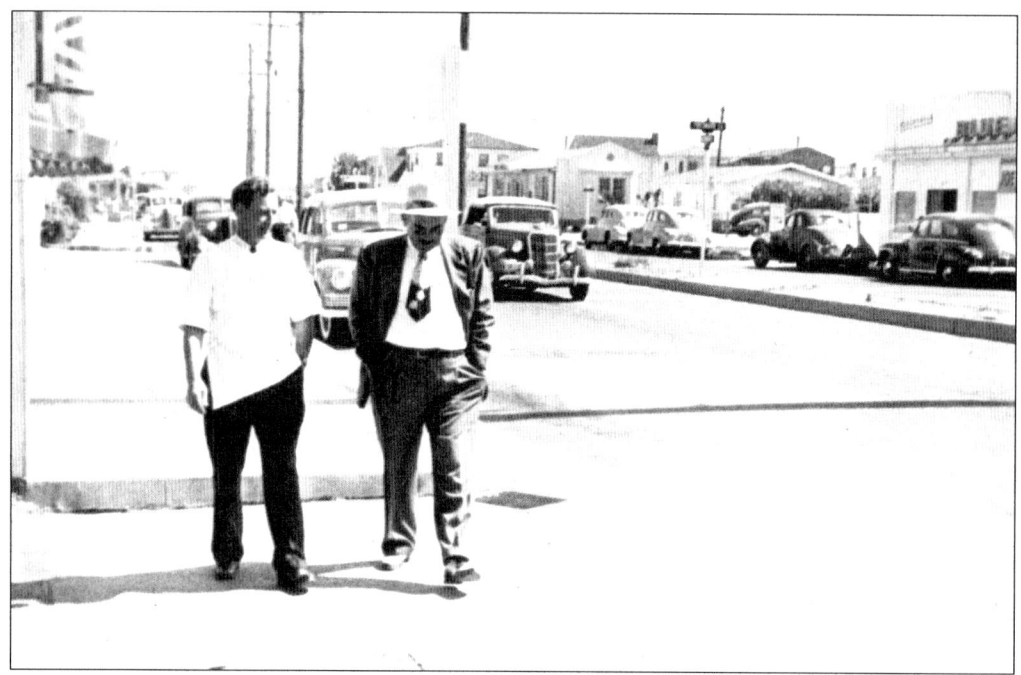

Walt the barber and an unidentified friend stroll Mission Boulevard in 1947. There were two barbershops—Walt's and Fred's (Wright)—in the Old Mission Beach business district. The sandy, salt-encrusted hair on the kids must have been a challenge when parents forced the kids to leave the beach for a few minutes to get their haircut. The building on the right is the Blue Pacific bar and restaurant. (Courtesy of authors.)

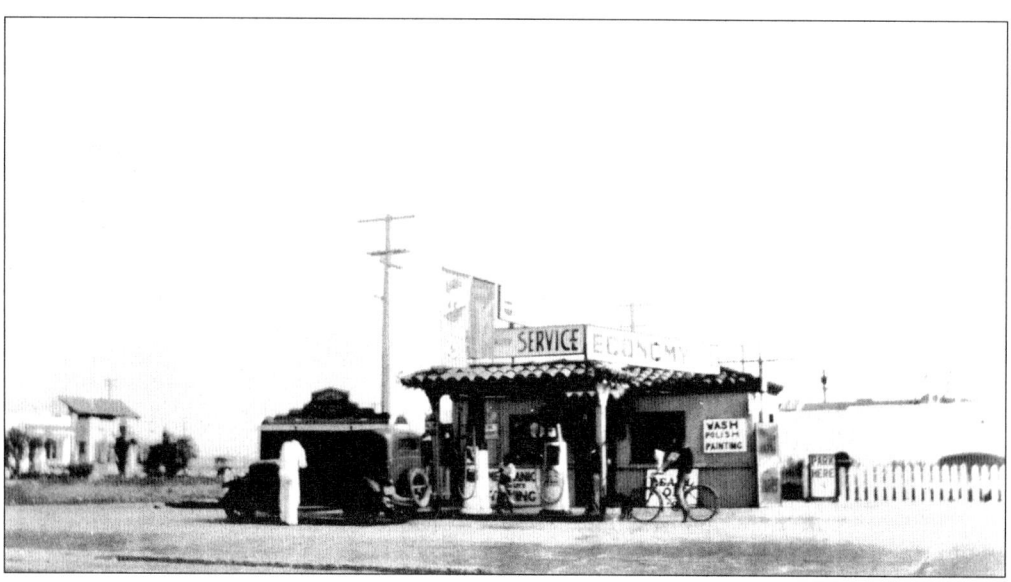

In 1936, the Bonita Cove Service Station sat at the northeast corner of Mission Boulevard and Ventura Place. Owner Ed Crie waits on a customer while one son, Don, fills the gas pump and the other, John, rides a bicycle. The building on the right is Crie's boat repair and part-time living quarters. (Courtesy of Don Crie.)

In 1939, huge storm waves and high tides caused extensive flooding and some damage in Mission Beach. Much rain and additional flooding from the San Diego River accompanied this January storm. To add to the confusion, hundreds of small water snakes washed down from the river making wading around quite interesting. High waters caused the wooden sidewalks on the courts to float away. They were soon replaced with the concrete walkways of today. (Courtesy of Don Crie.)

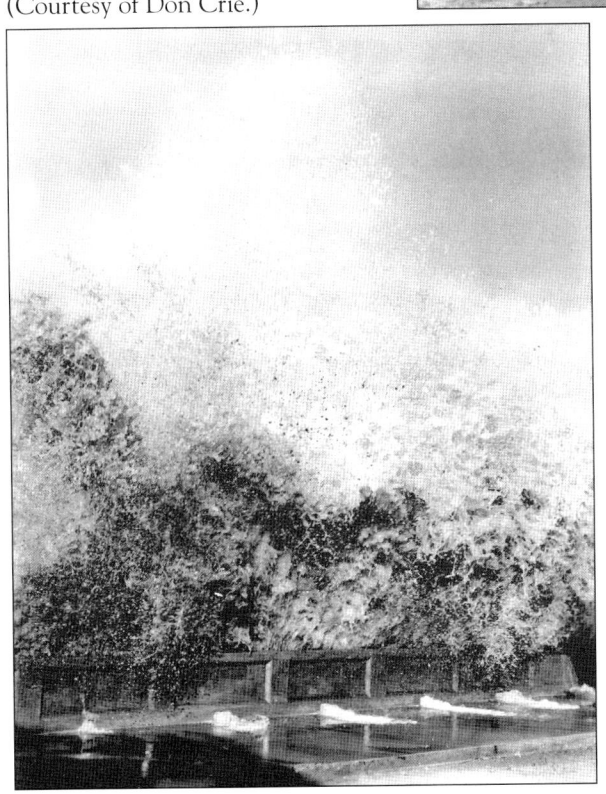

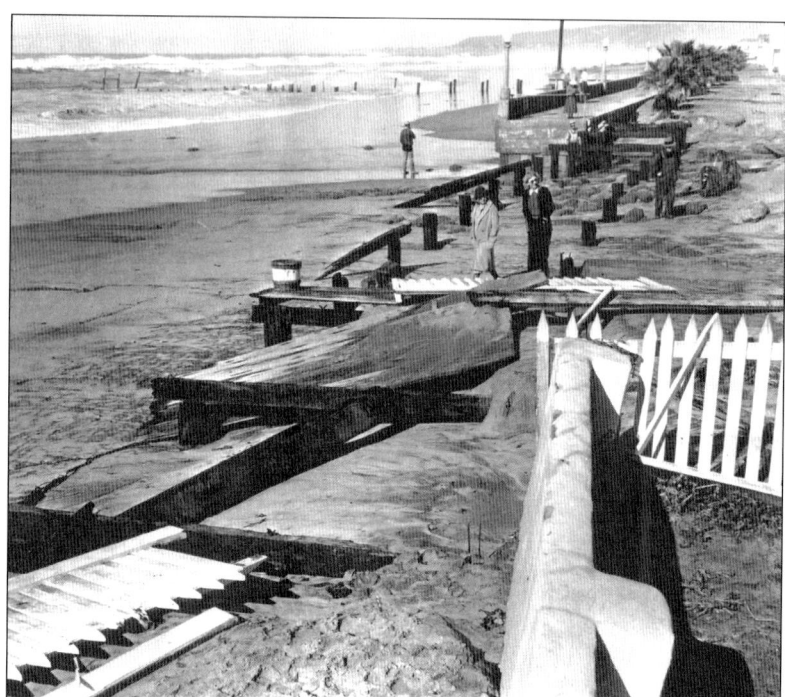

The oceanfront seawall stopped at Balboa Court in 1939, but it became apparent in the storm aftermath that the wall must be extended south to the end of Mission Beach. However, that extension was not completed until the 1960s. (Courtesy of John Chadwick.)

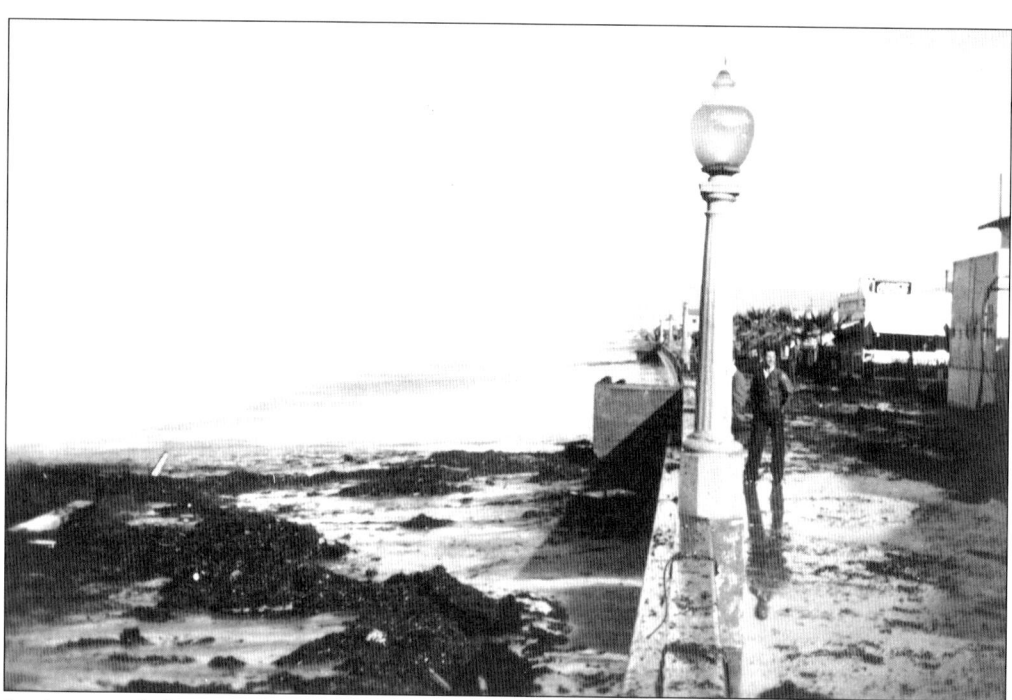

Looking north from Queenstown Court right after the storm shows the mess left by the flooding. The building in the right foreground is the Old Mission Beach Bathhouse, and the building behind it is Kay's Hamburger Stand. Both buildings survived undamaged thanks to the protection of the seawall. (Courtesy of authors.)

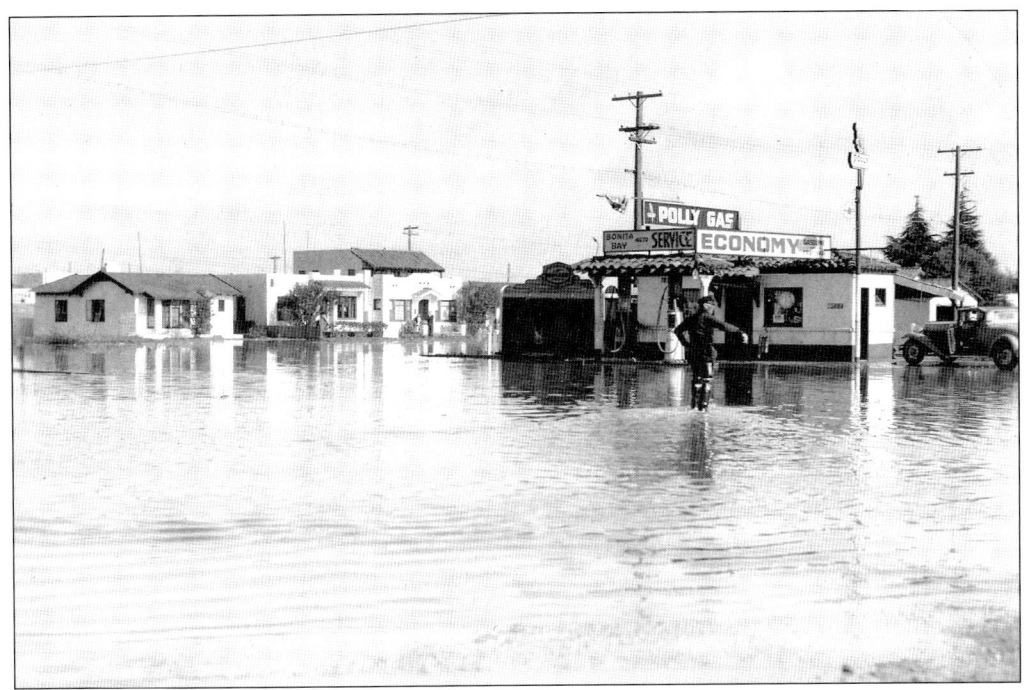

A policeman directs traffic during the flooding at Ventura Place and Mission Boulevard. Ed Crie's Bonita Cove Service Station has water up to the doorstep and does not appear to be open. The homes to the left are on Island Court. (Courtesy of Don Crie.)

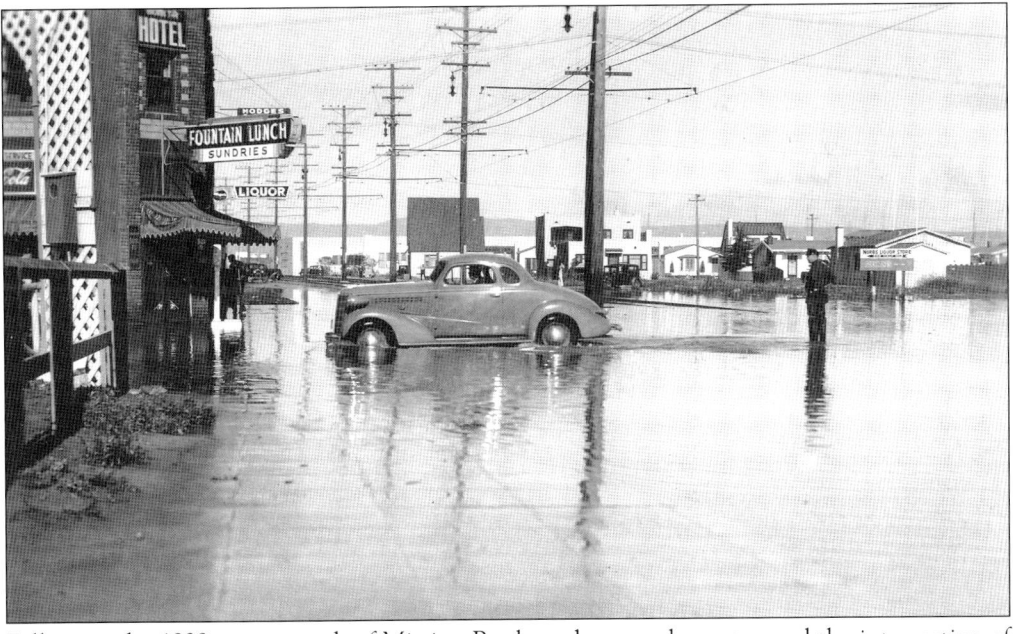

Following the 1939 storm, much of Mission Boulevard was under water, and the intersection of Ventura Place and Mission Boulevard was no exception. The policeman directs what little traffic there was. Not many drivers ventured out, unlike this person heading west on Ventura Place. The hotel and drugstore building on the left is on the northeast corner. Mission Beach School is in the background. (Courtesy of Don Crie.)

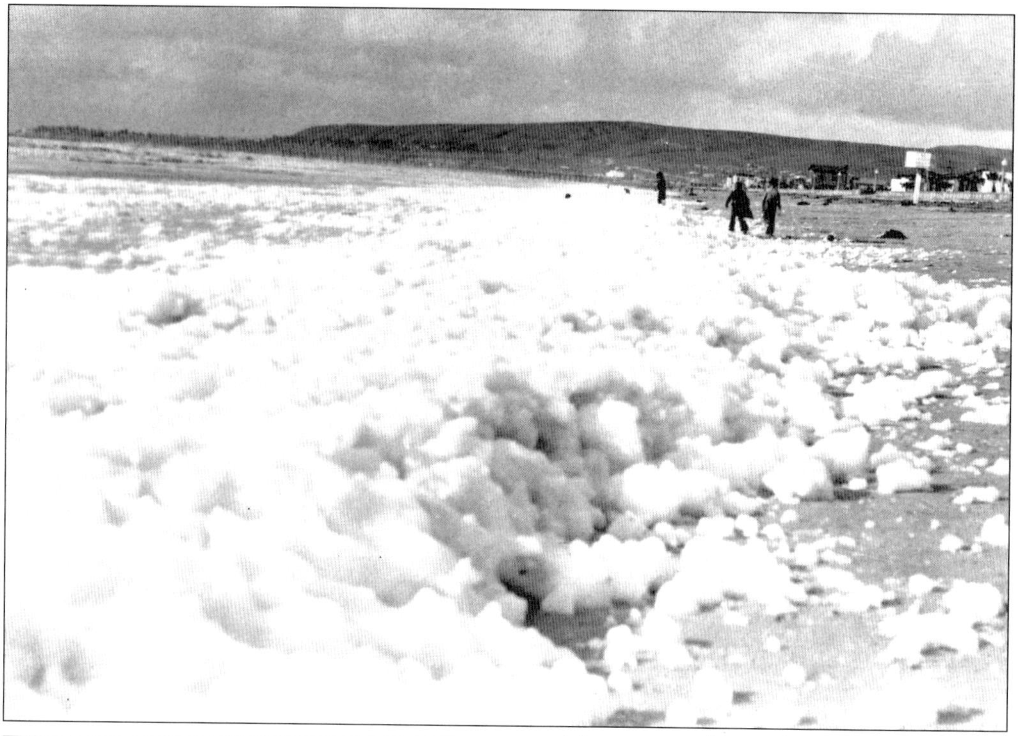

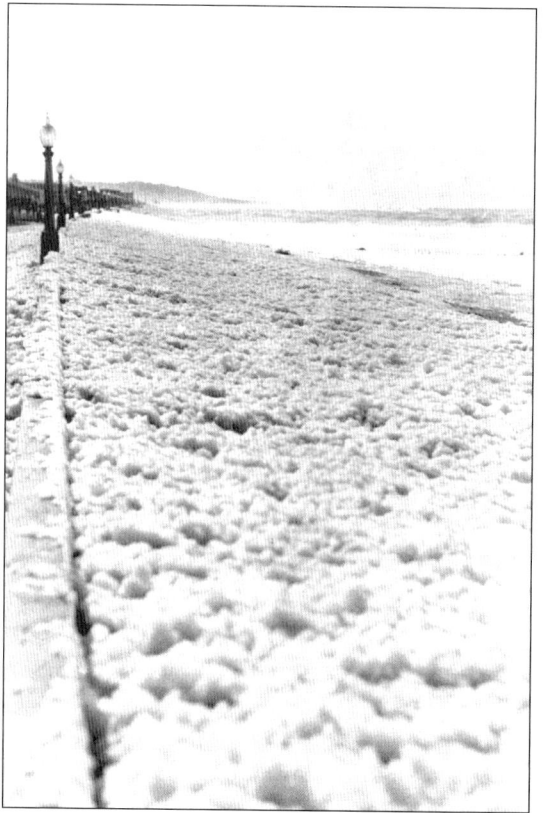

More storm aftermath created vast amounts of sea foam blown ashore by high winds. Residents strolled the beach in the upper scene. Later in the day, the winds had accumulated so much foam that it was stacked to the top of the seawall. Considering that much of the sand had been eroded away by the surf, the foam was 10 feet deep or more in places. It was quite a thrill for the beach kids to walk through the foam completely out of sight. (Courtesy of authors.)

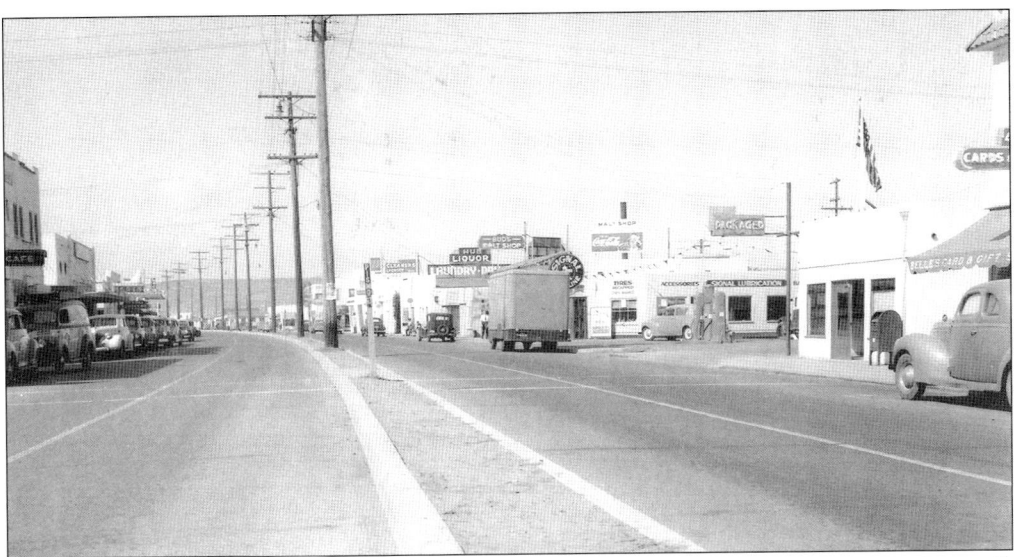

This view looks north along Mission Boulevard around Portsmouth Court *c.* 1946. The small, white building on the right at Pismo Court is the U.S. Post Office, and DiMarzio's Signal Station is directly beyond. Mission Beach was like many small towns, pretty much self contained, with enough stores and services to take care of its needs. Streetcar tracks were paved over in 1946.(Courtesy of Terry Polhamus Mendoza.)

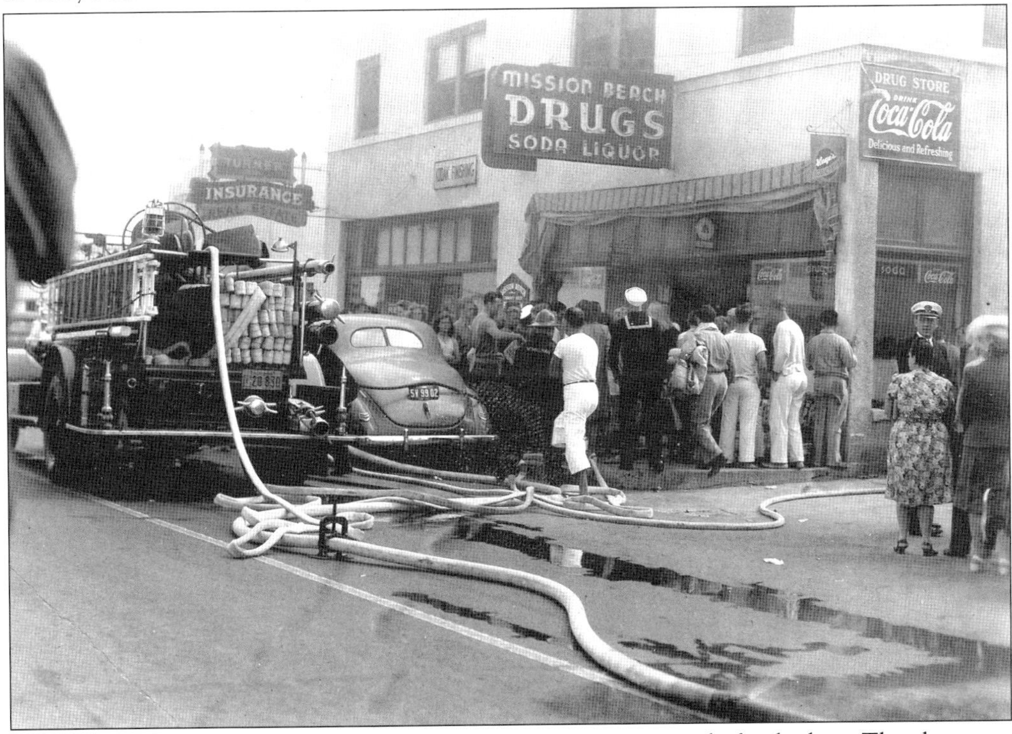

A 1947 fire in the Mission Beach Drugstore building draws a crowd of onlookers. This drugstore and old-fashioned fountain was a favorite hangout for the kids. Gordon Turner Realty and Insurance office is next door to the drugstore. The Turners were early residents of Mission Beach, and Kendall Turner was the first boy to be born here. (Courtesy of Ann Howe Mansfield.)

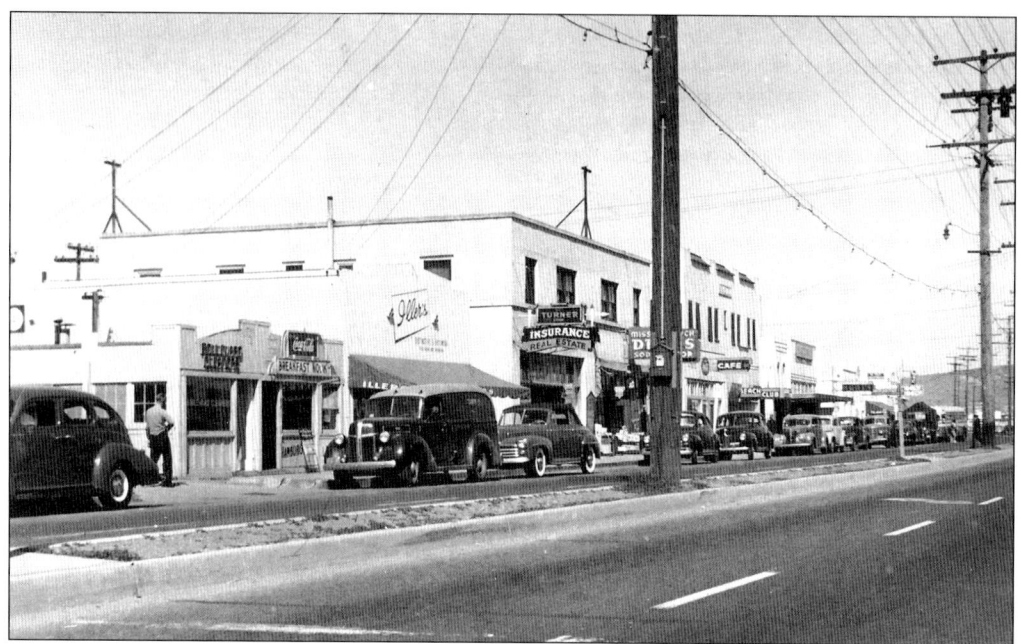

Everything that a small town needs is here in 1945. From left to right are a small café, Iller's Variety Store, Turner Realty and Insurance, and Mission Beach Drugstore and soda fountain. Beyond is Eckles' Steak House and Card Room, Beach Club Bar, Safeway market, Elledge's Meat Market, Ritz Bar (now Saska's), Claspell's Clothing Store, and Piggly Wiggly market. (Courtesy of Marge Harris.)

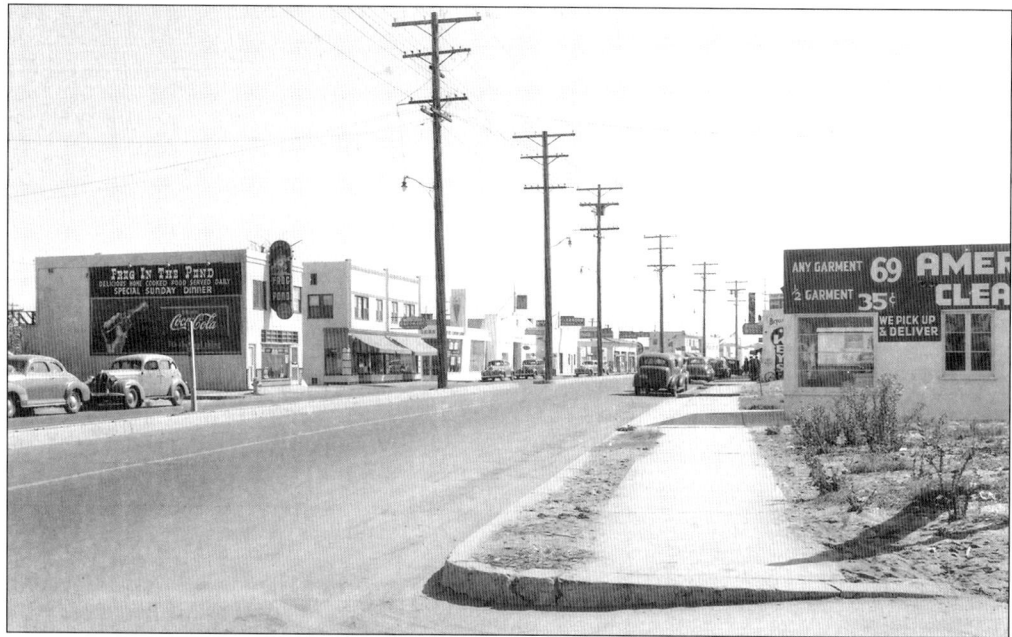

Looking south along the east side of Mission Boulevard from Salem Court are, from left to right, the Frog in the Pond Restaurant, Pappert's Hardware Store, Midway Malt Shop, and Al King's Garage. On the right is American Cleaners, where any garment could be cleaned for 69¢, half garment for 35¢, and they picked up and delivered. What a deal! (Courtesy of Terry Polhamus Mendoza.)

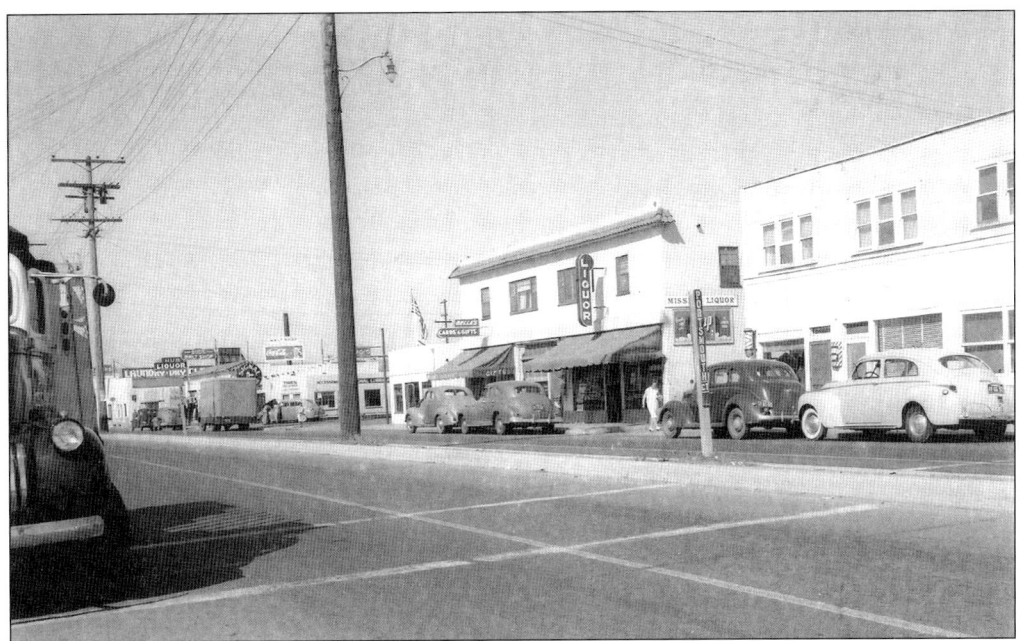

This c. 1946 scene shows the east side of the boulevard at Portsmouth Court. Originally Portsmouth Court was named Palm Court; it was later changed to conform to the theme of all the courts being named for seaside communities around the world. The courts are generally in alphabetical order, running from south to north. Portsmouth Court is an exception, due to the name change, coming before Pismo. (Courtesy of Terry Polhamus Mendoza.)

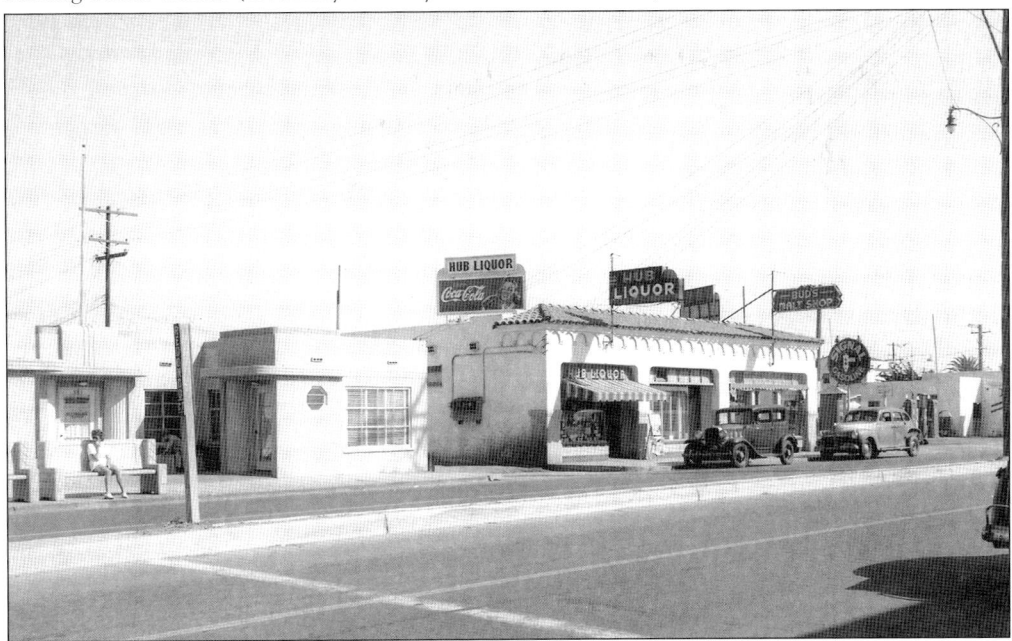

Right after World War II, in 1946, it was common to see 1930s vintage cars on the road. Auto manufacturers reconfigured their production lines to produce tanks, trucks, and jeeps necessary for fighting the war. It wasn't until 1946 that the new cars started hitting the market. Hub Liquor and DiMarzio's Signal Station are seen in this view. (Courtesy of Terry Polhamus Mendoza.)

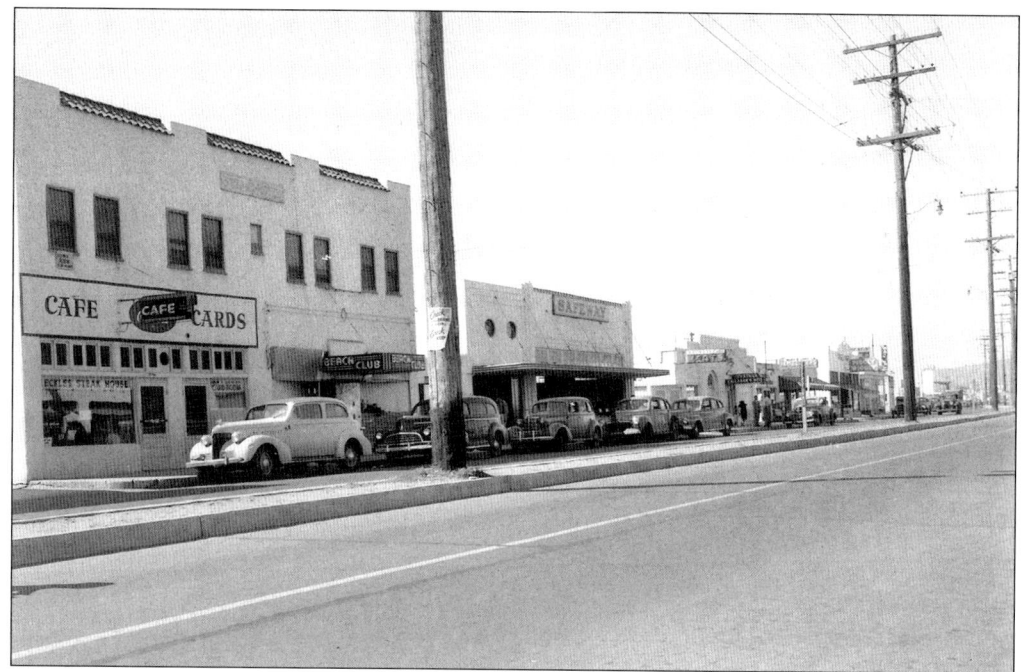

Pictured is the Safeway Market in 1946. The next building houses Elledge's Meat Market and the Ritz. Beyond is Claspell's Clothing Store, and the larger building at the end is the Piggly Wiggly market. Mission Beach really was a complete small town. (Courtesy of Terry Polhamus Mendoza.)

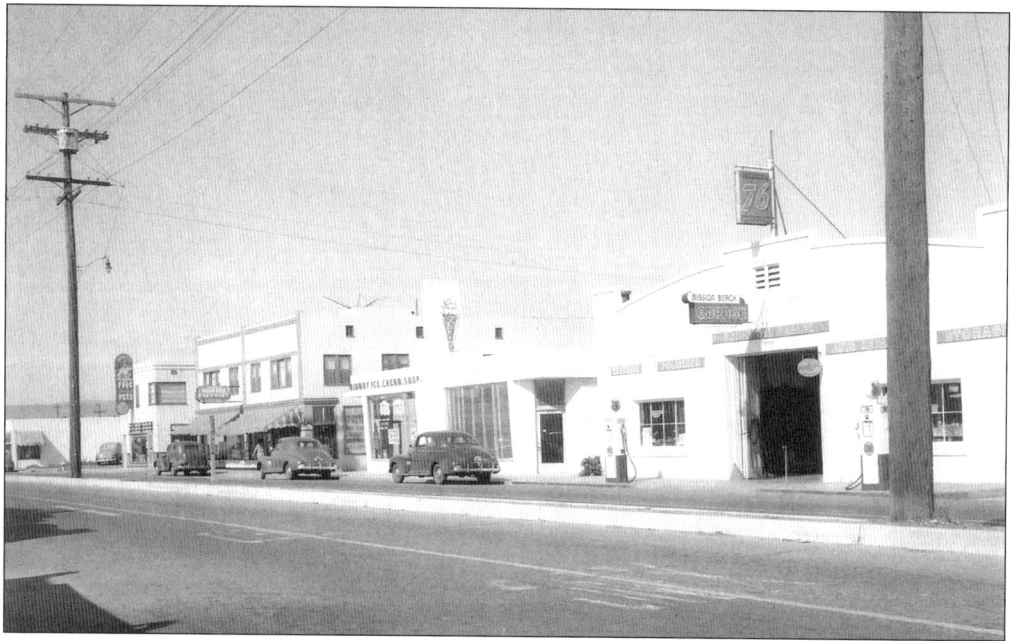

Al King operated the Mission Beach Garage for many years in the former home of Mission Beach Lumber Company. Midway Ice Cream Shop, Pappert's Hardware Store, and the Frog in the Pond Restaurant are from right to left beyond the garage in 1946. (Courtesy of Terry Polhamus Mendoza.)

Six
MISSION BAY

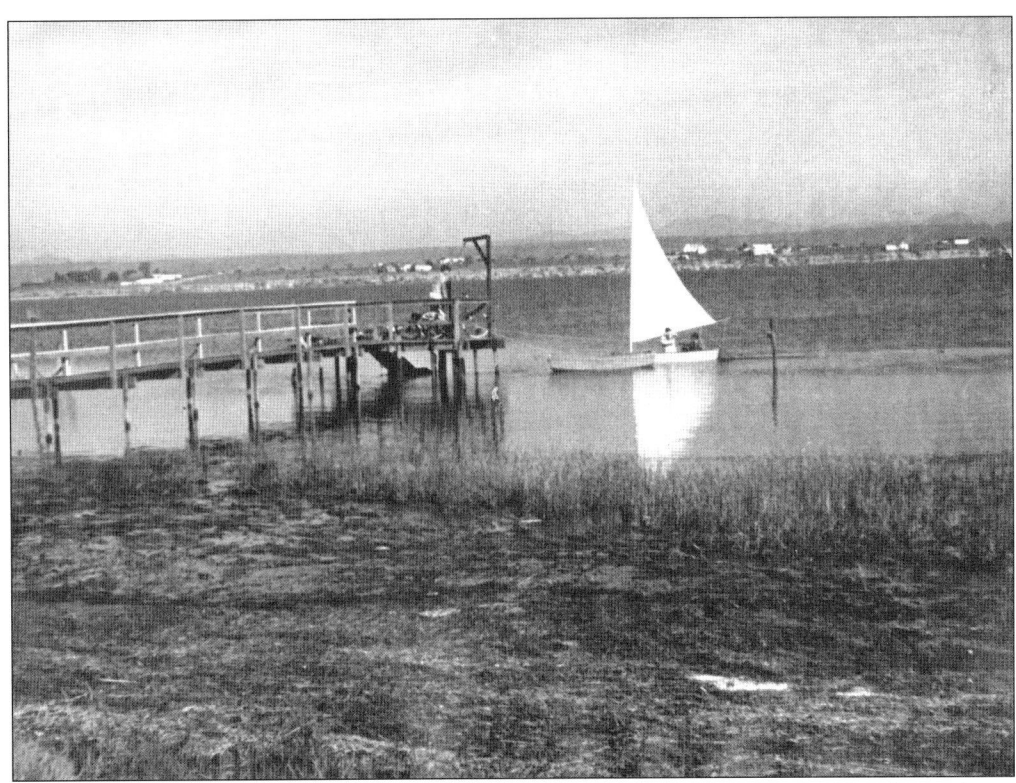

Mission Bay, prior to the dredging, was dotted with privately owned piers such as the Walton's pictured around 1939. The bay had a muddy bottom and shoreline that promoted the growth of the saltwater grasses. Clams, minnows, and larger fish were abundant. Crown Point, in the background, is sparsely populated with few houses. (Courtesy of Mike Curren.)

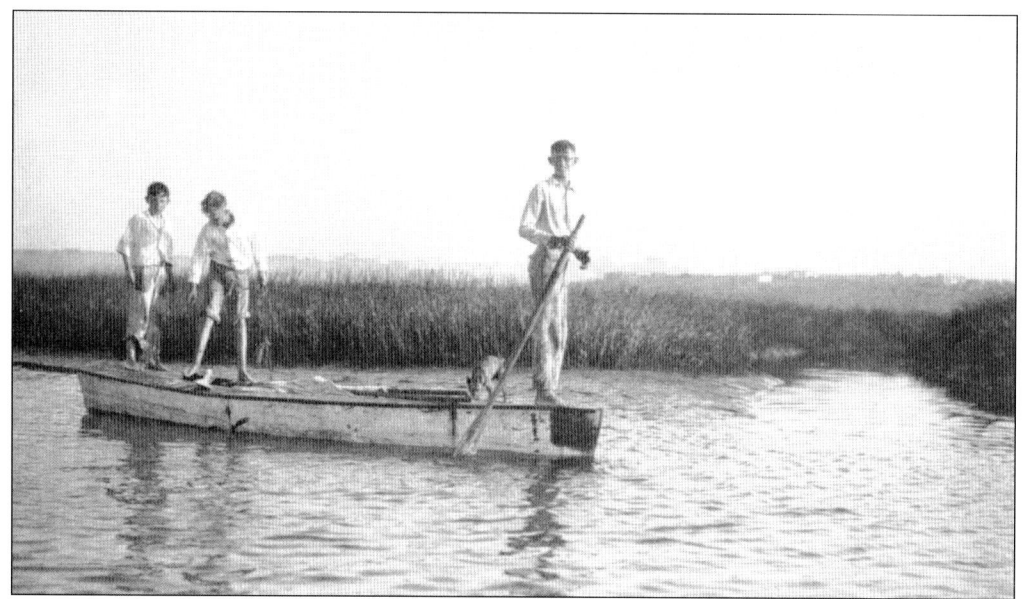

Three boys and a dog are trying to push their boat off the mudflats at low tide in this 1932 scene. It was only as a last result that one would get out and wade to push the boat free, due to the many stingrays that populated Mission Bay. Dredging in the late 1940s got rid of the reeds and mud, greatly reducing the number of rays. (Courtesy of Dee Lang.)

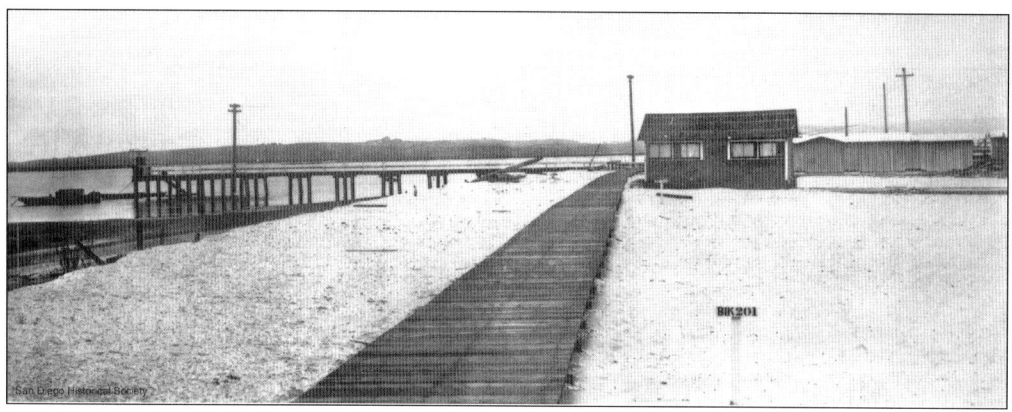

In 1915, Bayside Walk was constructed of wooden boards nailed to planks lying on the sand. Block 201 in the foreground was for sale; all that was needed was $1,000 or so per lot. Today each lot is worth $1 million to $1.5 million. Then, of course, there is the added cost of building the home. (Courtesy of SDHS.)

Al Harris and his daughter Elaine are showing off their catch of white sea bass, known locally as sea trout, from Mission Bay in 1925. The bay was a natural spawning ground for these fish, and they were a big favorite of the locals. (Courtesy of Marge Harris.)

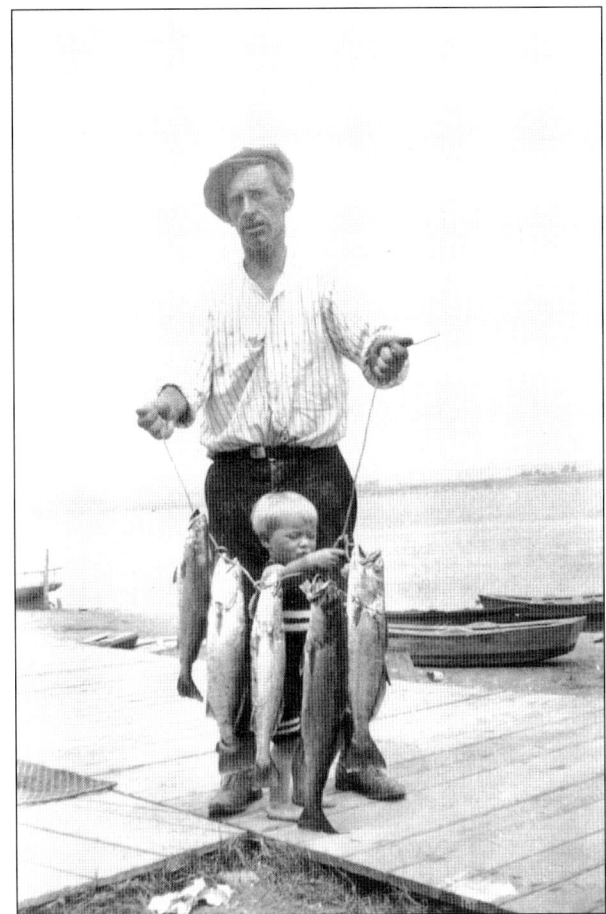

Foerster's pier was located at the southernmost end of Mission Bay, near the channel entrance. In 1941, the bay was undeveloped with a rocky and sandy shoreline. The rocky point just beyond the pier was typical along the bayfront. (Courtesy of Jackie Linstrom.)

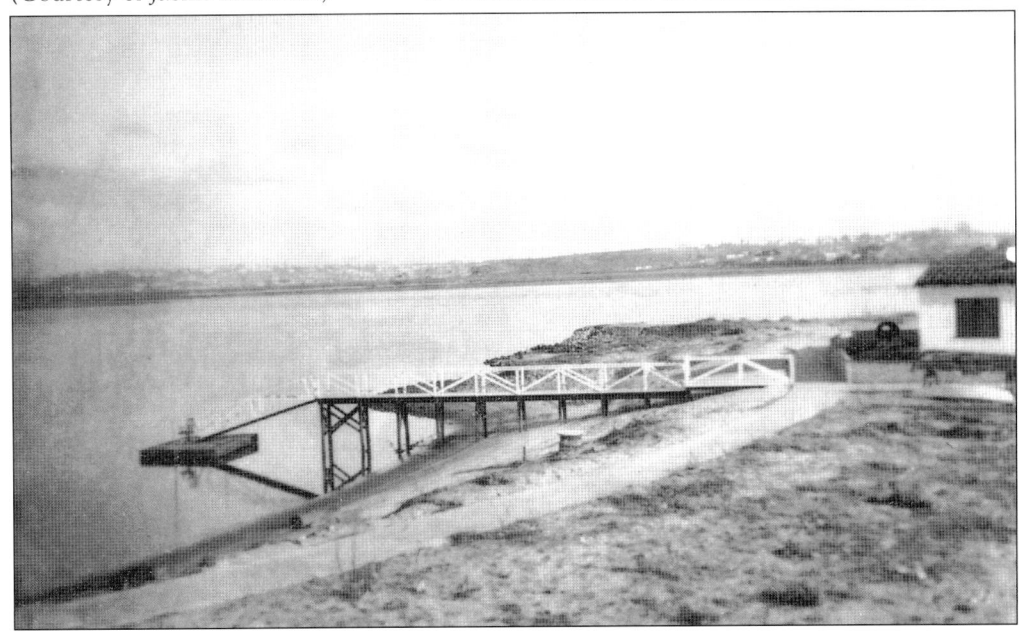

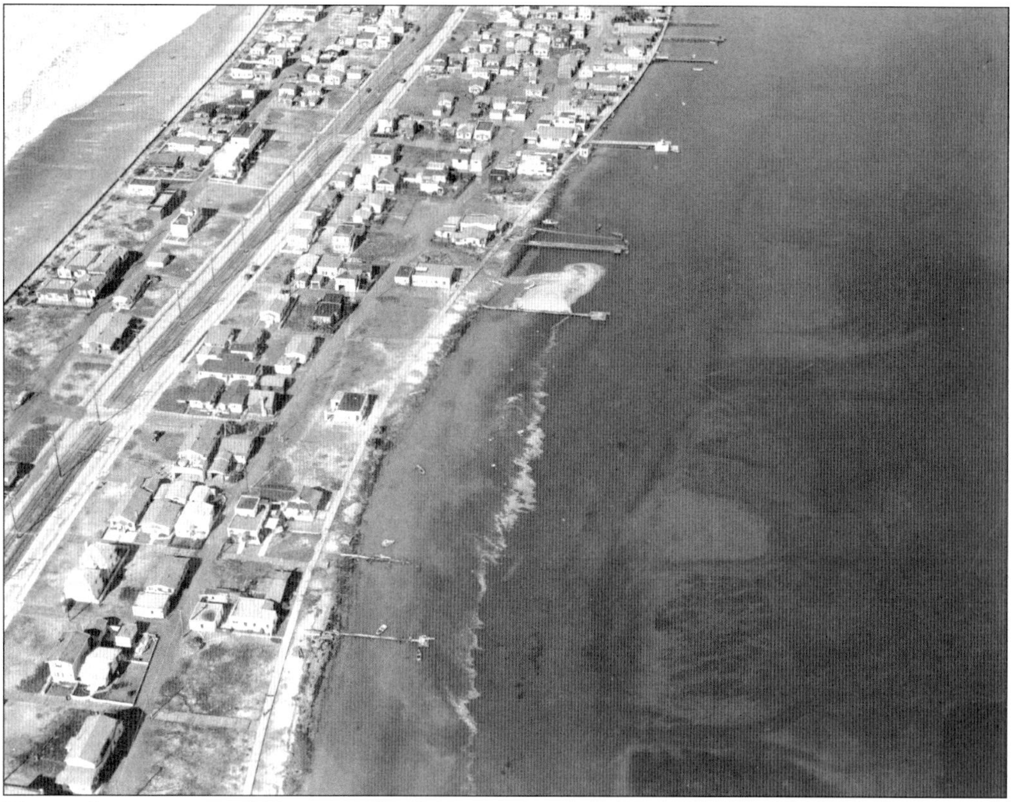

This early 1939 scene, looking north, shows Mission Beach and Mission Bay from around San Luis Obispo Place. Many private piers line the shore, and the mudflats are visible. The courts are still made of wood, and there are plenty of undeveloped lots. (Courtesy of SDHS.)

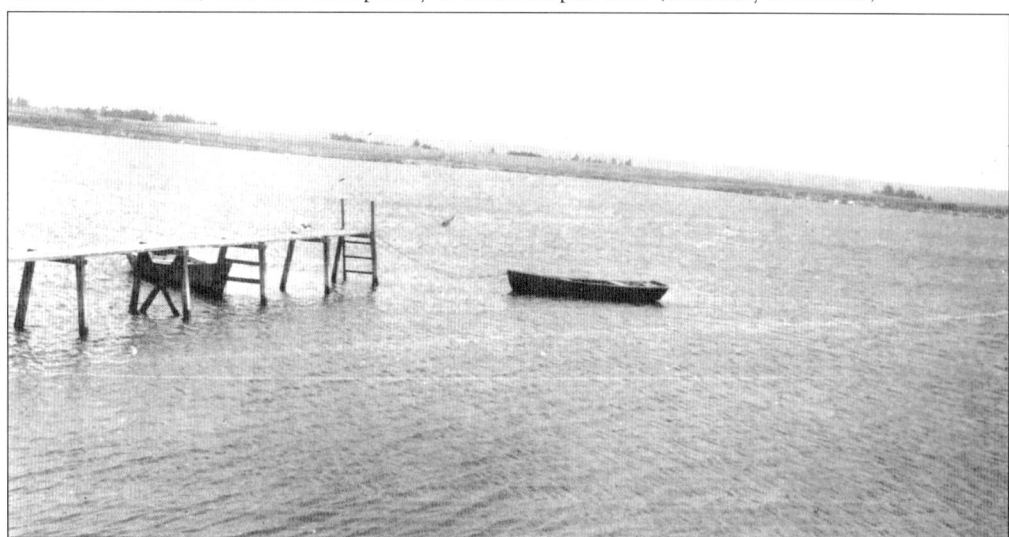

This ramshackle pier was near San Raphael Place in 1923. These piers were built by anyone who wanted to, and there were no construction or safety standards—people used the structures at their own risk. There are no buildings on Crown Point across the bay. (Courtesy of Ann Howe Mansfield.)

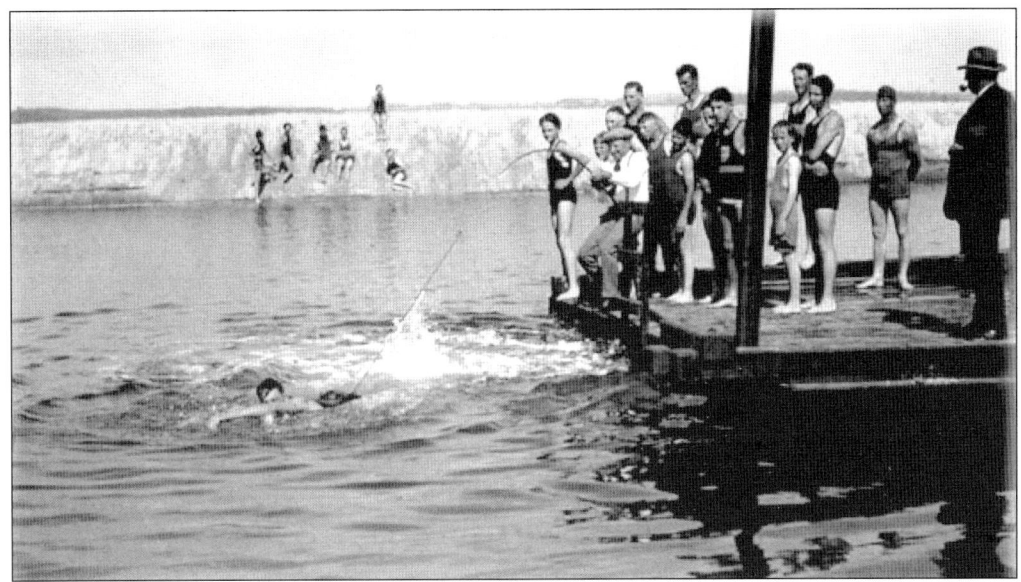

In the 1930s, swimming lessons were provided at Bonita Cove, opposite the Mission Beach Amusement Center. The instructor here attached a fishing line to the student and pulled hard to keep him near the dock. Note that a necktie was normal attire, even when reeling in the "big one." (Courtesy of authors.)

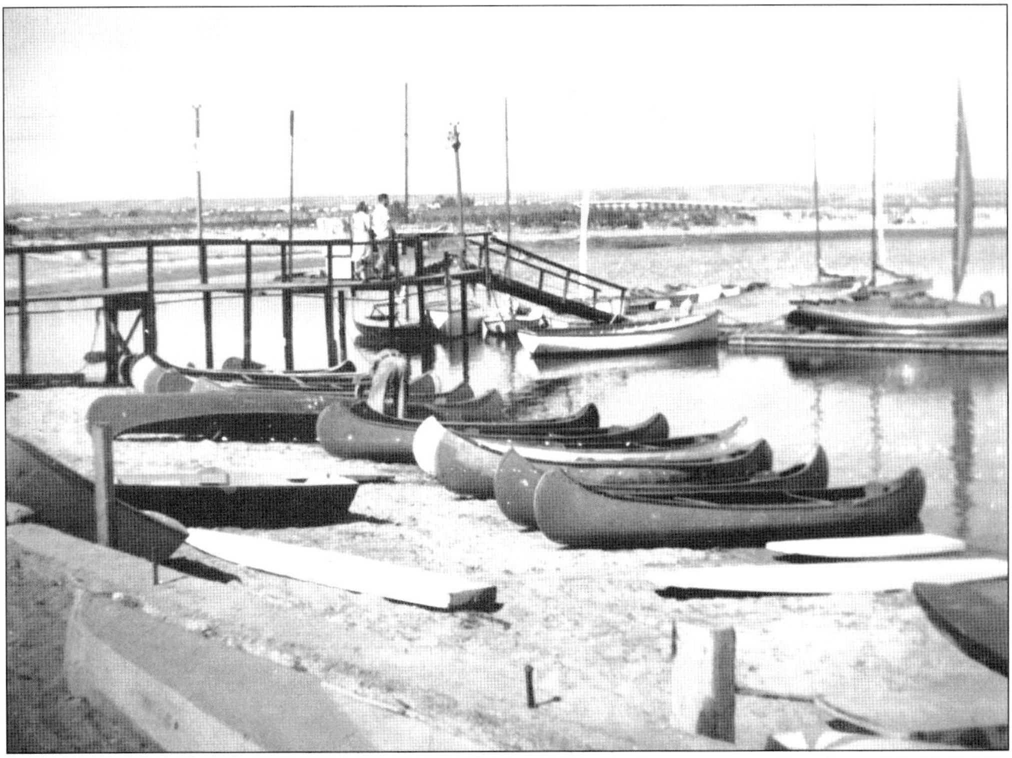

Ed Crie operated a boat and canoe rental service in Bonita Cove, pictured on June 26, 1942. He also ran a nearby gas station and boat repair business. (Courtesy of Don Crie.)

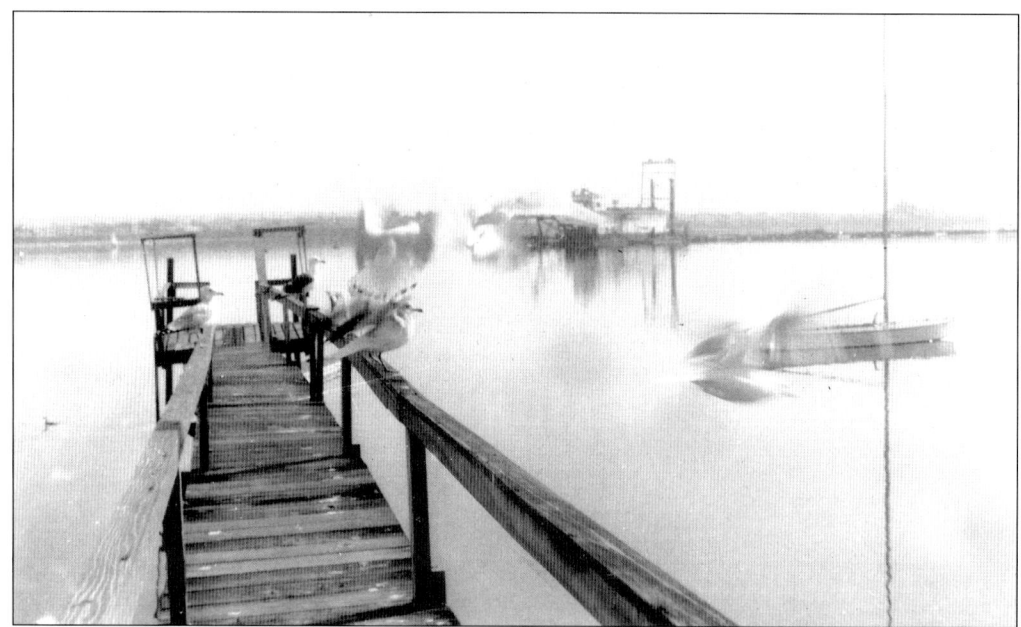

By 1946, dredging had begun in Mission Bay. Beyond this very shaky pier and the watchful seagulls, the dredge is beginning to deepen Mission Bay, remove the mudflats, and transform the bay into a beautiful, fully usable recreation area. The blurred images are seagulls taking flight. (Courtesy of Ann Howe Mansfield.)

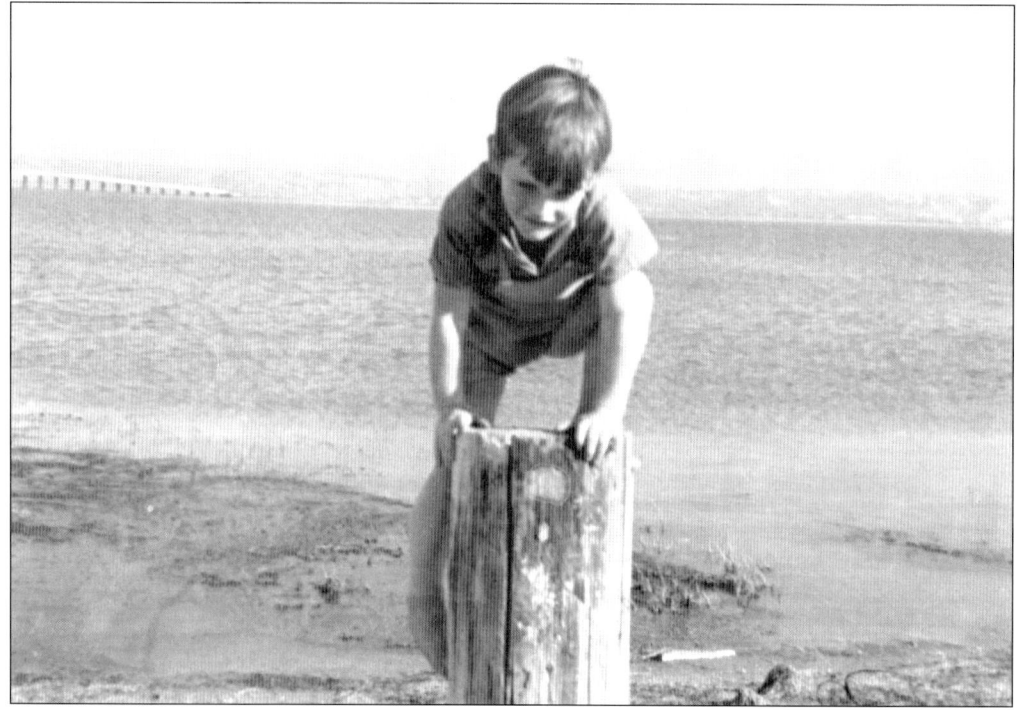

Five-year-old Terry Curren scales an old pier piling in 1939. A great place to grow up, Mission Beach was a wide, open playground with unlimited opportunities for exploration. The kids could swim, fish, build rafts, and run free in those carefree days. (Courtesy of Mike Curren.)

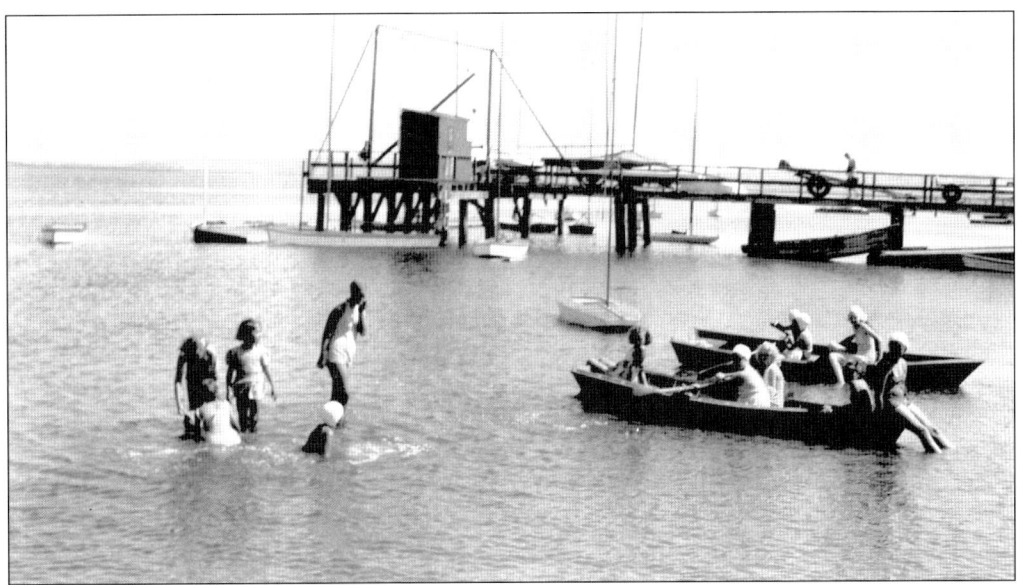

Ann Howe celebrates her birthday in 1945, a year before the dredging began. Asher's pier is now also the docking area for the boats of Mission Bay Yacht Club. (Courtesy of Ann Howe Mansfield.)

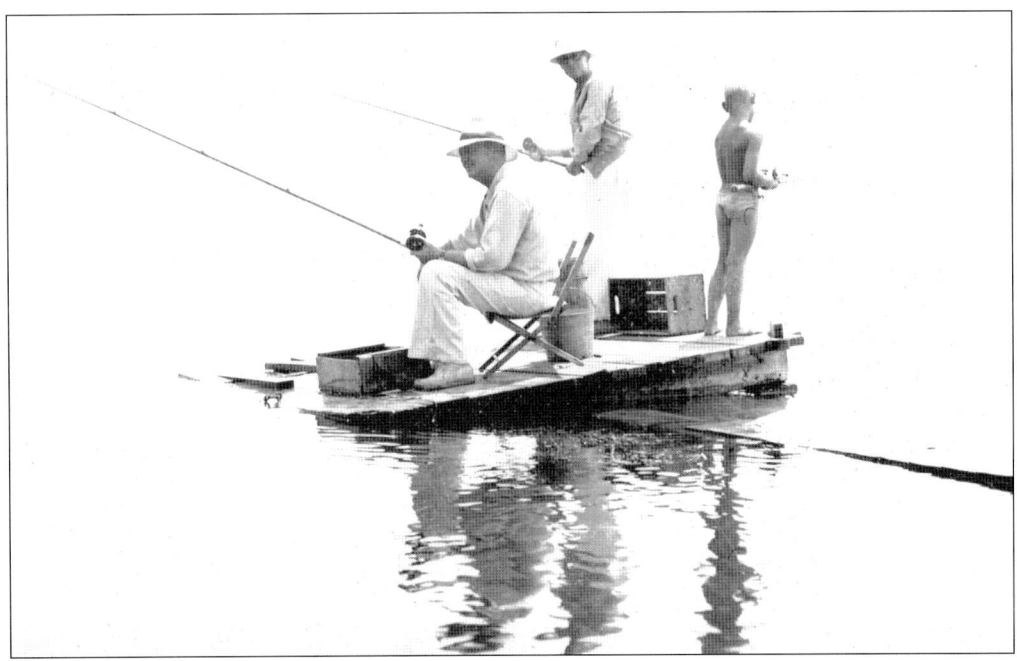

A listing float, partly awash, is no deterrent to these fishermen. Seen here c. 1945 are, from left to right, Roger Howe, Stan Howe, and Skipper Smith. The walkway to the float does not appear to be very safe, but people were not worried about lawsuits then. (Courtesy of Ann Howe Mansfield.)

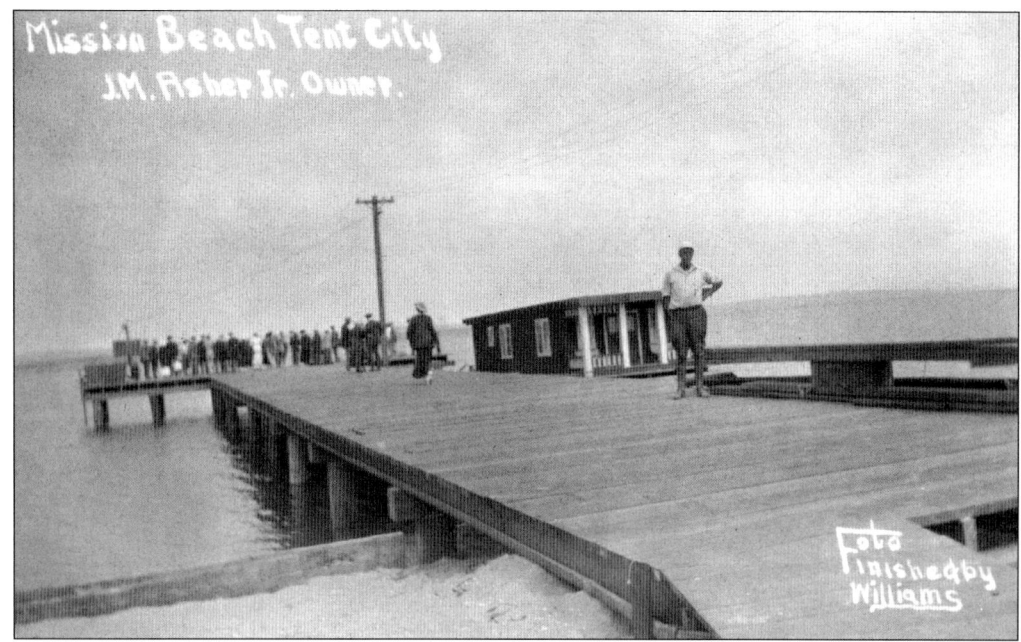

J. M. Asher Jr. stands on his newly built pier, and many visitors admire the vista of Mission Bay. This early scene shows the pier prior to the construction of railings and a boat landing. Asher subdivided and developed all of Mission Beach north of Santa Clara Place. (Courtesy of Willie Skinner.)

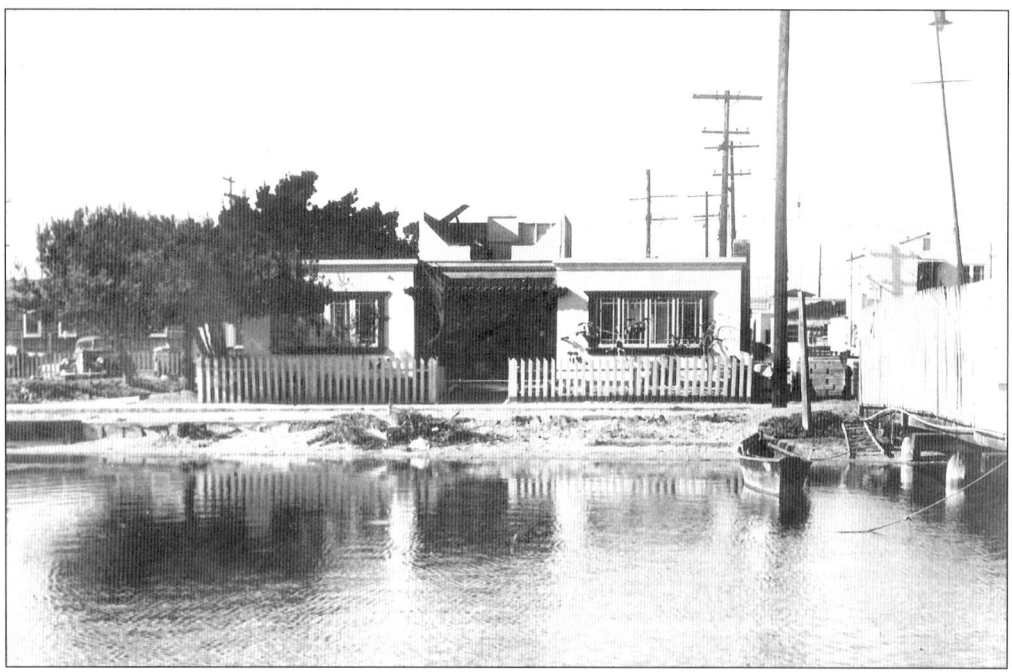

This is J. M. Asher's home around 1938. Asher's pier is to the right of the photograph. High tide has brought the water near the wooden walkway. Wood shoring is visible at left, trying to prevent erosion of the shoreline and to protect the walkway. The storms of 1939 washed out the walks and led to permanent concrete ones. (Courtesy of Willie Skinner.)

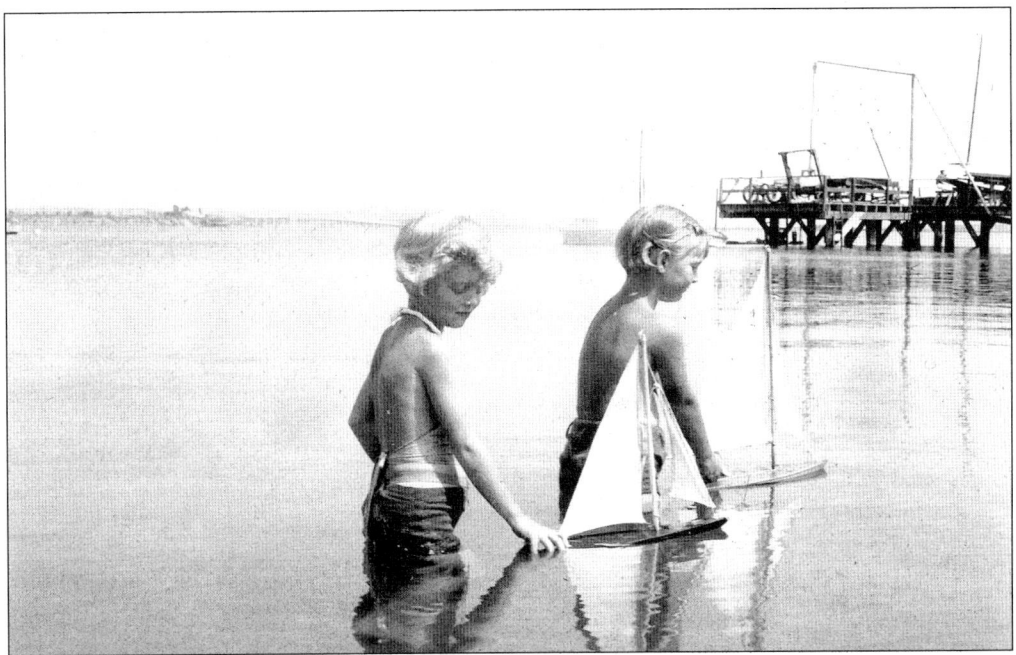

Kids with toy sailboats enjoy a calm day on Mission Bay in 1937. The bay provided a marvelous playground where children could let their imaginations run. There were no television or video games to occupy the youngsters, so they created their own entertainment. (Courtesy of Ann Howe Mansfield.)

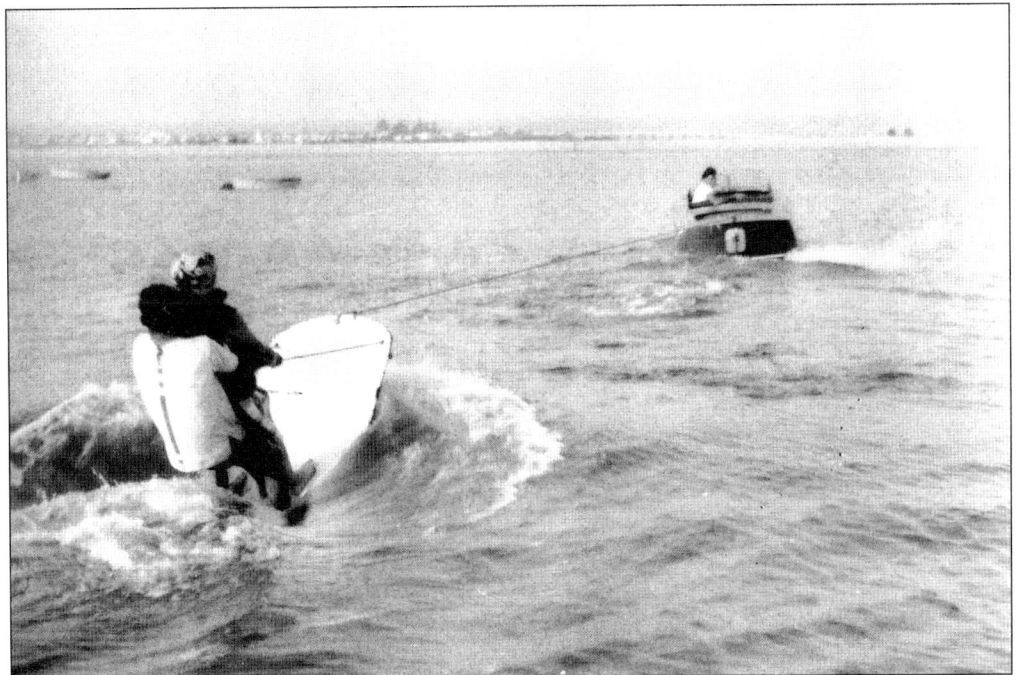

Before the introduction of water skis, aquaplaning was the thrill of the day. Here, c. 1940, Ed Crie is driving the boat as an instructor teaches a student the technique of the sport. Before long, the aquaplane was considered too easy, and along came water skis. (Courtesy of Don Crie.)

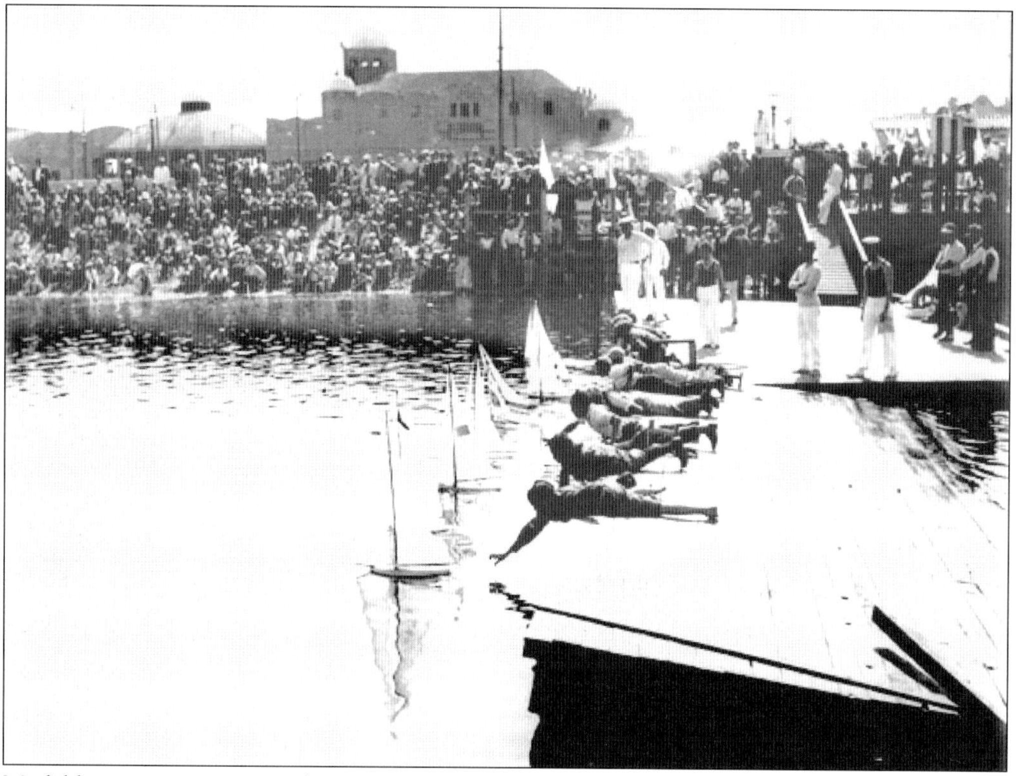

Model-boat racing was a popular activity around 1927. Here in Bonita Cove, hundreds of spectators line the shoreline to watch the contest. Looking west, the amusement center is in the background. (Courtesy of authors.)

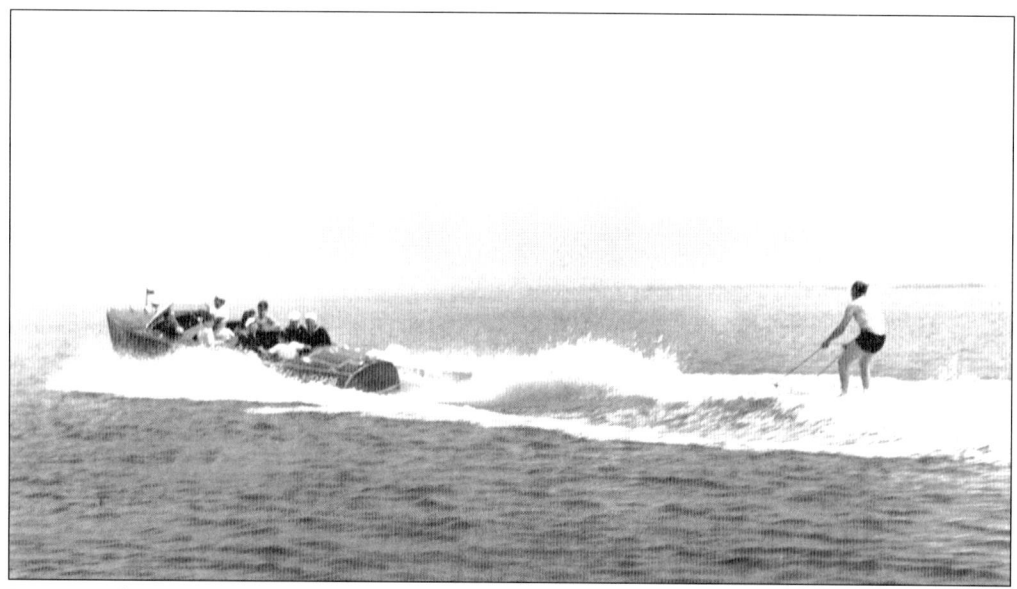
In 1942, Ed Crie is in the driver's seat of his speedboat *Buckaroo*, previously owned by Hollywood actor James Cagney. The man on the aquaplane appears somewhat uncertain but is hanging on. (Courtesy of Don Crie.)

By 1945, water skis had replaced the aquaplane. This group is using the dock as a takeoff spot. The Causeway Bridge to Crown Point is visible in the background, and a tall pole marks the beginning of the shallow water covering the mudflats. (Courtesy of Marge Harris.)

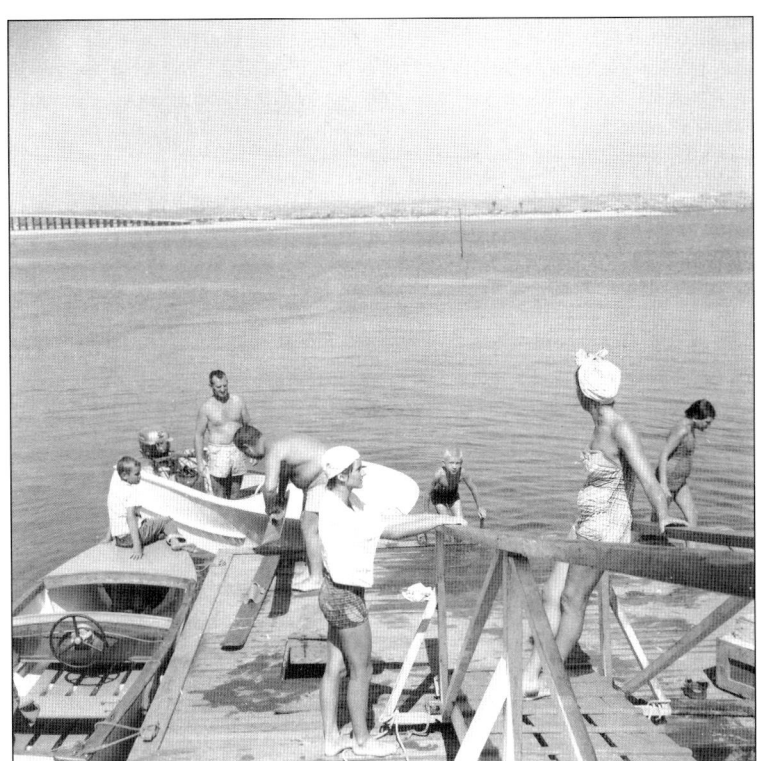

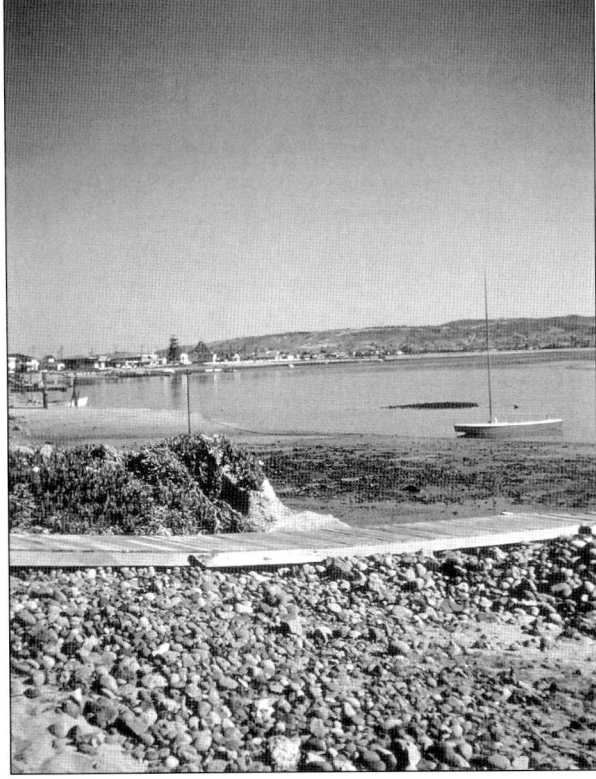

Looking north from the south end of Mission Bay c. 1946, the rocky shoreline would soon be covered with new sand dredged from the bay and channel, creating wonderful beaches and shorelines. The walkway was used to cross the rough beach to the water. At very low tide, as pictured, there was still an unpleasant walk through the grass and mud. (Courtesy of Jackie Linstrom.)

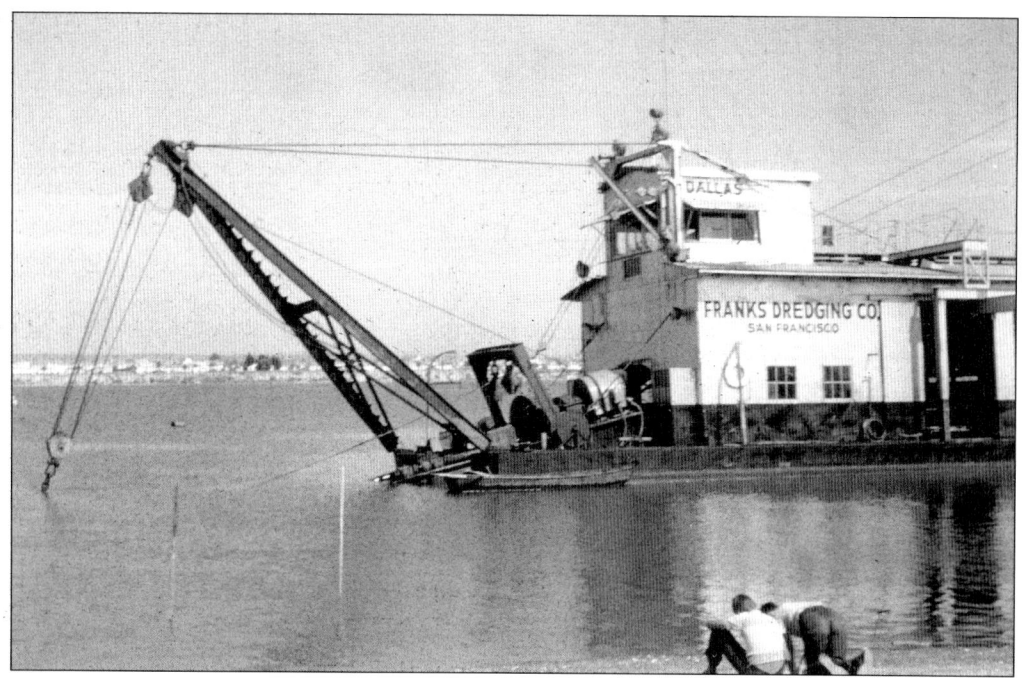

After several years of planning, the development of Mission Bay began in 1946. Frank's Dredging Company was hired by the City of San Diego to dredge the bay, develop the shoreline, create peninsulas into the bay, and open the bay to the ocean. One of the goals was to make the entire bay and channel navigable for larger boats. (Courtesy of Ann Howe Mansfield.)

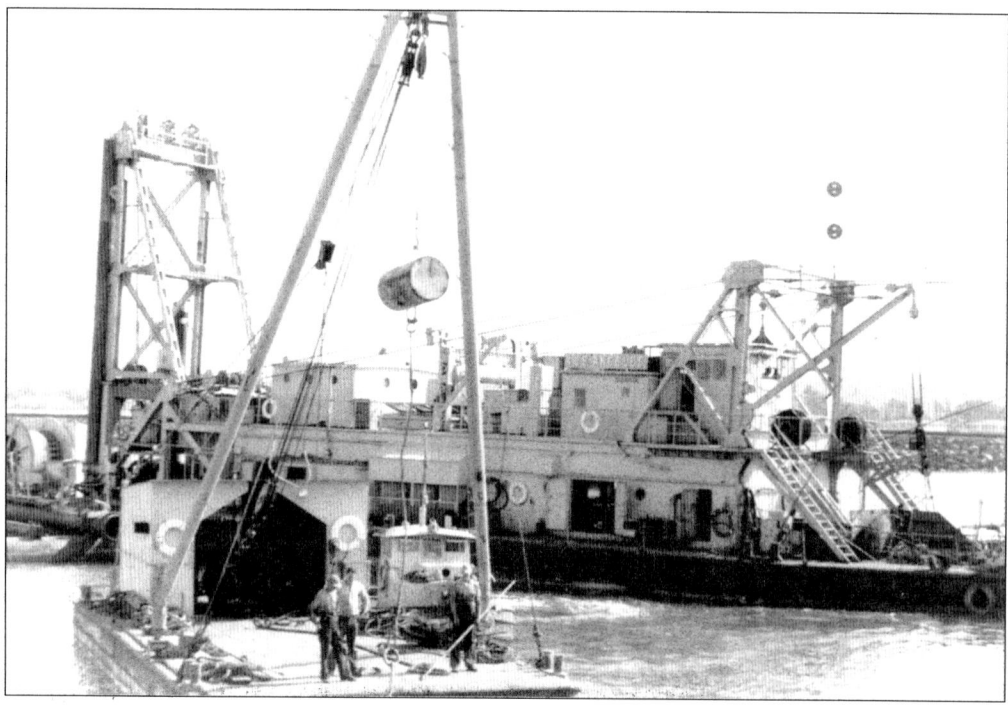

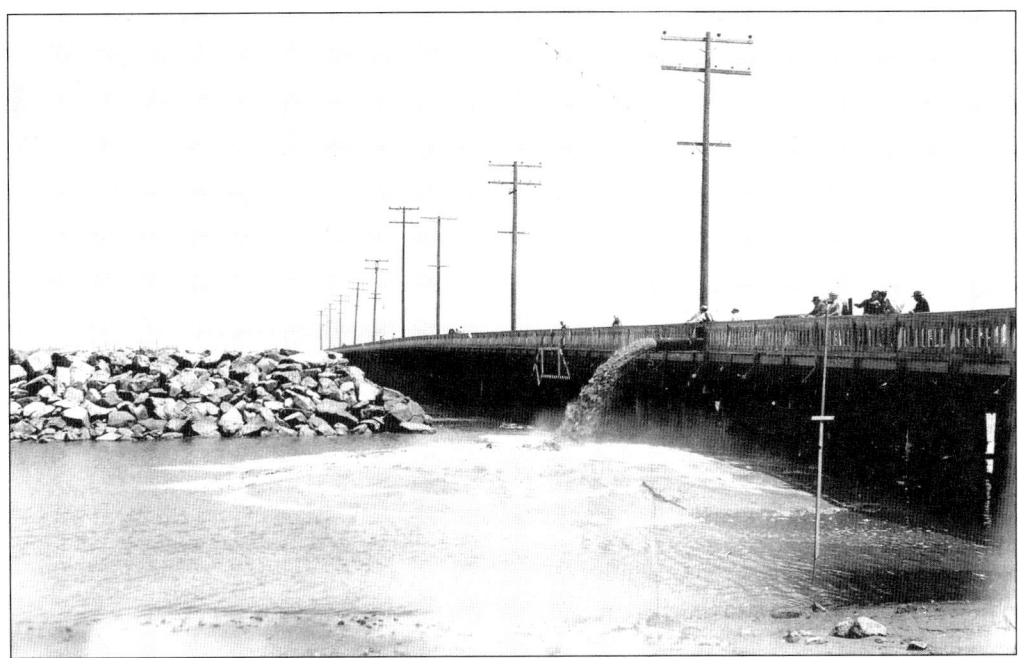

The Ocean Beach Bridge was scheduled for demolition as soon as the new Ventura Bridge could be built. New land was created with the dredge fill as seen around 1946. Miles of white-sand beaches would soon replace rocky and muddy shores. The small crossbar on the white pole indicates the future sand level. (Courtesy of authors.)

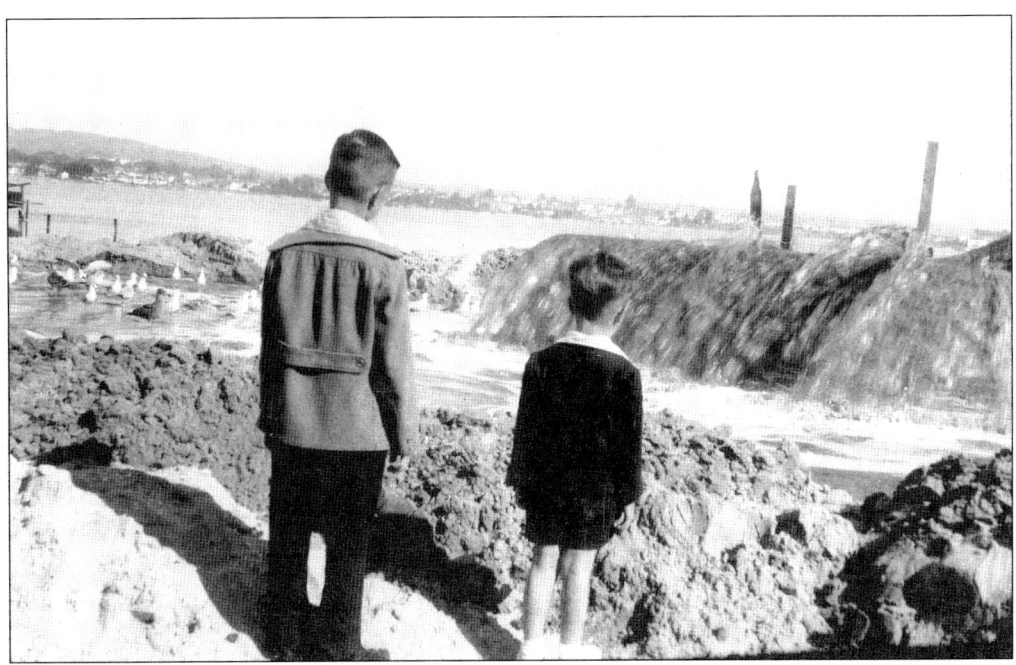

Two young boys, Albie (left) and Johnny Fitzpatrick, dressed in their Sunday best, are fascinated by the dredging operation on November 27, 1946. The sand-laden water gushing from the dredge pipe gradually built the beaches. (Courtesy of Ann Howe Mansfield.)

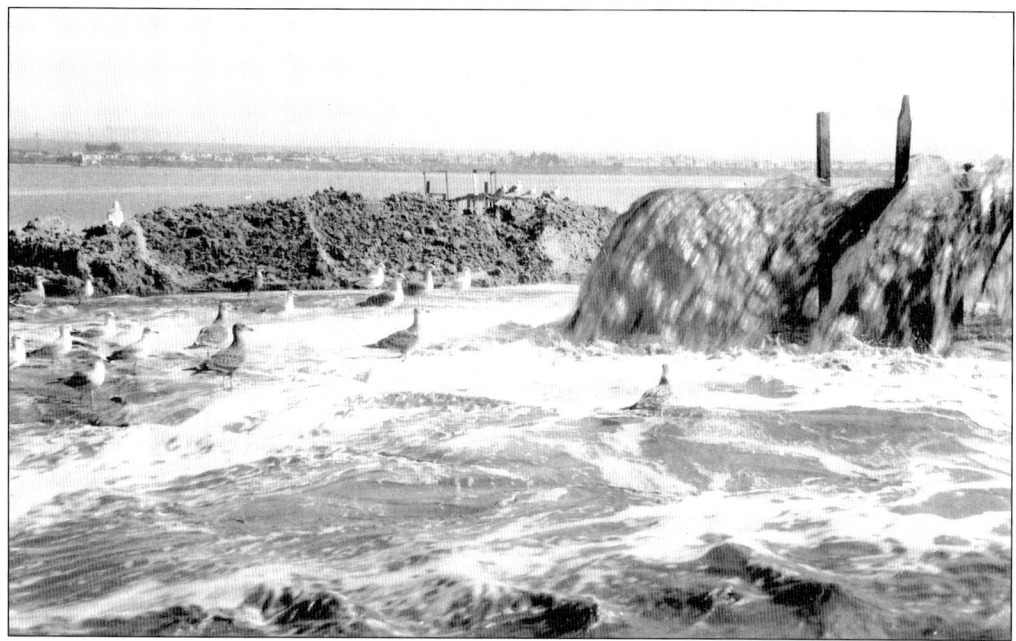

Clams, dredged up with the bay bottom and sent through the pipes, emerged cracked and broken, a ready-to-eat meal for the waiting seagulls. (Courtesy of Ann Howe Mansfield.)

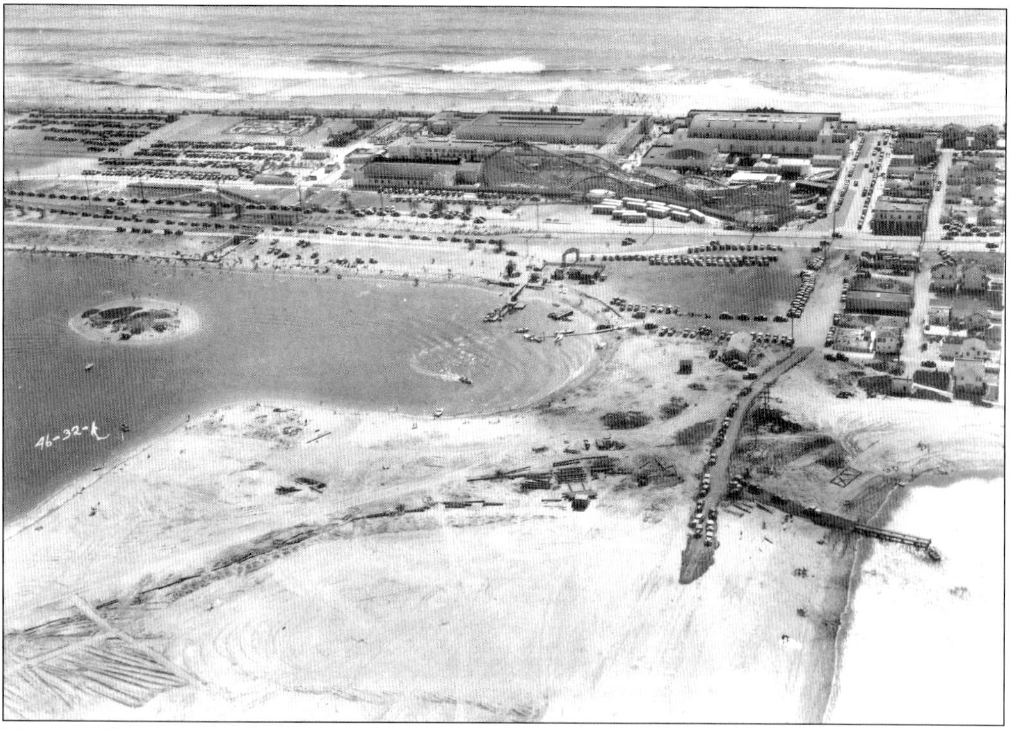

Ventura Place now extends into Mission Bay as the new land is formed c. 1947. Dredge pipes are laid out across what will become Mariners Point. The pier on the right is near the site of the yet-to-be-built Bahia Hotel, with Belmont Park pictured on a busy day in the background. The parking lots are full, and the streets are lined with cars. (Courtesy of Chuck Whitmarsh.)

A strong, outgoing tide pushes through the surf line in this 1947 aerial. The Ocean Beach Bridge is the most direct route from downtown to Mission Beach. The dredging, though well underway, has a long way to go before boaters need not fear running aground in the shallow waters of the bay. (Courtesy of Ann Howe Mansfield.)

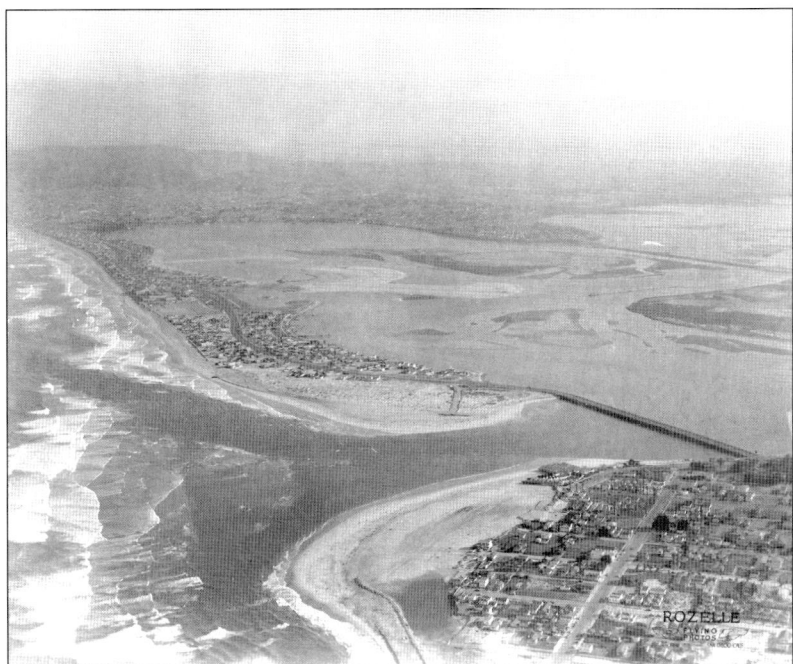

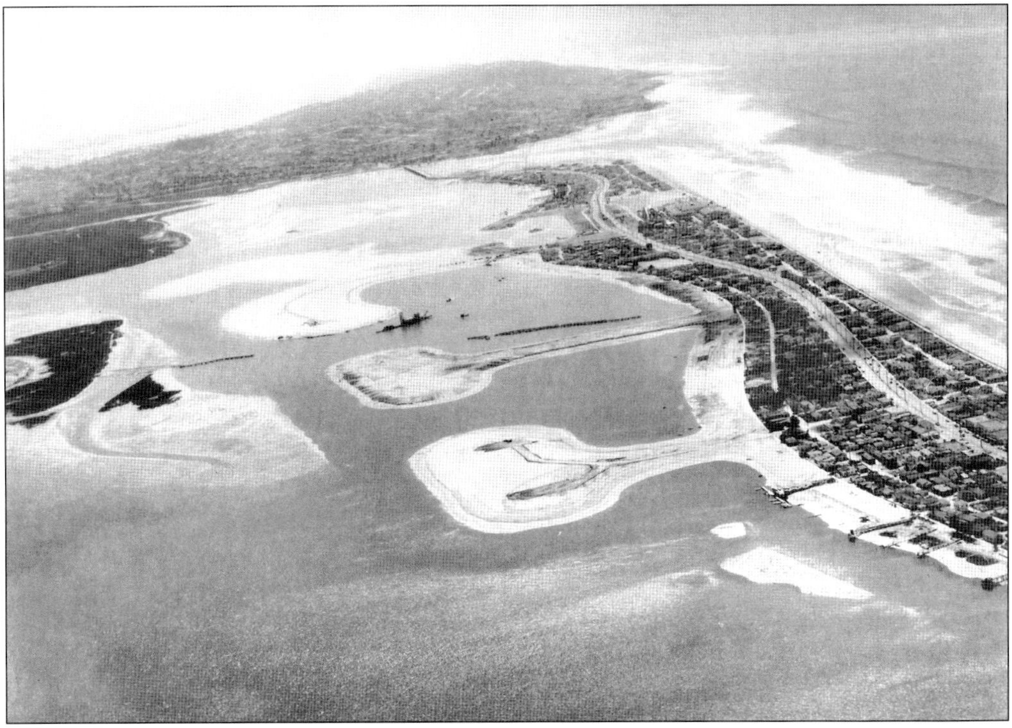

A new landscape is emerging in Mission Bay. Pictured around 1948, Santa Clara Point is complete in the foreground with El Carmel Point just beyond. The dredge is operating at the north end of Gleason Point, the future home of Bill Evans's Bahia Hotel. The Ocean Beach Bridge is visible, linking Mission Beach to Ocean Beach and Point Loma in the background. (Courtesy of Ned Huntington.)

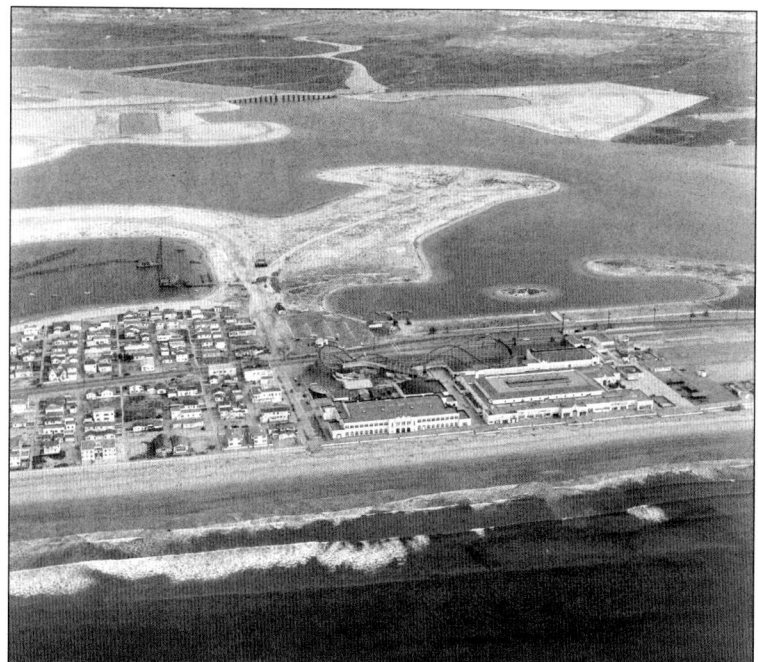

Looking east, this June 15, 1949, view gives another perspective on the bay development. The dredge is working in Gleason Cove, center left. The rectangular shape in the upper left is the Model Yacht Basin located near Ingraham Street and the southern causeway bridge. The Ventura Bridge will span the open channel in the upper right. (Courtesy of Chuck Whitmarsh.)

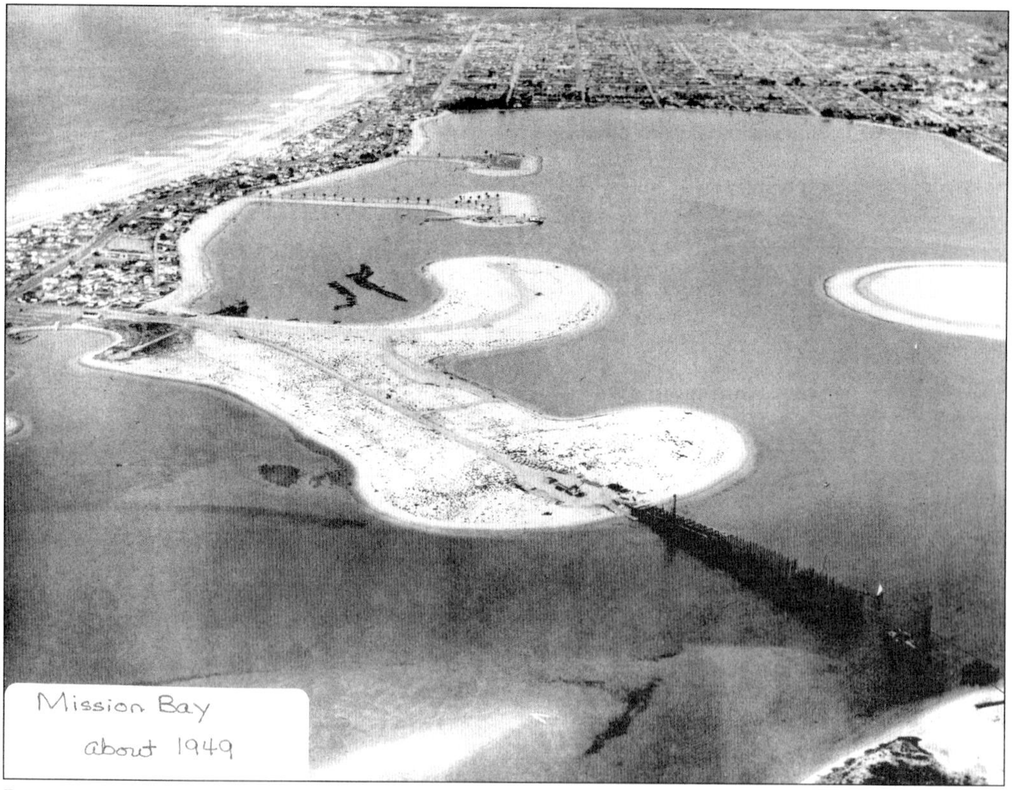

By 1949, much had been accomplished. The new Ventura Bridge is under construction in the right foreground, El Carmel Point is now the home of Mission Bay Yacht Club, and Santa Clara Point, the northernmost point, now has a new dock and boat launching ramp. (Courtesy of Burke Royale.)

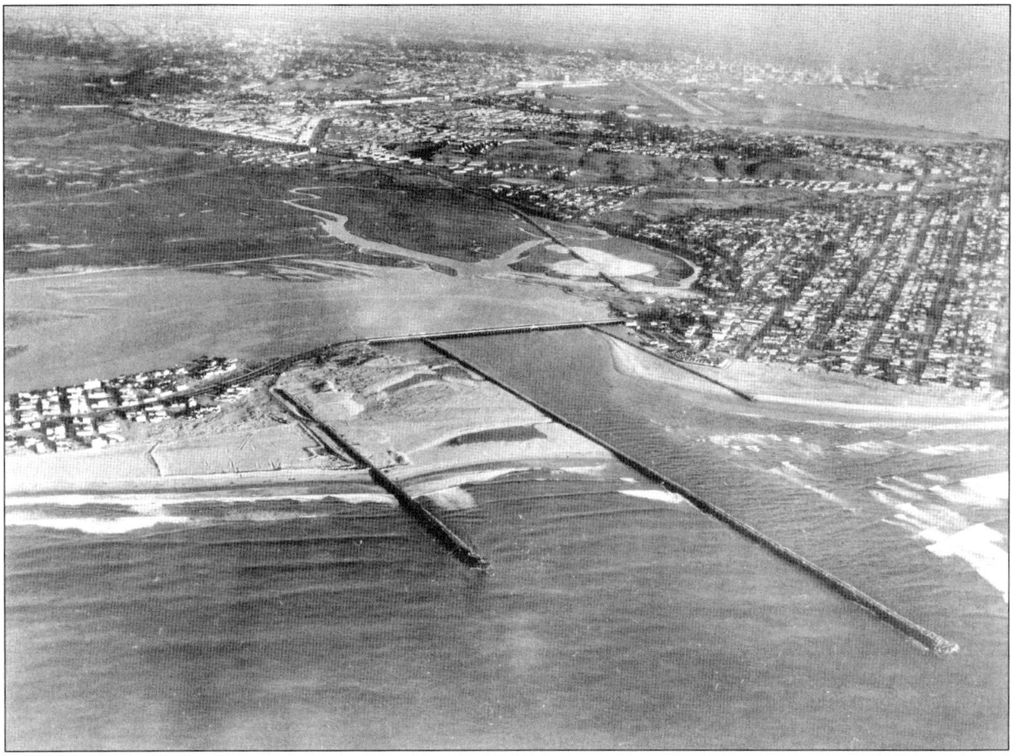

The middle jetty has been completed westerly, and the north and south jetties are halfway there. The land between the middle jetty and the north jetty, left, will be dredged out to create the new Mission Bay Channel and entry to the bay. The middle and south jetties will continue inland to create the San Diego River flood-control channel. (Courtesy of Ned Huntington.)

By 1951, the jetties are complete, the Mission Bay Channel is open, and most of the sand has been removed between the jetties. The Ocean Beach Bridge closed to traffic in April 1950 and was demolished in January 1951. The new Ventura Bridge, on the left, now carries traffic to and from Mission Beach. (Courtesy of Burke Royale.)

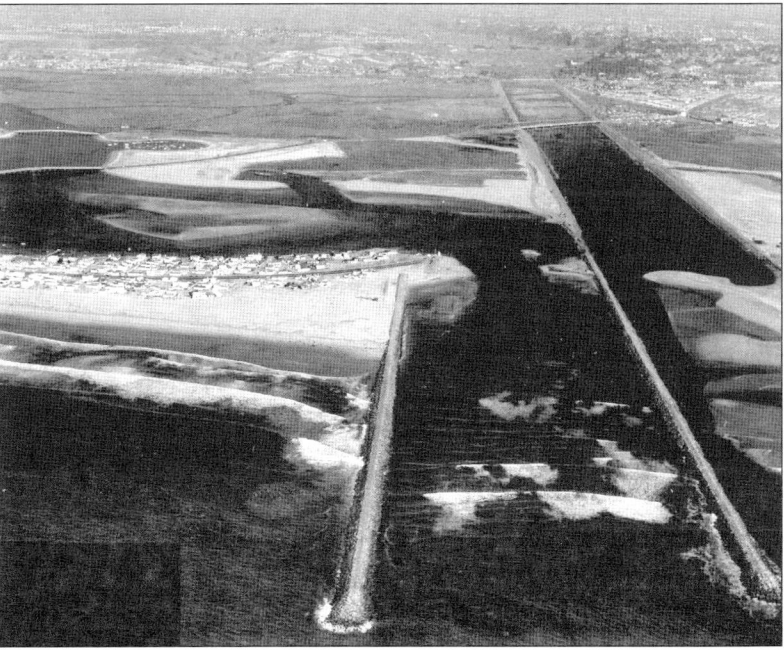

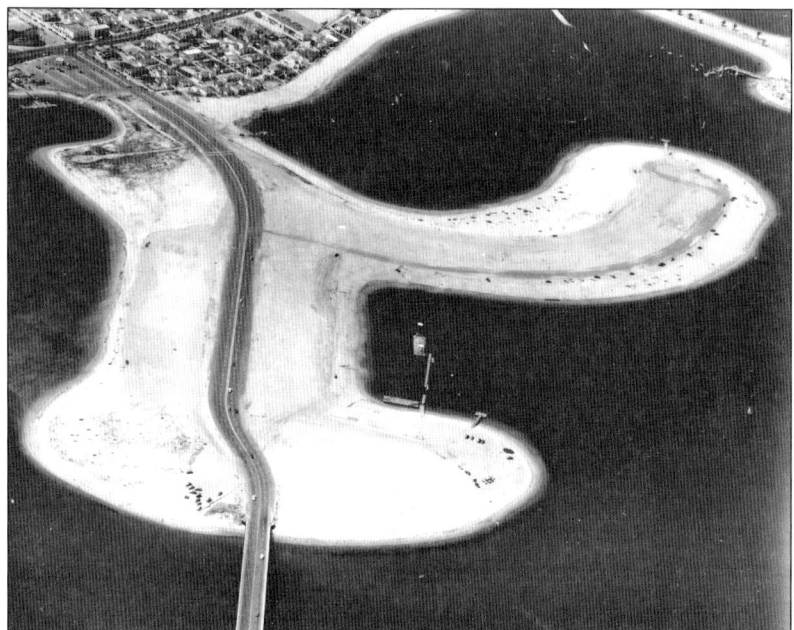

West Mission Bay Drive (Ventura) connects with the new bridge and a more direct route is open to downtown San Diego c. 1950. A vacant Gleason Point is ready for the construction of the Bahia Hotel. The pier visible at upper right is part of Mission Bay Yacht Club on El Carmel Point. (Courtesy of Ann Howe Mansfield.)

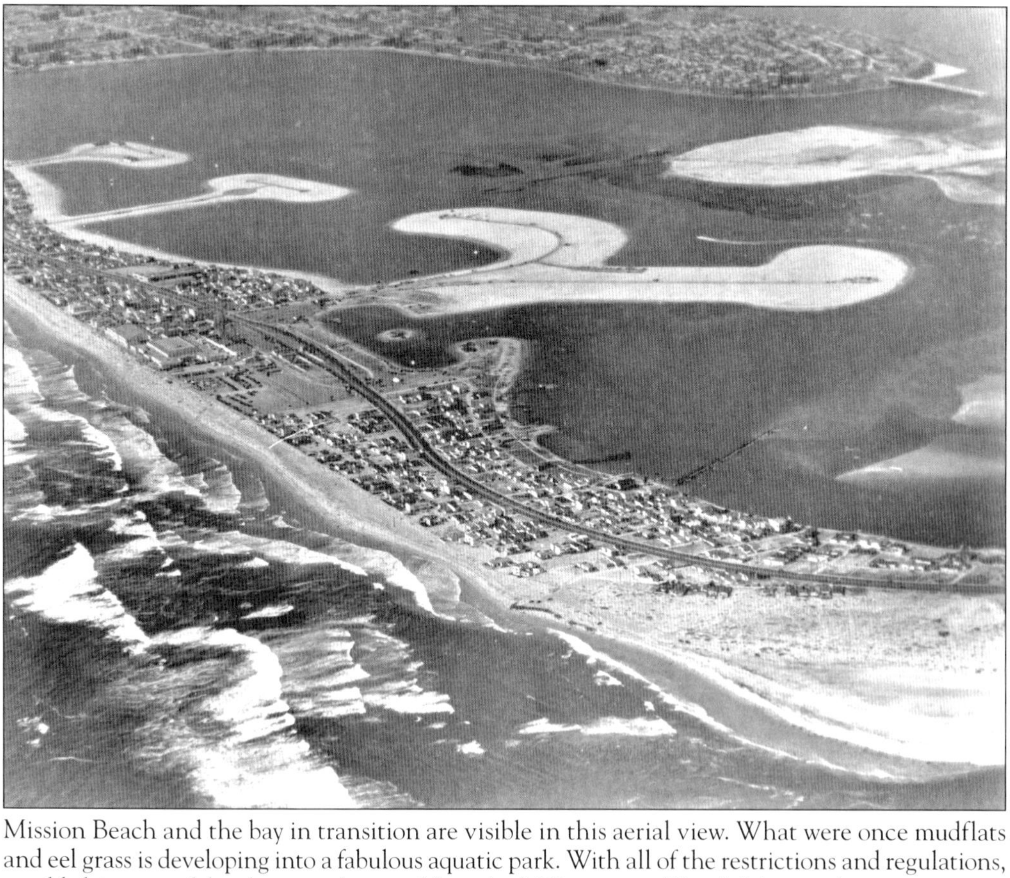

Mission Beach and the bay in transition are visible in this aerial view. What were once mudflats and eel grass is developing into a fabulous aquatic park. With all of the restrictions and regulations, would this type of development be possible today? (Courtesy of Frank Munson.)

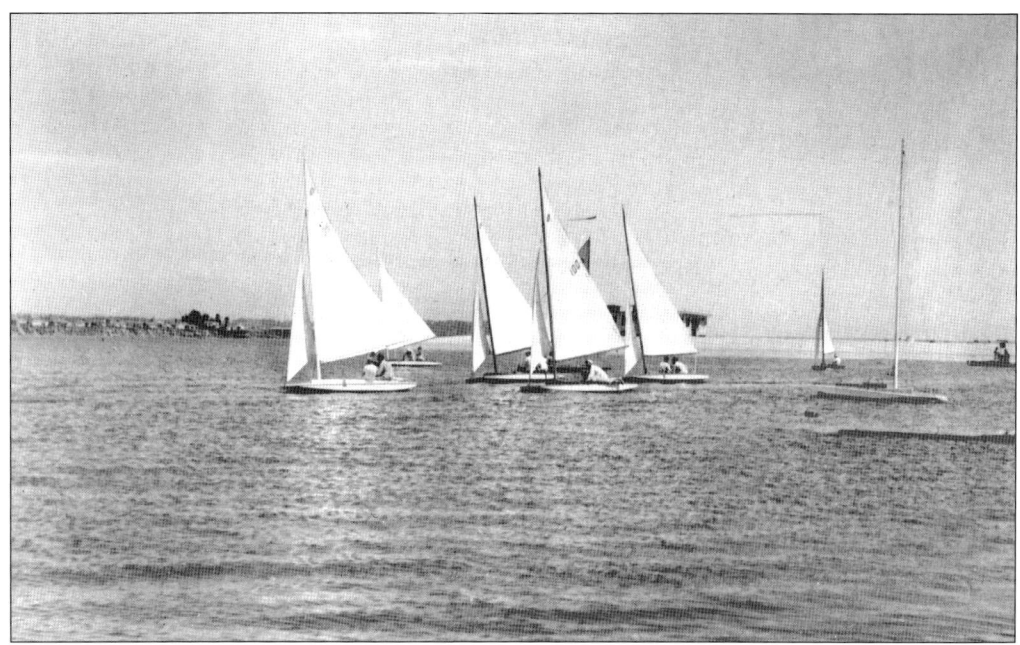

Skimmer-class sailboats from Mission Bay Yacht Club race on June 8, 1947. These boats were among the fastest around at the time, well before Hobie Catamarans and the high-tech watercraft of today. The more the bay was dredged, the wider the range of the sailboats and motorboats. There was no more concern about coming to an abrupt stop aground on the mud. (Courtesy of Ann Howe Mansfield.)

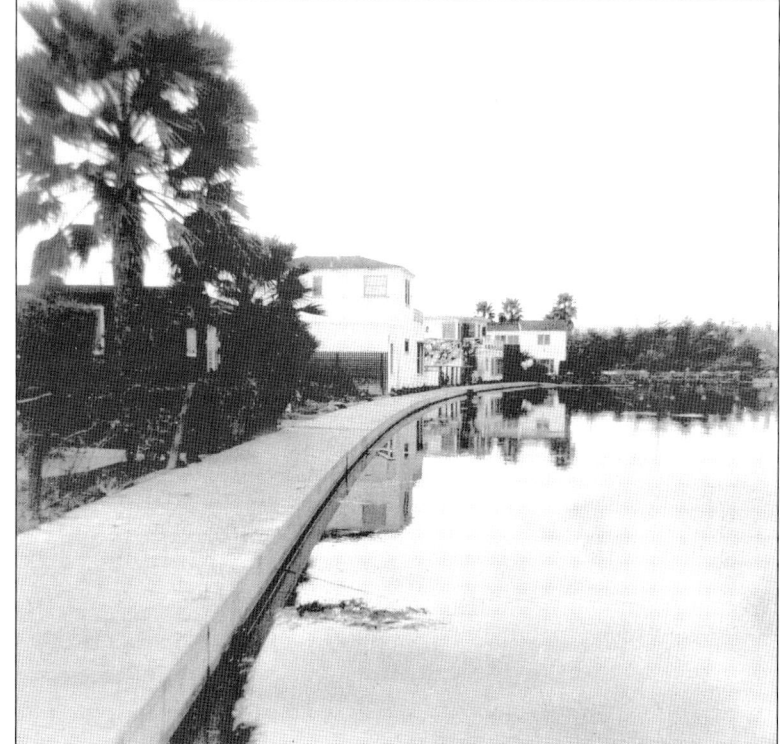

High tide could still be a problem, as seen in this June 26, 1948, photograph. The water has reached Bayside Walk at the far north end of Mission Beach. Since this shot was taken, the beach has been widened considerably, and flooding along the bayfront is rare. During the winter months, city crews build a sand barrier to further guard against damage. (Courtesy of Sterling Suhre.)

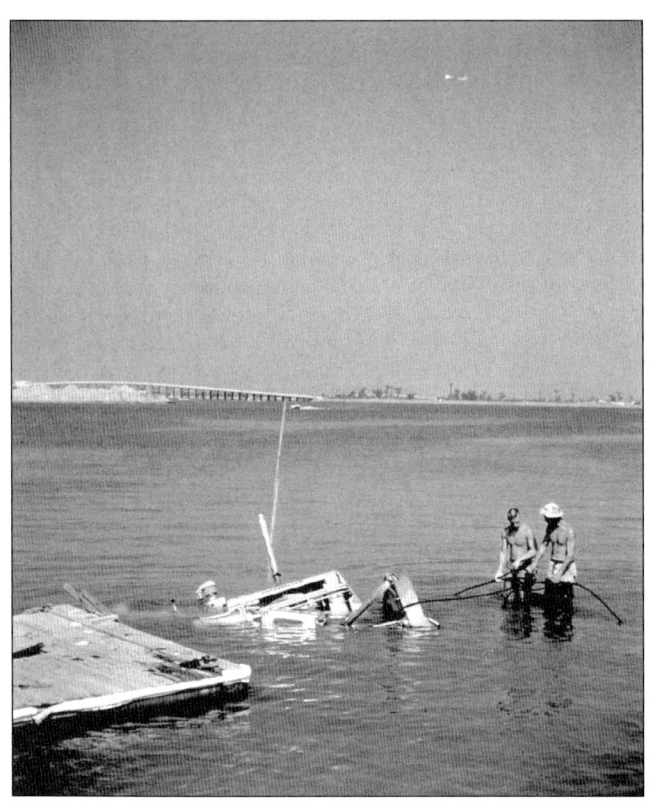

Dredging and beach construction did not always go smoothly, as is visible in these 1948 scenes. Somehow, the bulldozer fell into the water and became a major headache for the crews. Two men attach cables to the submerged tractor, and it is lifted out by crane. Saltwater is not the recommended environment for this type of equipment, according to Caterpillar Inc. (Courtesy of Jackie Linstrom.)

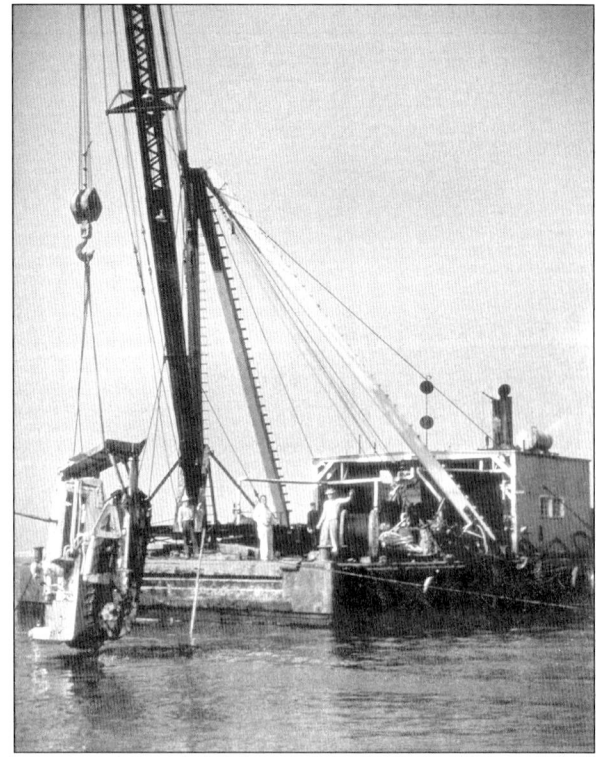

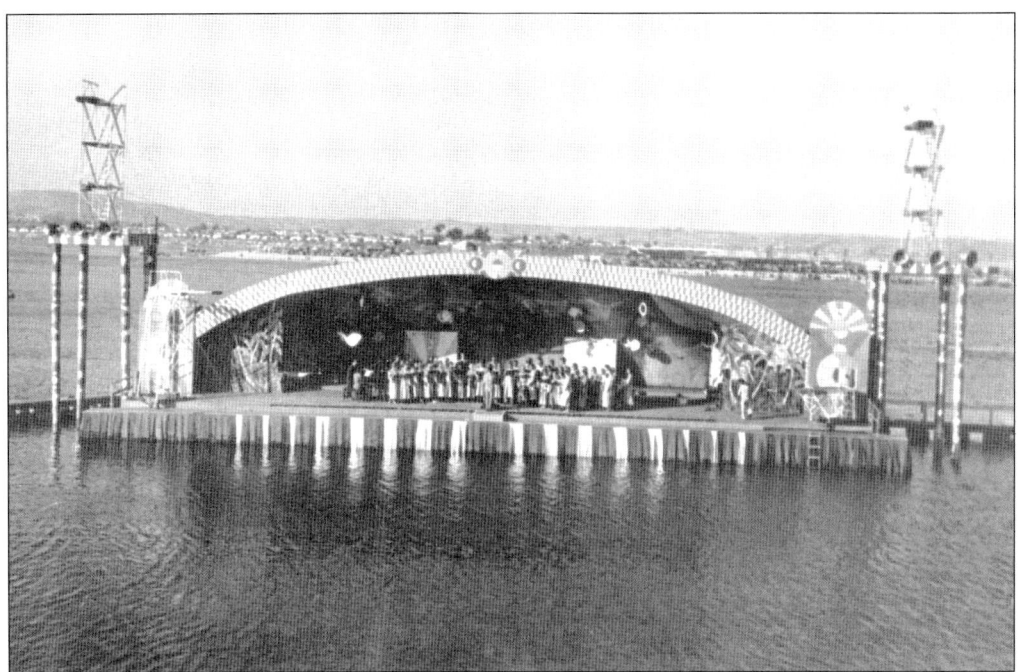

To celebrate the completion of the Mission Bay development, the City of San Diego, along with Olympic swimmer Buster Crabbe, produced a fabulous water festival called Fiesta Del Pacifica on Labor Day weekend in 1949. A large stage, erected on barges just north of Ventura Boulevard, was flanked by high-diving platforms. There were swimming and diving events, concerts, boat races, and many exhibitions. (Courtesy of Frank Munson.)

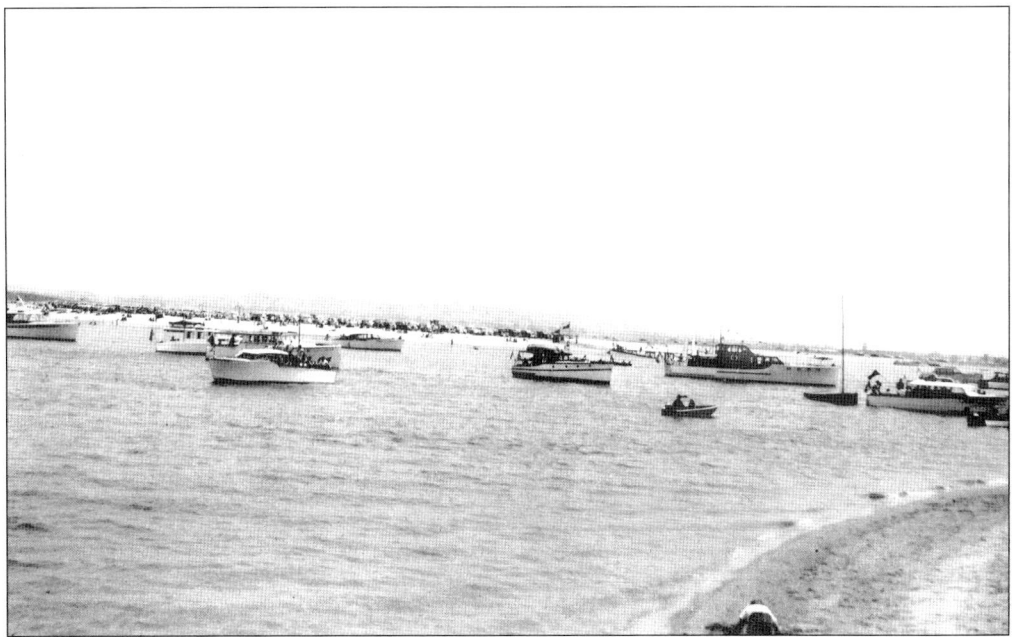

The grand opening of the Mission Bay Channel was cause for a parade of boats in 1951. It was now possible for large vessels to navigate the channel where previously, passage was prevented by the low channel bridge and shallow waters. (Courtesy of Ann Howe Mansfield.)

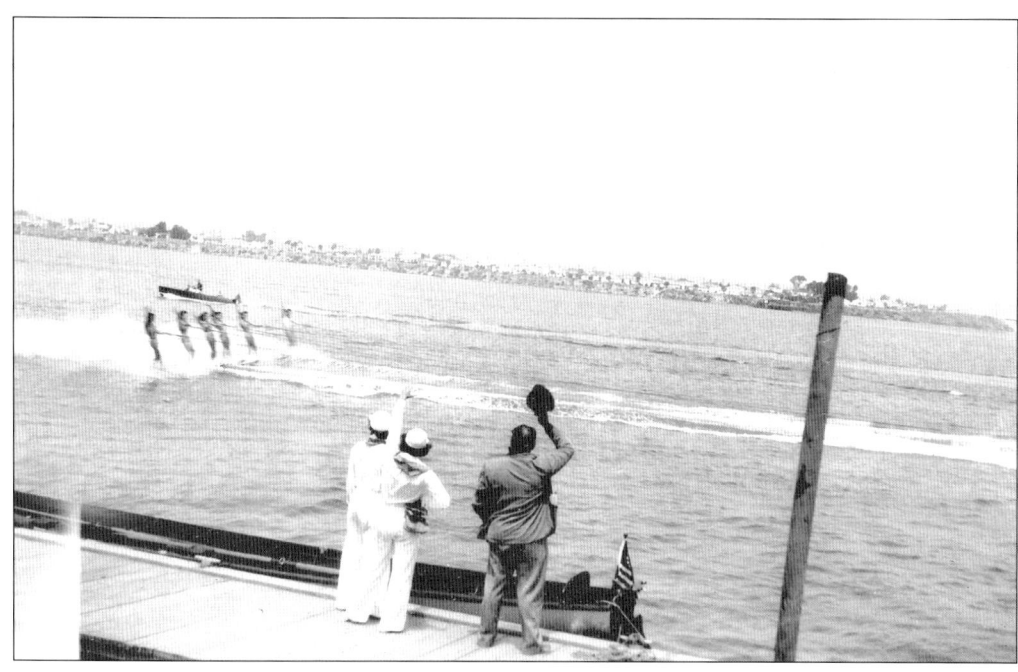

Waterskiing exhibitions by the six young ladies seen in the top photograph were part of the grand celebration. Here the skiers are passing by the Mission Bay Yacht Club dock at the tip of El Carmel Point. Below, canoe jousters battle it out near Santa Clara Point, and it appears that the team on the left has just lost its gladiator to the water. (Courtesy of Ann Howe Mansfield.)

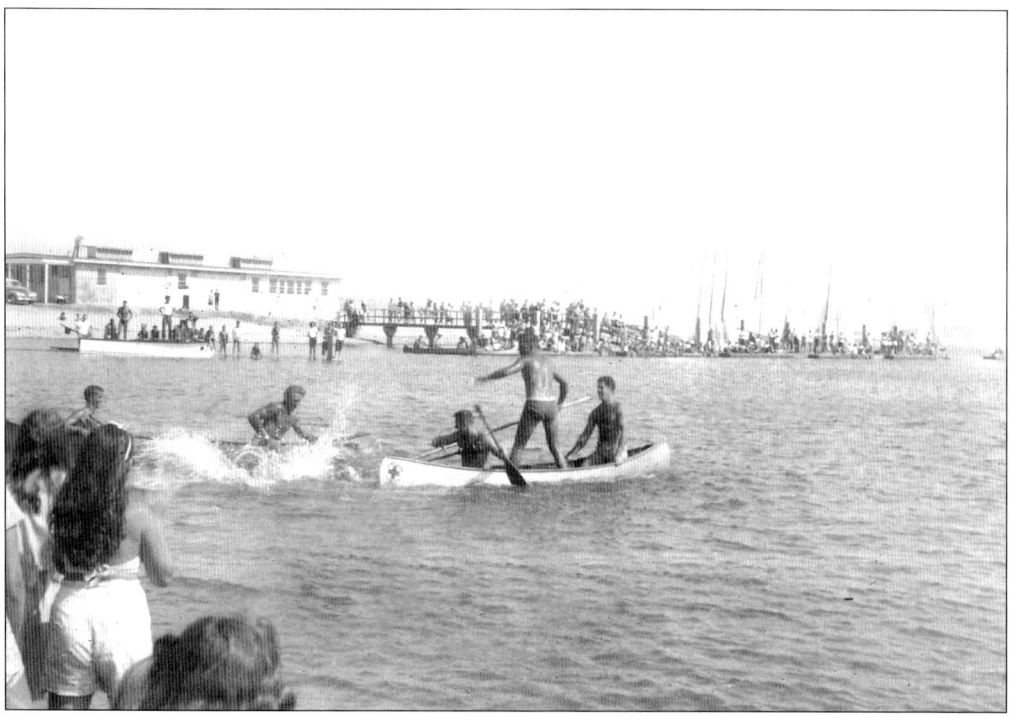

These scenes show SeaWorld in its infancy in 1956. The crowds were small and the facilities were basic, yet the leaping dolphins were fun to watch. SeaWorld has grown into a world-class tourist attraction, luring millions of visitors every year. Bay Park in the background has very few homes; the hills are bare. (Courtesy of Jackie Linstrom.)

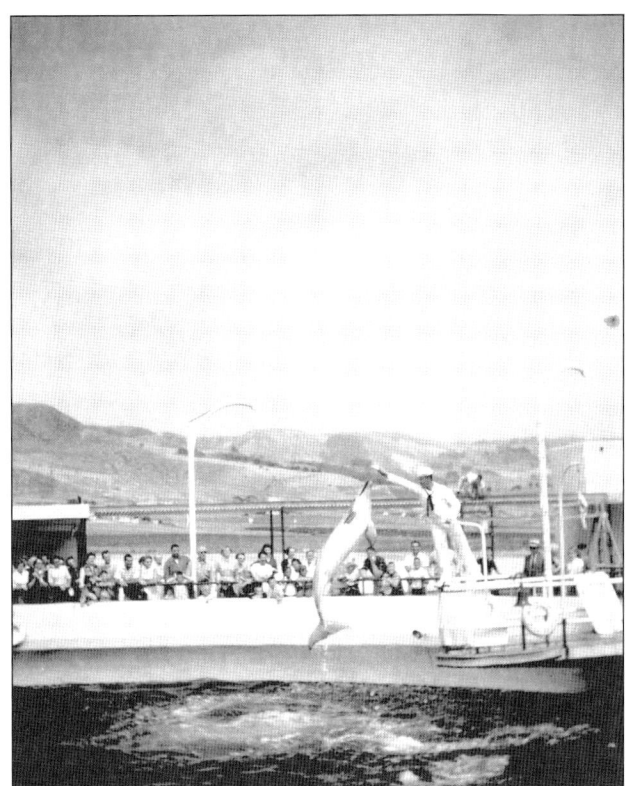

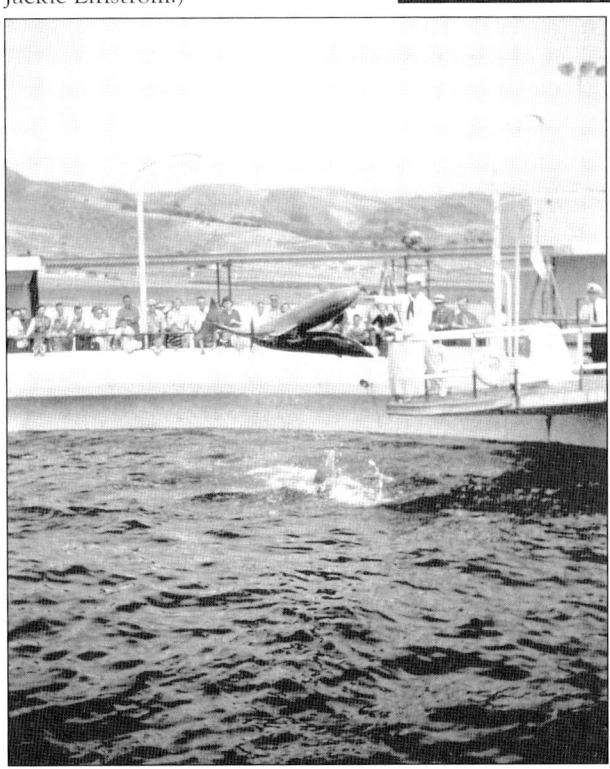

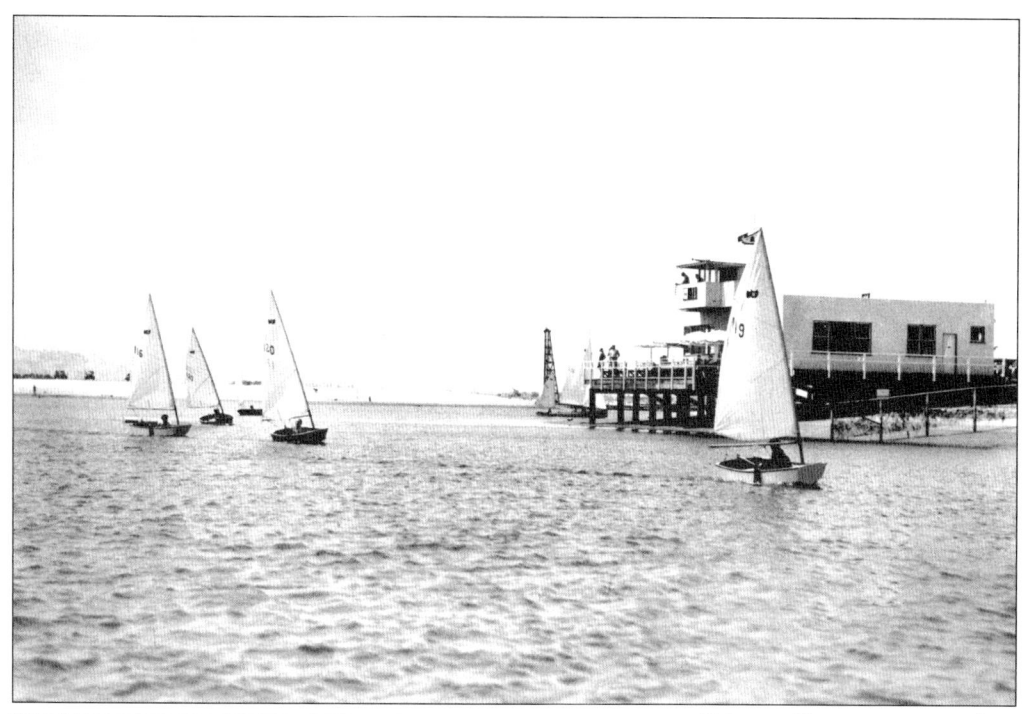

Sabot sailboats are racing by Mission Bay Yacht Club as race officials and spectators watch the action. The City of San Diego Park and Recreation Department also offered lessons, teaching thousands of youngsters the techniques of sailing. The city had dozens of Sabots available for their classes. (Courtesy of Mission Bay Yacht Club.)

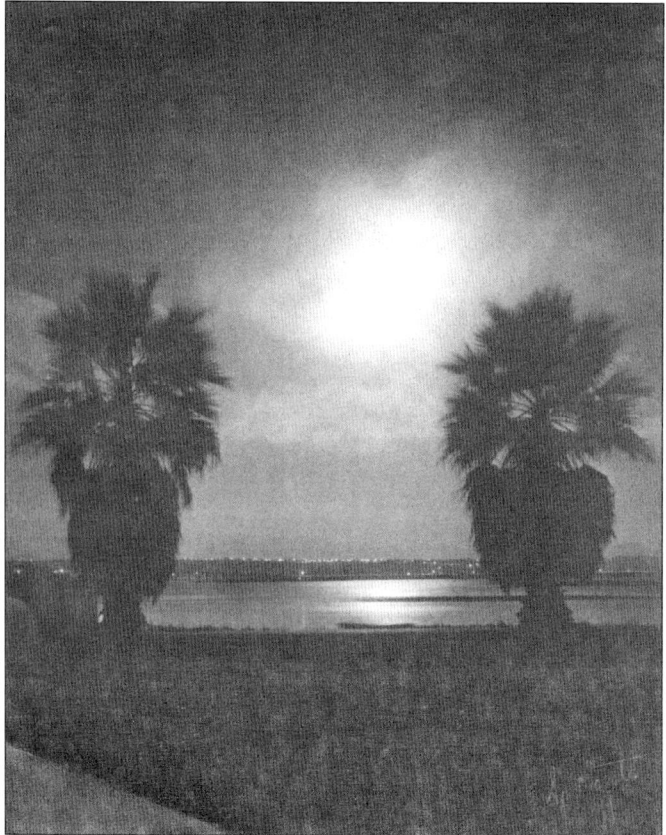

The chapter on Mission Bay closes with a full moonlit view between the palm trees. Calm waters and city lights are a main reason that Mission Beach properties are in such demand. (Courtesy of Mike Curren.)

Seven
OLD MISSION BEACH

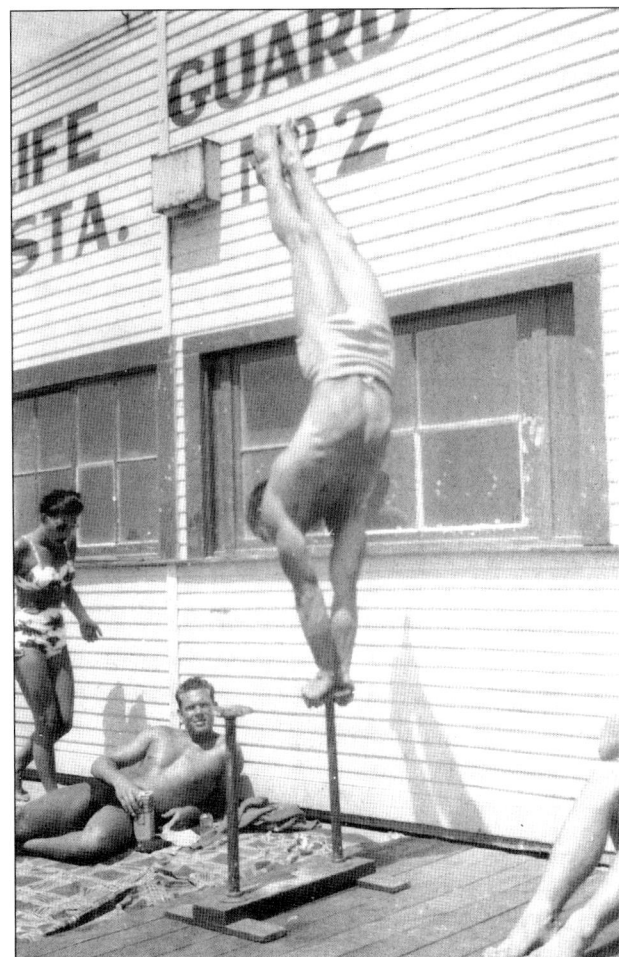

The beachfront area between Queenstown Court and Redondo Court was the gathering place of choice for most of the young beachgoers in the 1930s, 1940s, and 1950s. High school and college kids from all over San Diego County gathered here on most summer days, forging close friendships that have endured to this day, some 60 or more years later. Athletic activities were ongoing daily. (Courtesy of Sterling Suhre.)

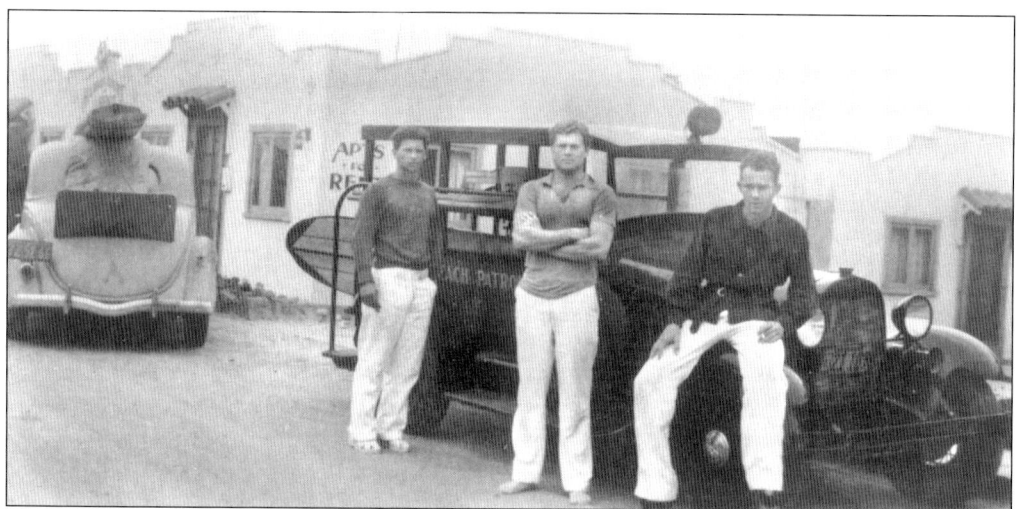

Lifeguards Dorian Paskowitz (left), Don Pritchard (center), and Dick "Stormsurf" Taylor are pictured at Queenstown Court in 1938. Al Harris's bungalows are in the background. The surfboard in the back of the truck was the latest advance in design and only weighed about 100 pounds, some improvement over the older, heavy models. Today surfboards weigh just a few pounds. (Courtesy of Norma Griffin.)

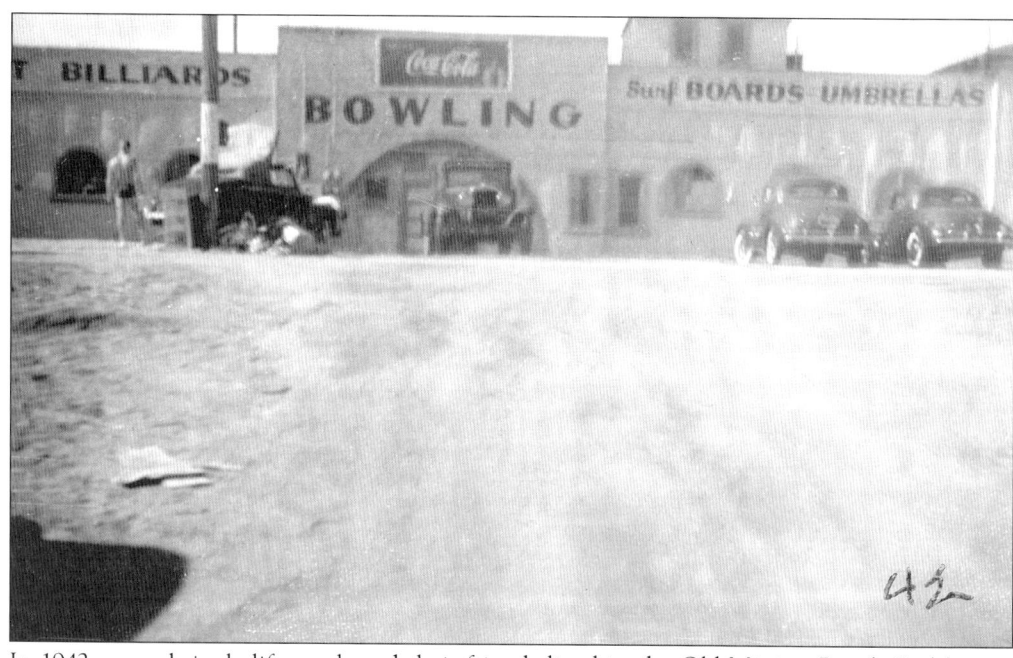

In 1942, several single lifeguards and their friends lived in the Old Mission Beach Bathhouse, now converted into a bowling alley. An apartment, nicknamed "Skunk Hollow," was built on the right side of this photograph just below the Surf Boards sign, and became party headquarters. The stories told cannot be repeated in polite company. (Courtesy of Sterling Suhre.)

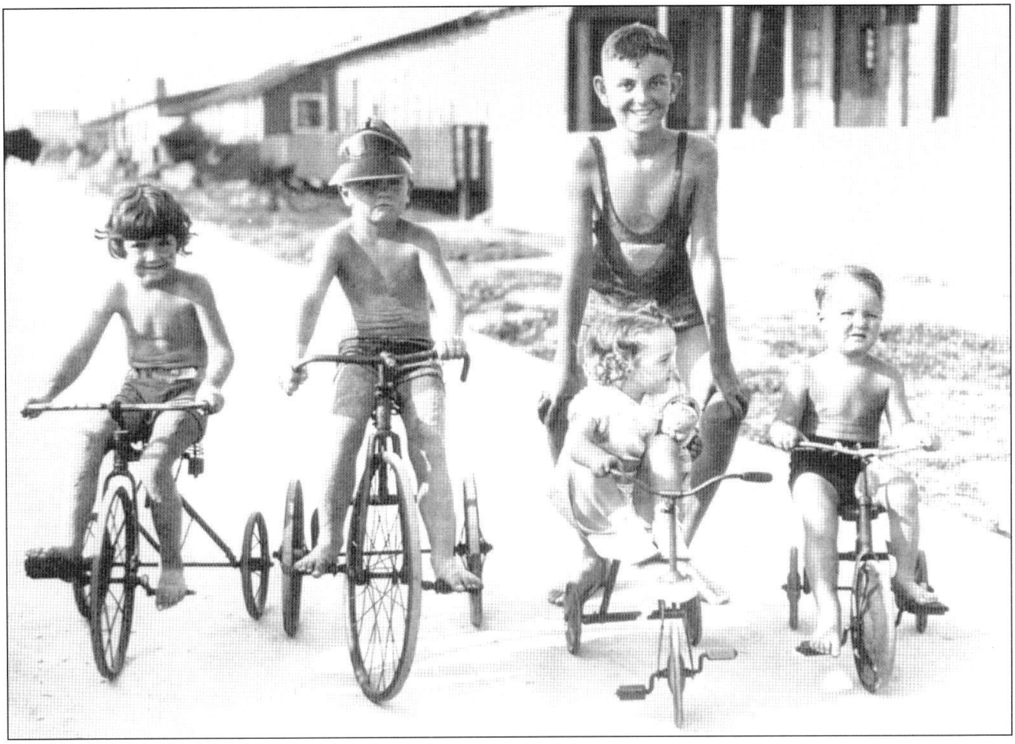

From left to right are Marilyn Royale, Ed Fletcher, baby Sharon Steen, Burke Royale, and Michael Fletcher in 1934. Growing up in Mission Beach was a great adventure with plenty to keep kids busy—swimming, surfing, sports of all kinds, and riding tricycles, as are the five in this photograph. Burke Royale became a lifeguard lieutenant while attending college and later had a long career as a dentist. (Courtesy of Marilyn Brucker.)

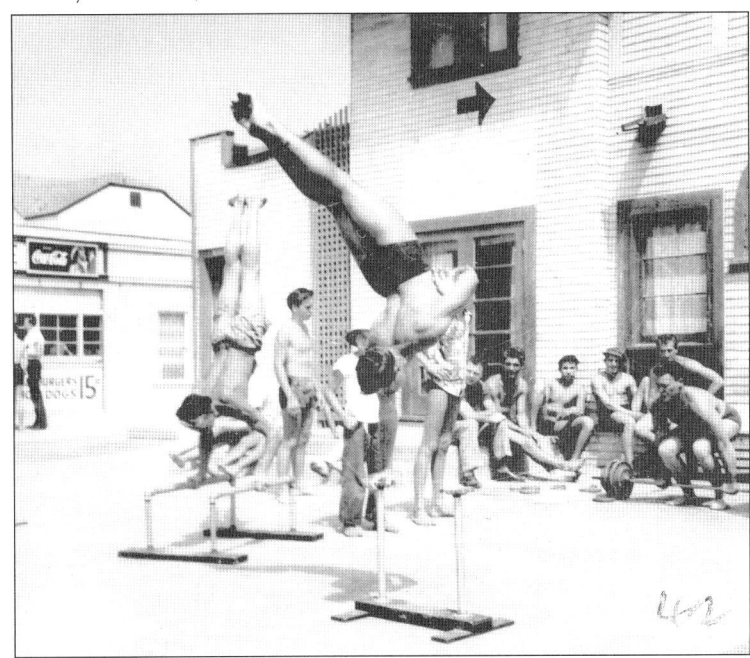

In 1942, Warren Hall executes a perfect, one-arm handstand as a group of young admirers look on. Gymnastics and weight lifting were a popular pastime at Old Mission. The building on the left was Kay's Place, home to the best hamburgers on the beach. (Courtesy of Sterling Suhre.)

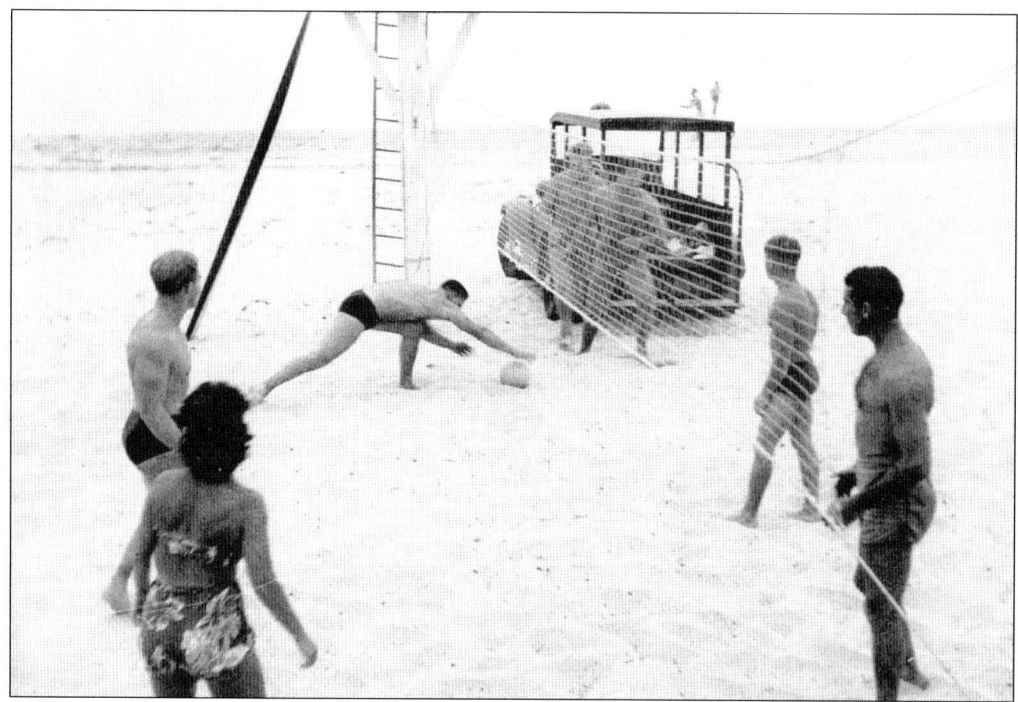

The lifeguard tower post became one side of the volleyball court in this 1942 scene. Two-man and four-man volleyball was very popular and, at times, the wait to get on the court could be quite long. The game "Over-the-Line" was developed at Old Mission Beach and was played to pass the time while waiting a turn on the volleyball court. (Courtesy of Sterling Suhre.)

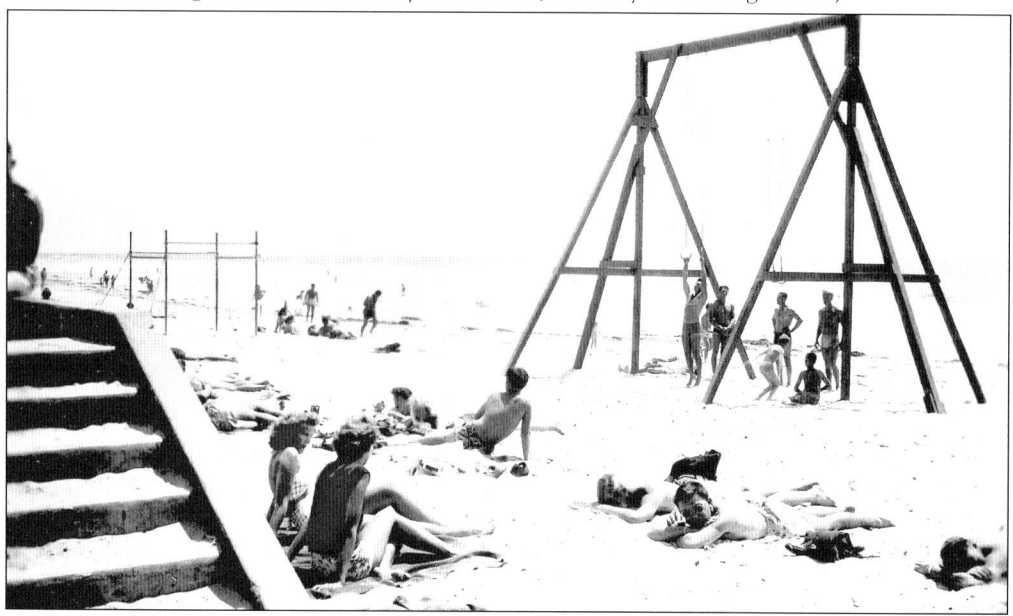

Sterling "Suzy" Surhe, along with some of his buddies, built the swinging rings pictured in 1946. Rumor has it that the lumber for this structure was "discarded" by one of the local outdoor advertising companies. The young boys soon learned the basics of gymnastics, and many became very proficient. A set of horizontal bars can be seen on the left. (Courtesy of Sterling Suhre.)

They started them young, as seen in this 1940s scene. Mother and baby seem to be having a great time as part of this three-high human pyramid. Today the two adults would probably be arrested on child endangerment charges. Life was easier back then. (Courtesy of Sterling Suhre.)

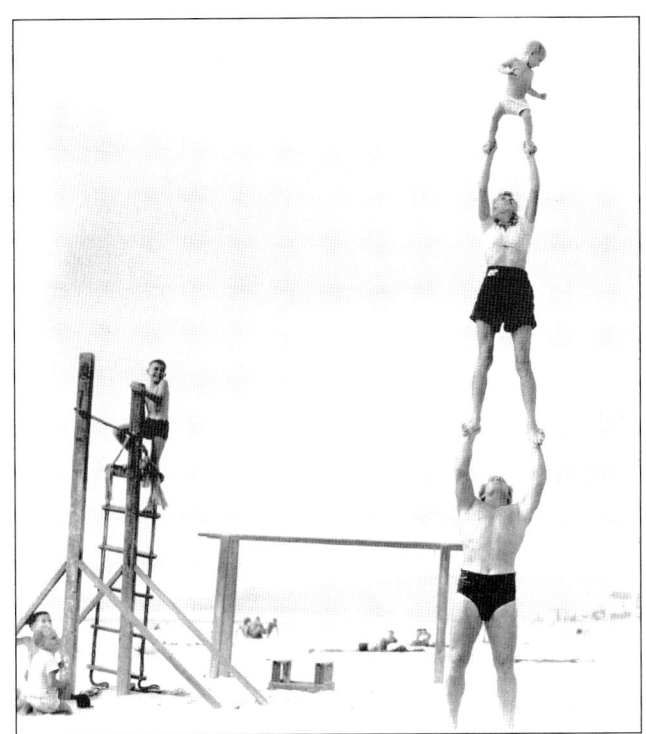

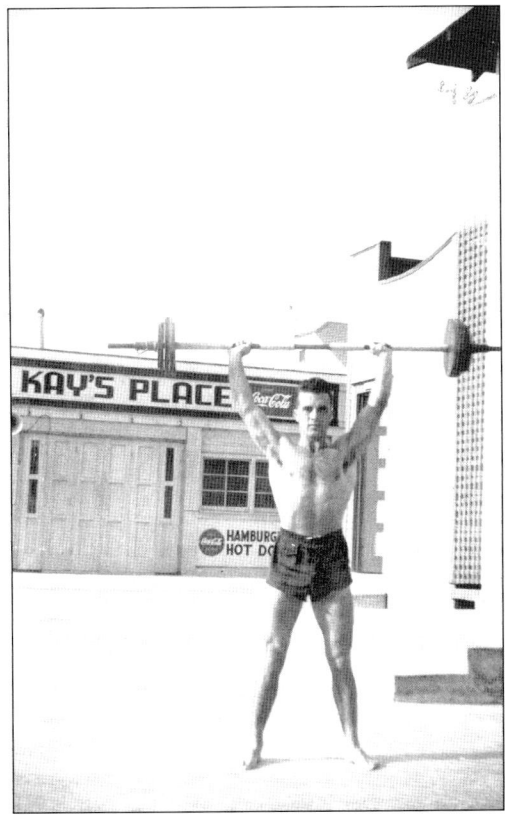

A buffed out Mickey Aguirre lifts weights in front of Kay's Place in 1942. Mickey, a top San Diego baseball player who played with Ted Williams at Hoover High School, continued playing the game until he was over 80 years old. It must be early in the day as Kay has not yet opened her doors. It was not uncommon for the guys to arrive at the beach by 8:00 a.m. and not go home until dark. (Courtesy of Sterling Suhre.)

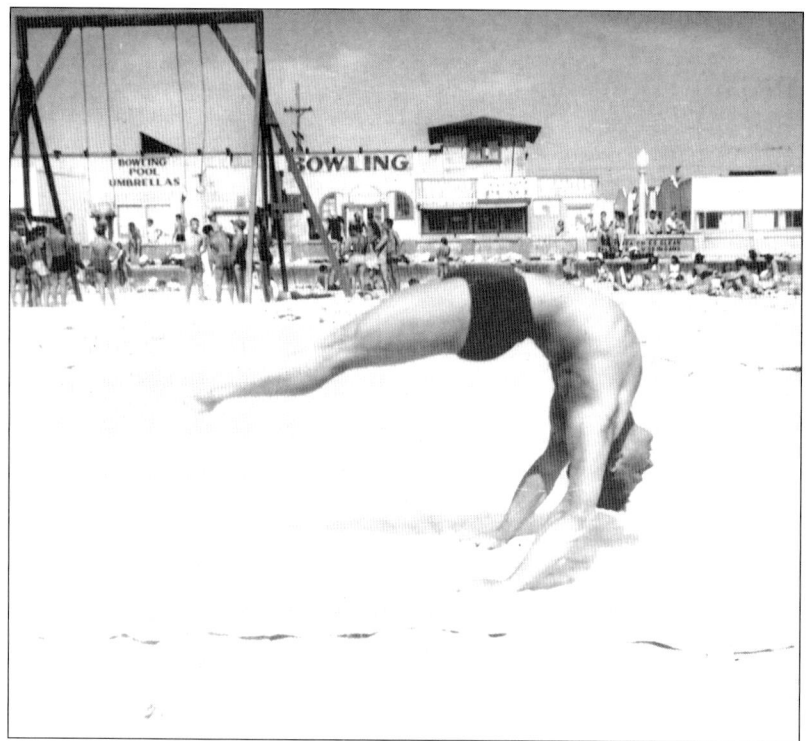

The human body is not supposed to bend like this. This gymnast is performing in front of the bowling alley building in 1944. Besides bowling, beachgoers could rent umbrellas and beach gear or find lots to eat and drink at the beachfront food stands. Directly across from Queenstown Court, right, are Al Harris's beach cottages. (Courtesy of Sterling Suhre.)

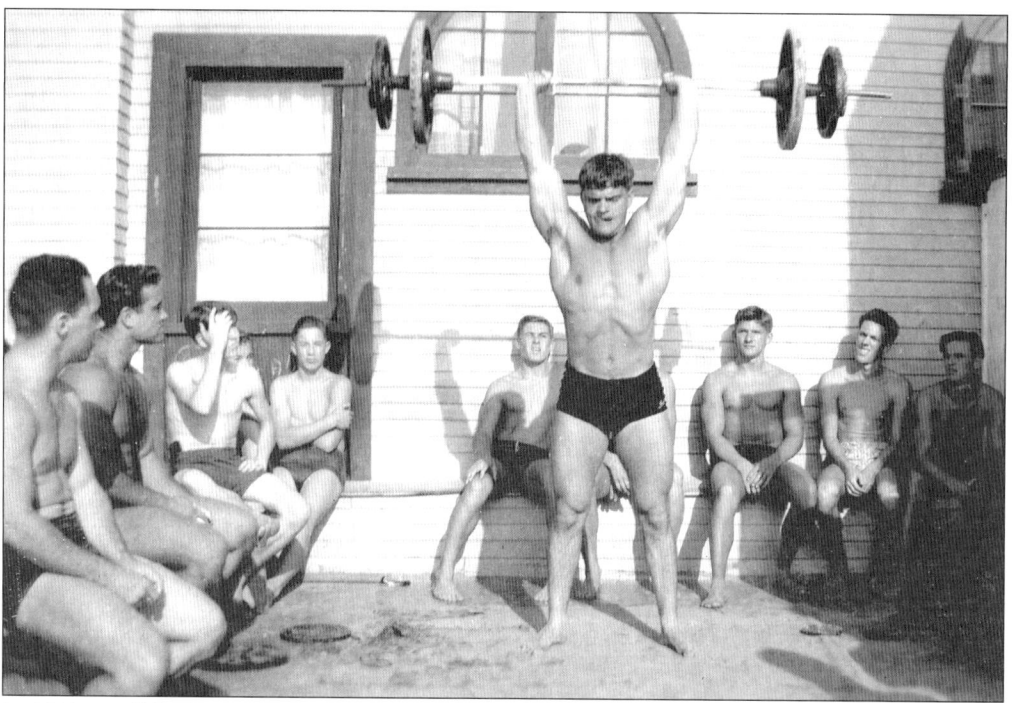

In 1942, a well-built young man shows his strength as others wait their turn. Coauthor Phil Prather is pictured second from the left. The lifeguards had space in the building, and the young athletes often stored their gear in the facility. (Courtesy of Sterling Suhre.)

A young Hughie Lyons flexes his muscles on the beach in the early 1940s. Lyons was adept at both weight lifting and gymnastics and later performed with his wife on stage in Las Vegas. He also owned and operated a successful taxidermy business in San Diego. (Courtesy of Sterling Suhre.)

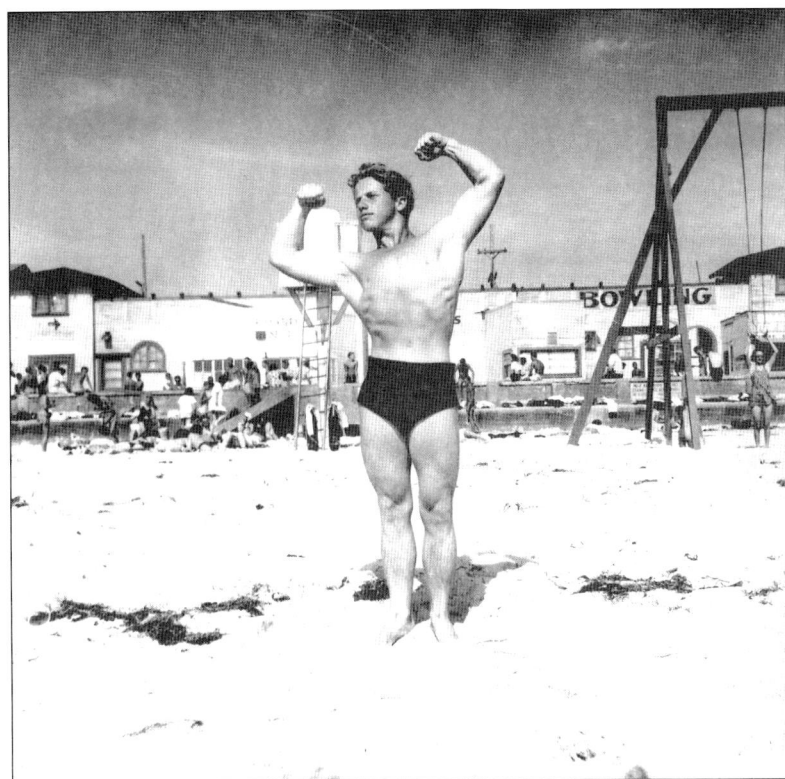

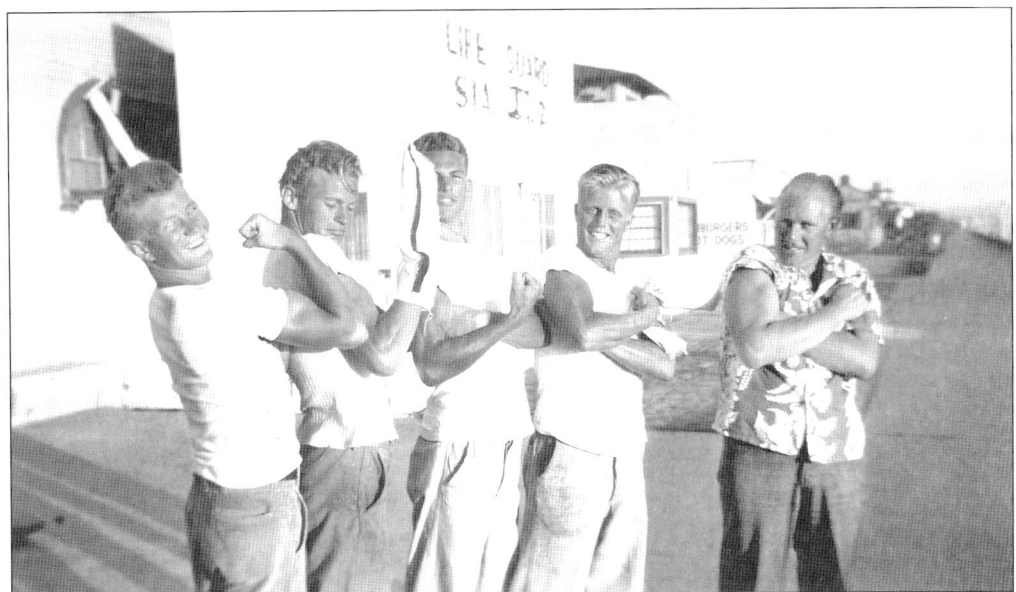

Not to be out done by Hughie Lyons (above), these guys show off their biceps in June 1943. From left to right are Ed Teagle, Bill Goldsmith, Bob Goldsmith, "Suzy" Suhre, and Earl Russell. Suhre retired after a long career with the San Diego Fire Department and is known around the beach as "Captain Suzy." (Courtesy of Sterling Suhre.)

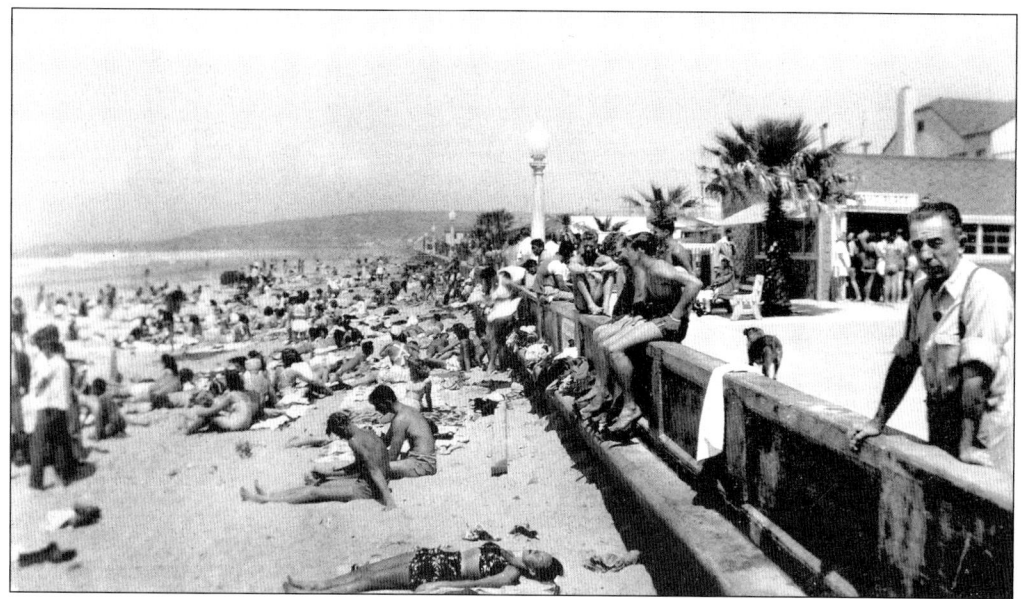

This Easter 1944 scene illustrates the popularity of Old Mission Beach. This is the birthplace of the Old Mission Beach Athletic Club, known as OMBAC, sponsors of the annual World Over-the-Line Championships for some 55 years. OMBAC was formed in 1954 with 35 members and has grown to nearly 500 in 2007. (Courtesy of Sterling Suhre.)

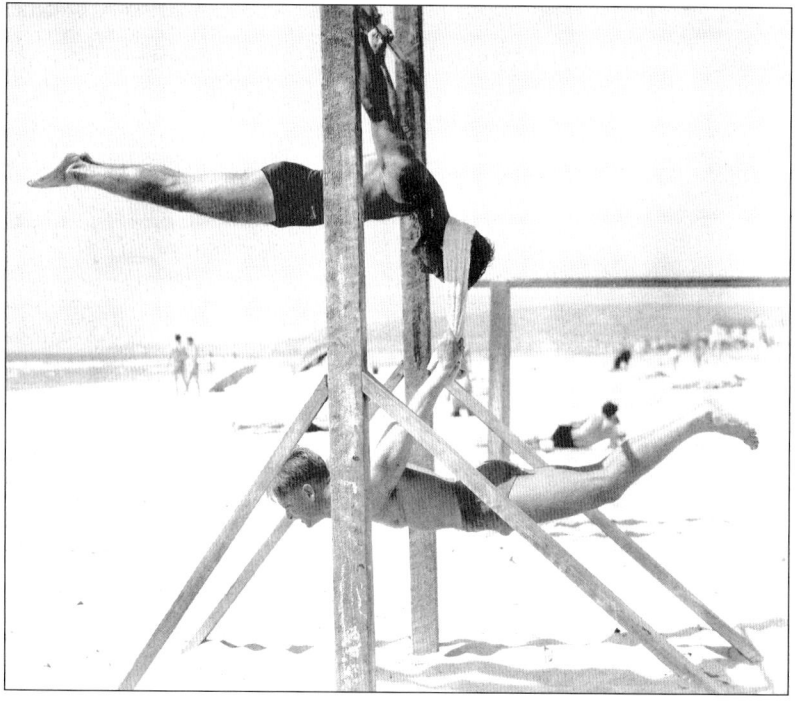

Ouch! What a pain in the neck. The young athletes probably attempted any stunt they could think of in 1944, hoping not to sustain any permanent damage. Right after this picture was taken, the man on the bottom lost his grip and ended up face down in the sand, while his friend rotated up and cracked his head on the bar. (Courtesy of Sterling Suhre.)

The young man in the foreground is getting some pointers on how to hold a handstand on the parallel bars while others perform on the rings in the background. In 1946, the beach kids led a very active lifestyle, playing sports of all sorts and always doing something. (Courtesy of Sterling Suhre.)

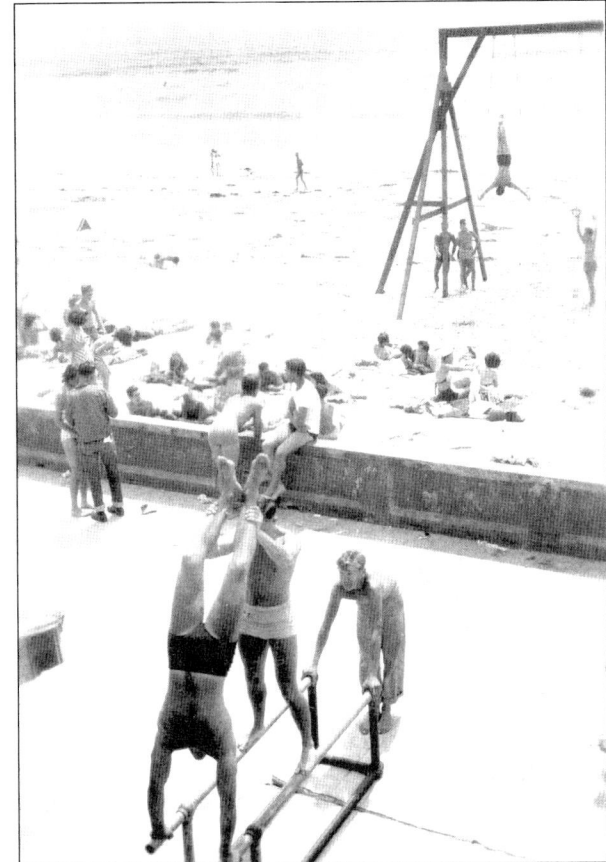

A volleyball game is in progress on a busy day, June 2, 1946. With only one court and volleyball so popular, a long list of challengers was always ready to take on the game winners. As long as a team continued to win, they could stay on the court. (Courtesy of Sterling Suhre.)

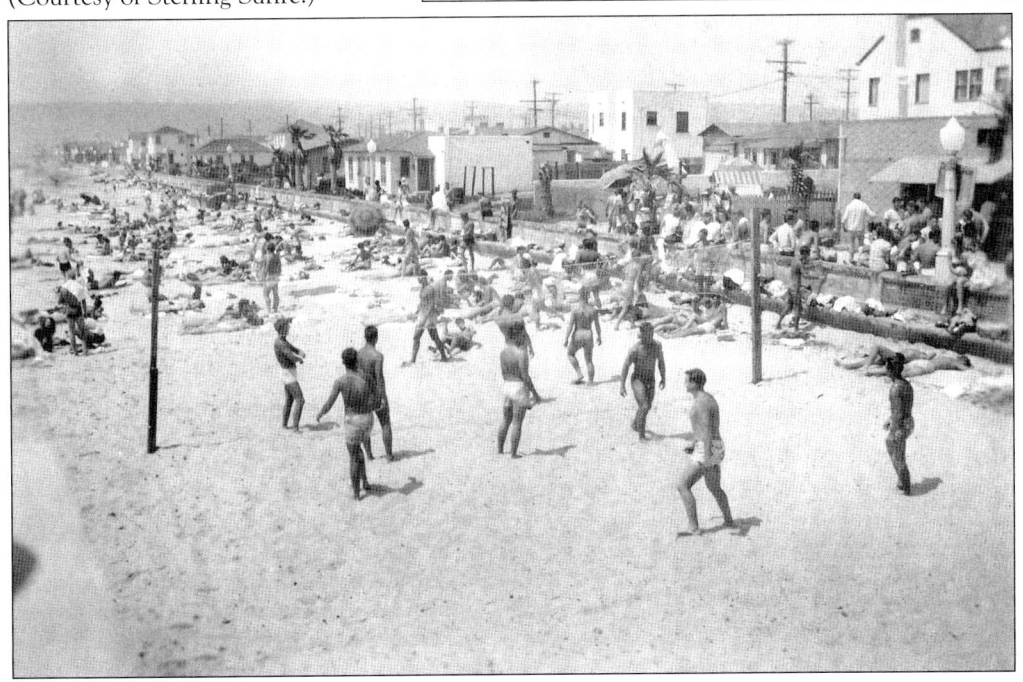

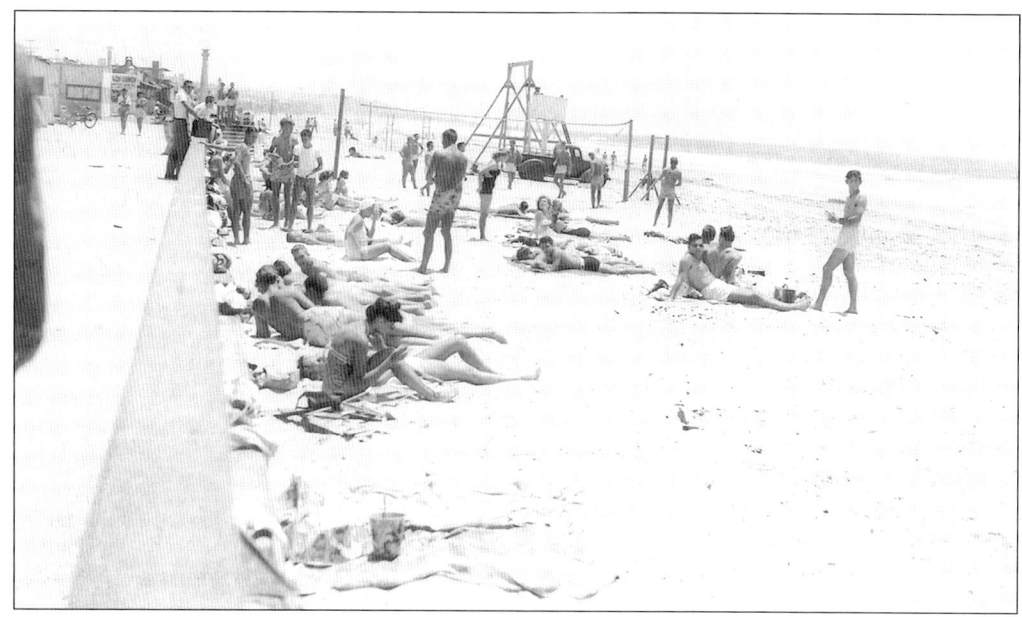
Looking south from Rockaway Court in 1947, one gets a good, overall view of Old Mission Beach. Soaking up all the sun possible, unaware of potential skin damage, beachgoers wanted to acquire the darkest tans possible. (Courtesy of Terry Polhamus Mendoza.)

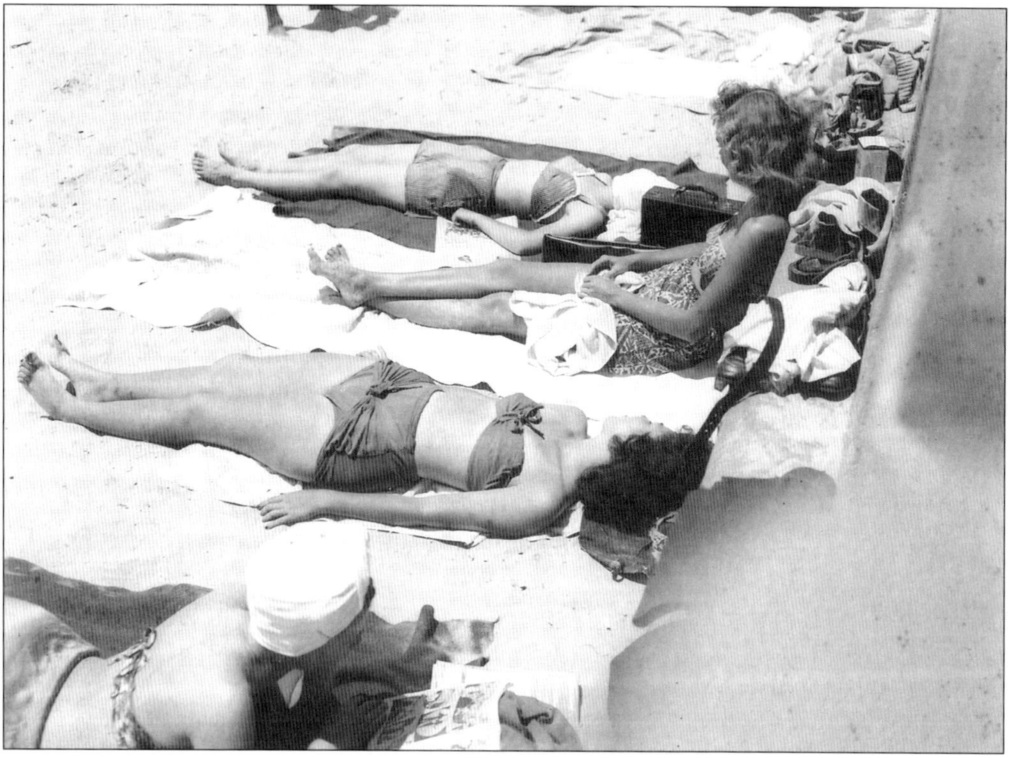

Pretty girls are enjoying the sunny beach in 1949. The girl in the foreground is catching up on the latest comic book heroes, but the one sitting at the wall is more interested in the real-life action around her. (Courtesy of Terry Polhamus Mendoza.)

Eddie Teagle—lifeguard, athlete, high school coach, and best friend to many—is pictured spiking the ball in a two-man game in 1947. Ed, the first president of OMBAC, was elected in 1954. Reb's Hamburger Den replaced the old bathhouse building that was torn down earlier in the year. (Courtesy of Terry Polhamus Mendoza.)

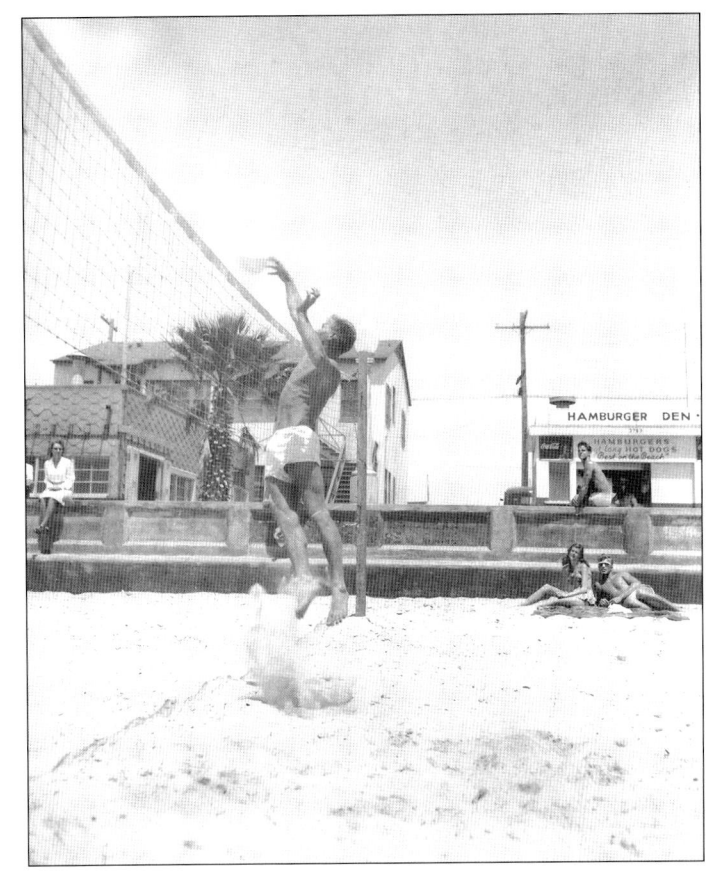

In 1947, this young lady is using a mattress cover to ride the waves. Once the material was wet, the mattress cover was filled with air by running along the shore, quickly closing and tying the opening when the bag was full. Before manufactured beach toys were commercially available, innovation and imagination filled the need. (Courtesy of Terry Polhamus Mendoza.)

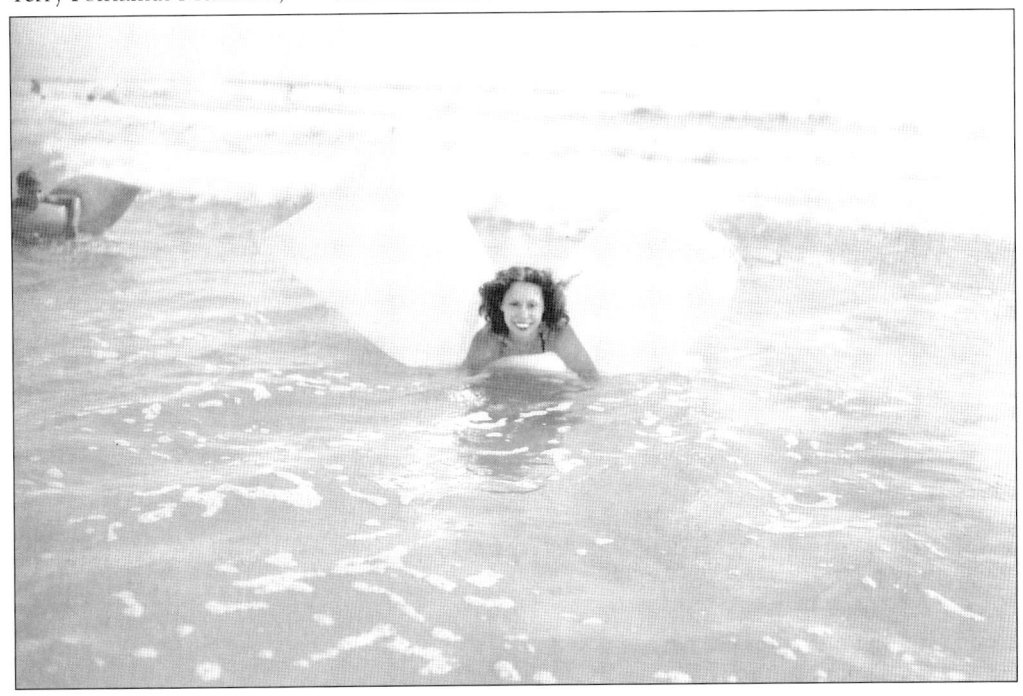

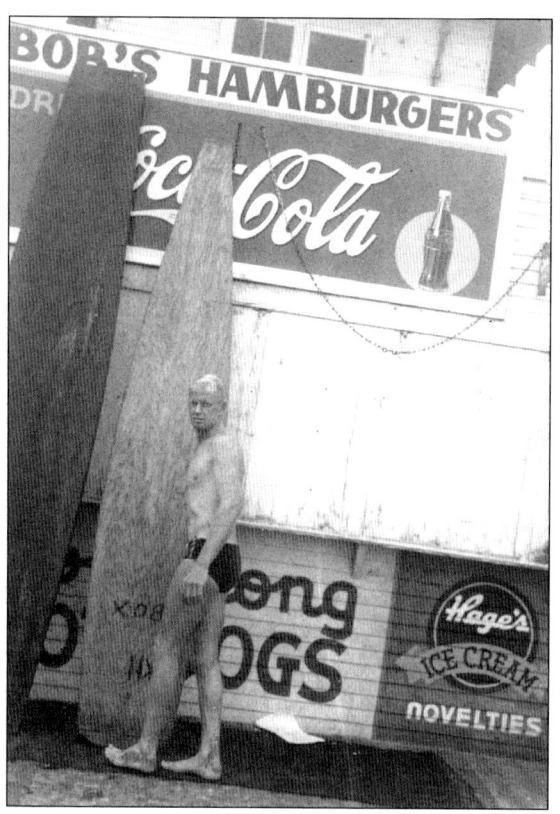

J. B. Asher, son of developer J. M. Asher Jr., is pictured at Old Mission Beach with a pair of unwieldy looking surfboards. J. B. is standing in front of a hollow board called a kukai box. J. B. served aboard the submarine USS *Corvina* and perished along with all hands on November 16, 1943, when the vessel was sunk by the enemy near Truk Island. (Courtesy of Norma Griffin.)

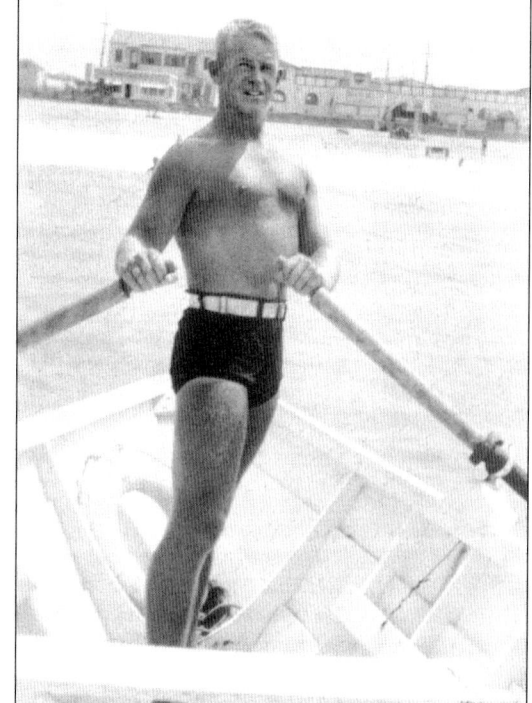

In 1938, Bill Rumsey stands offshore in the dory with Old Mission Beach in the background. Rumsey went on to develop the San Diego County Lifeguard service. (Courtesy of Norma Griffin.)

Eight
THE LATER YEARS

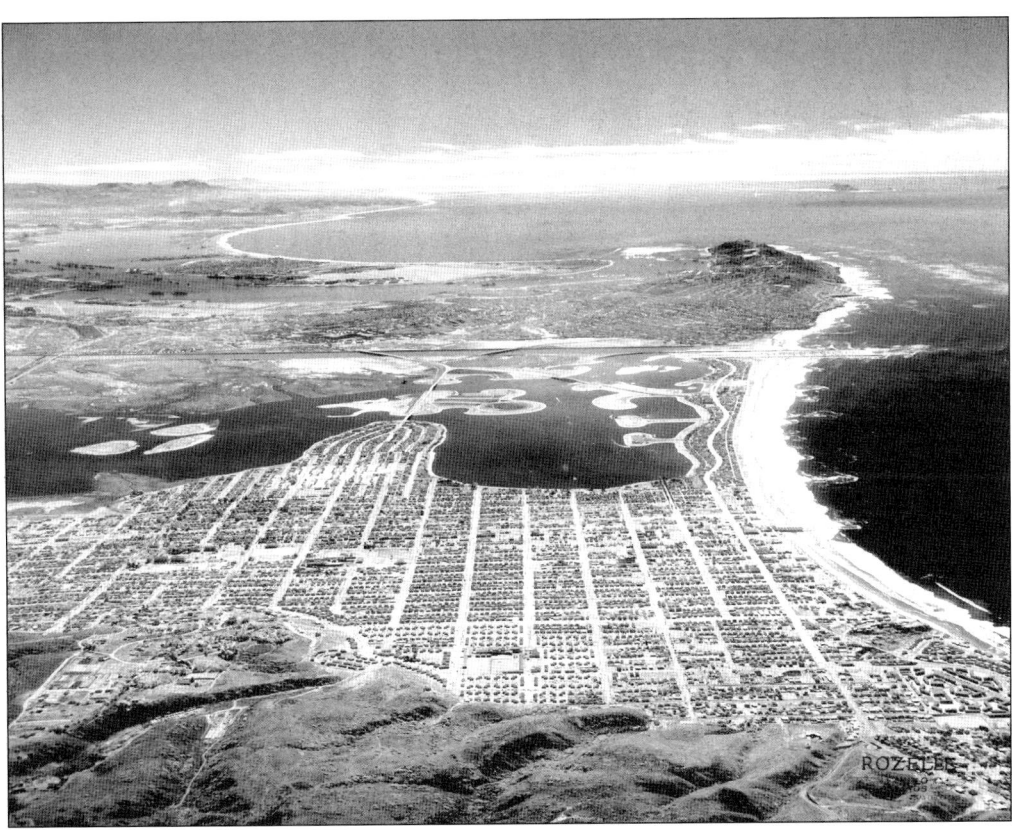

This fabulous 1952 aerial view shows San Diego from the hills of La Jolla, past Mission Beach and Mission Bay to Point Loma, San Diego Bay, and beyond, all the way to Mexico. Mission Beach is the narrow strip of land separating Mission Bay (center) and the Pacific Ocean (right). The Coronado Islands in Mexico are visible the distance. (Courtesy of Ann Howe Mansfield.)

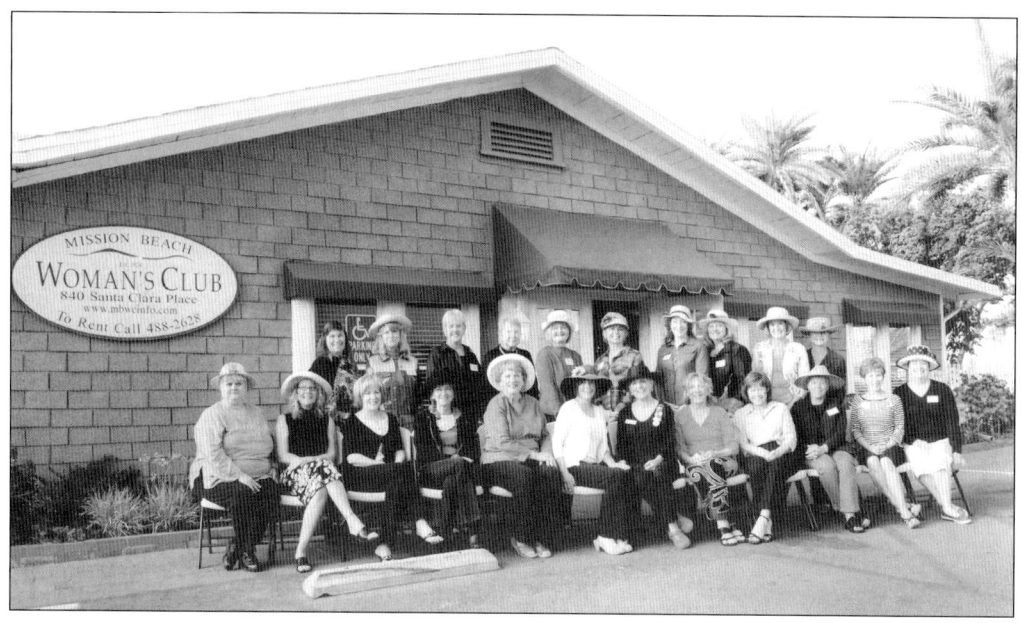

Keeping with the tradition of the Mission Beach Woman's Club, 2007 members pose to replicate the photograph of the ladies in 1926, below. The organization has served the needs of Mission Beach since 1921, raising money for pet projects throughout the community. Pictured in the December 20, 1926, photograph below are, from left to right, (first row) Mrs. Jackson, Flora Hunt, Meelund Blade, Elaine Harris (young girl), first president Alice Wonder, Beth Painter, and Mrs. Baumgartner; (included in the second row) Ruth Garner, Mrs. Huffman, Mrs. Jones, Mrs. Rynes, and Billie Harris Jenkins, mother of Elaine; (third row) Helma Edwards, unidentified, and Dorothy Warren. Little Elaine Harris was the first girl to be born in Mission Beach at Glenwood Sanitarium Hospital, located at 3624 Bayside Walk. (Courtesy of Mission Beach Woman's Club.)

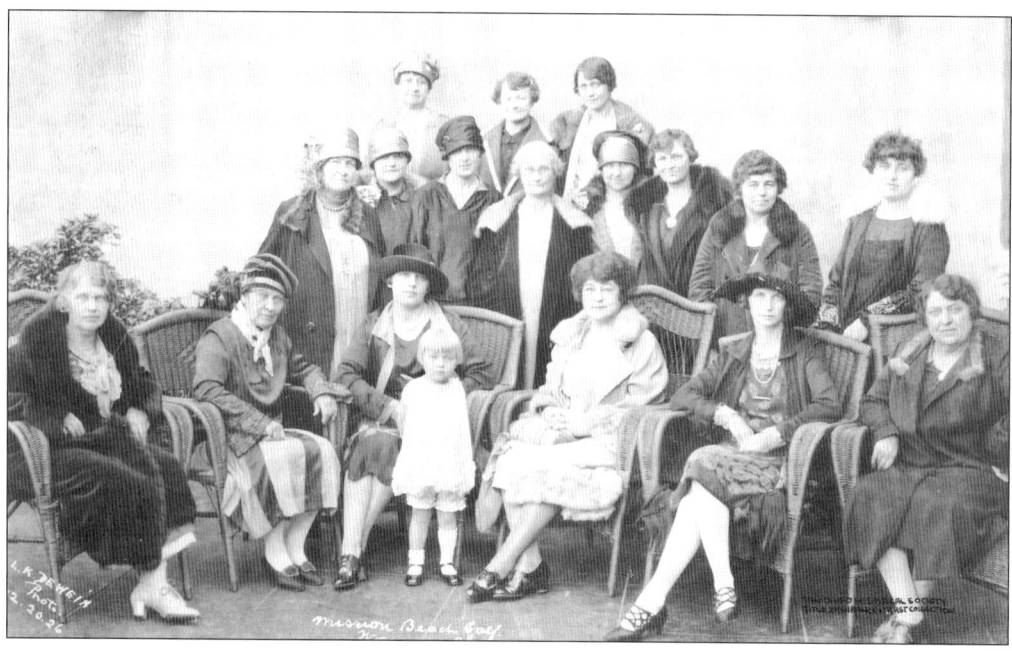

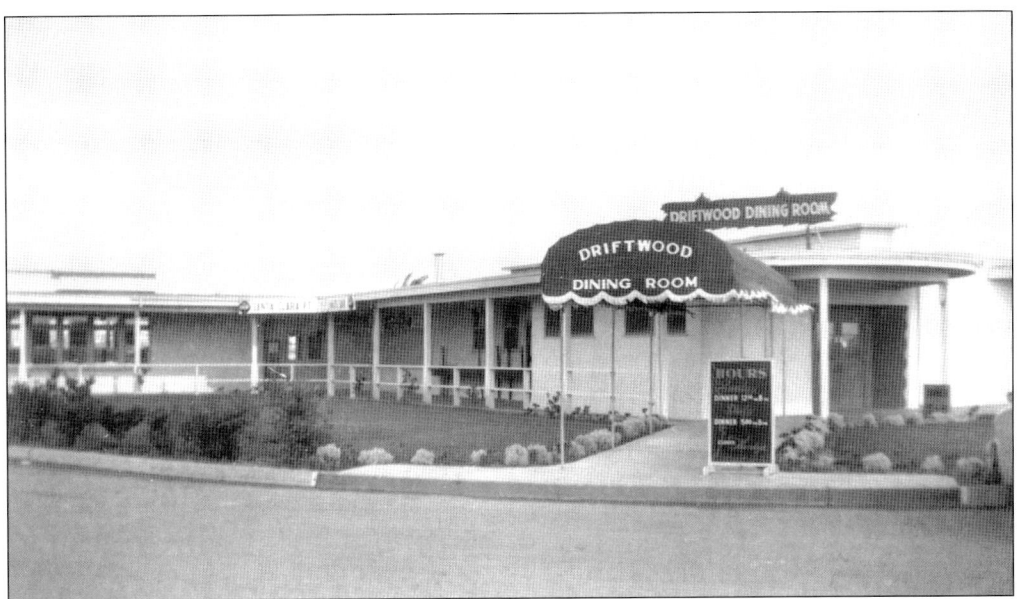

The Driftwood Dining Room, owned by Ben and Doris Hansen, occupied a wing of the Santa Clara Recreation Center from 1951 to 1961. This was a beautiful location with wonderful bay views, but the Hansen's were forced to close after a lengthy battle over a liquor license. (Courtesy of Paul Hansen.)

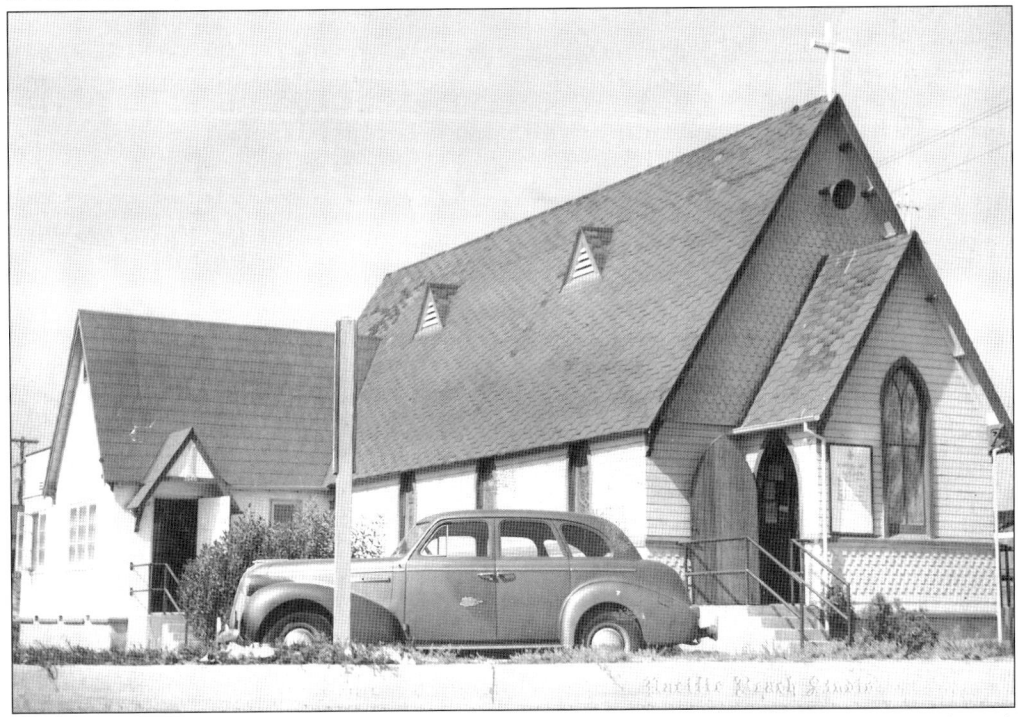

St. Andrew's by-the-Sea Episcopal Church was located on Toulon Court at Mission Boulevard. This church was moved from Logan heights to Mission Beach in 1946 and served the community only until 1948. The Mission Beach site proved to be inadequate for the needs of the church, so the structure was relocated to Pacific Beach. (Courtesy of Ralph Roblee.)

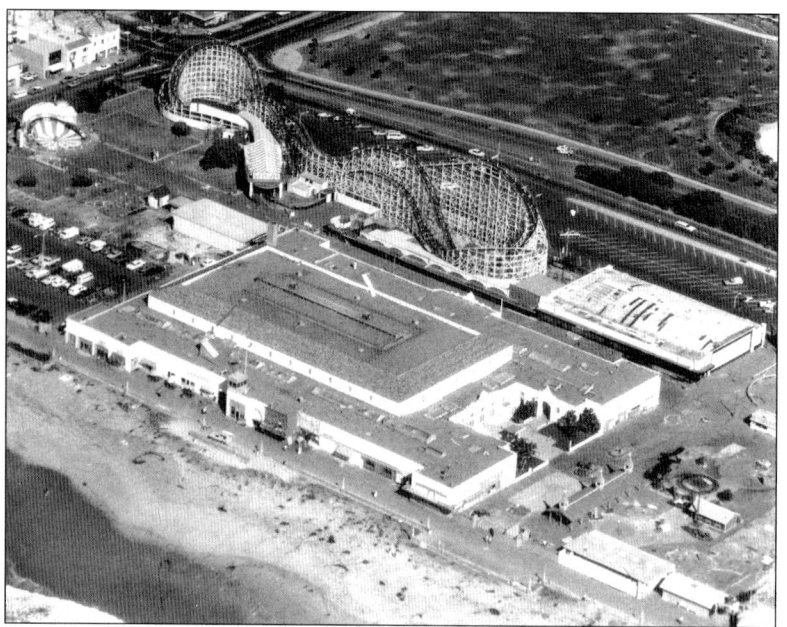

Belmont Park, with the exception of the Mission Beach Plunge, was closed in December 1976 due to declining business. This October 1977 photograph shows an empty midway and only a few cars in the north parking lot. The Plunge building is the large structure in the foreground, and the roller rink is at center right. (Courtesy of the authors.)

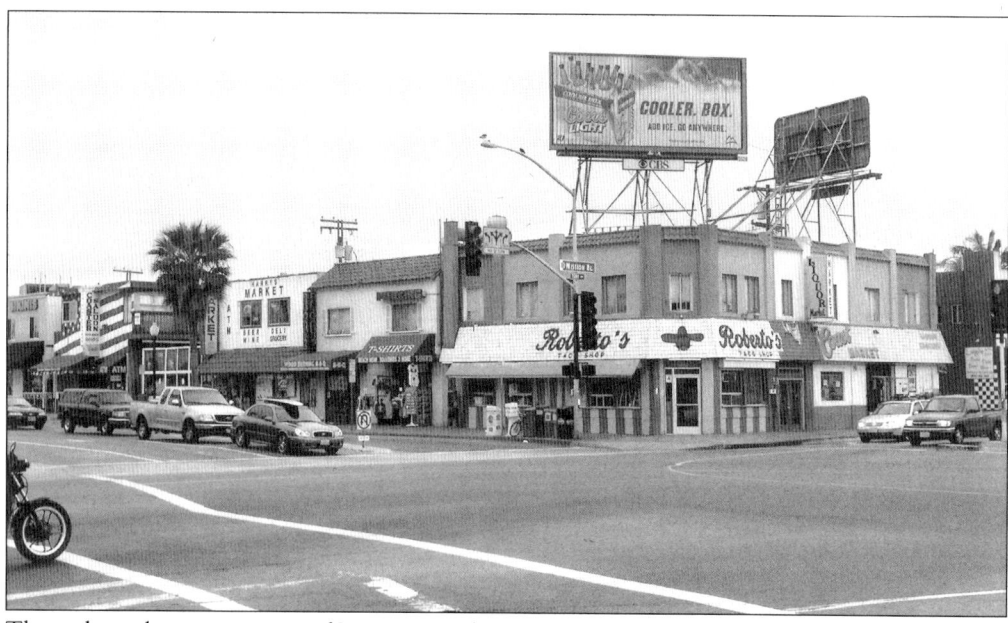

This is how the intersection of Mission Boulevard and Ventura Place looked on April 5, 2007. The corner building once housed a drugstore, two restaurants, Sam's Cheesecake Company, and an ice-cream parlor. Even though the brick facade is gone, the building looks much the same as it did in 1930. (Courtesy of authors.)

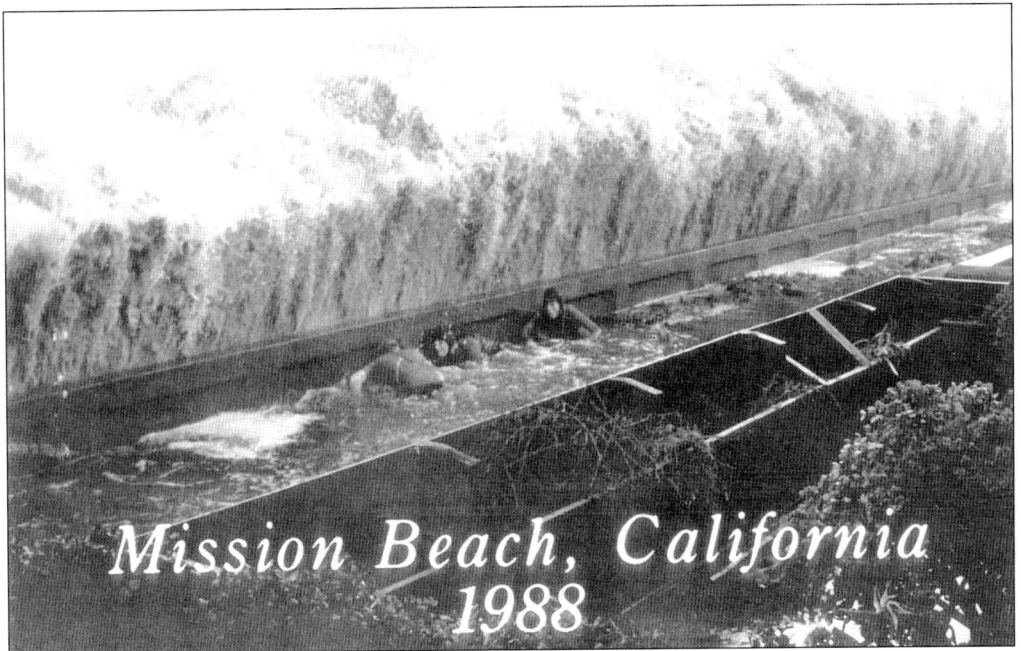

Some things never change. Every few years, Mission Beach gets hit with huge surf and high tides as pictured in 1988. Three young men are crouched behind the seawall as a wave crashes over the top. They are really wet but appear to be enjoying themselves. (Courtesy of John Chadwick.)

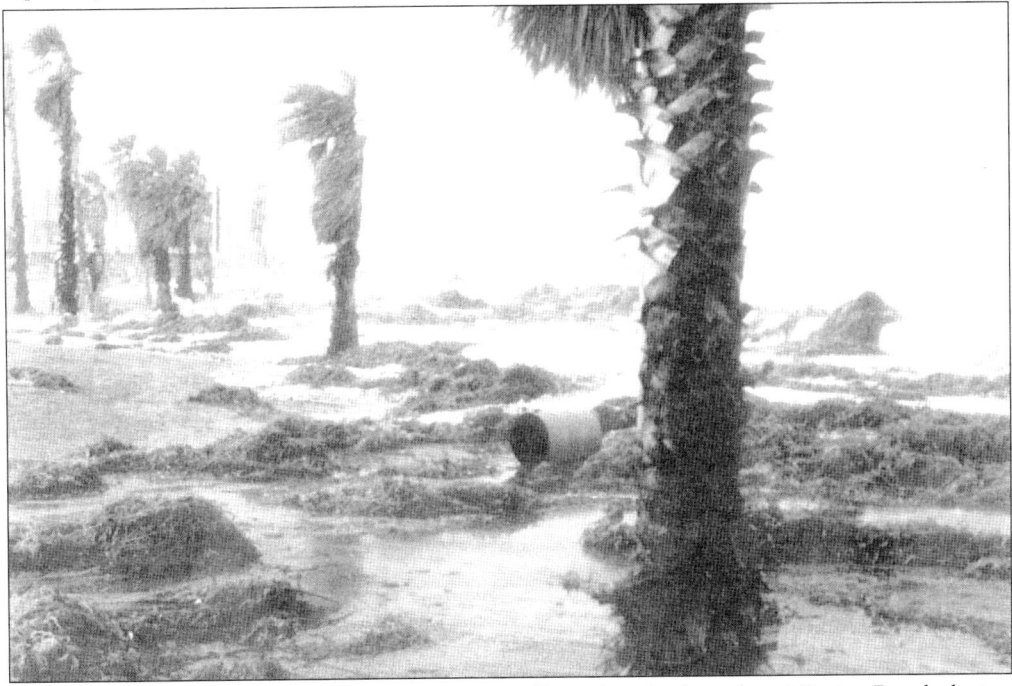

Tons of kelp was torn from the sea bottom at La Jolla and washed south to Mission Beach during a 1988 storm. Saltwater, seaweed, and trash barrels litter the oceanfront walkway, looking much like the aftermath of a hurricane. This view is looking at the park, just south of Belmont Park. (Courtesy of John Chadwick.)

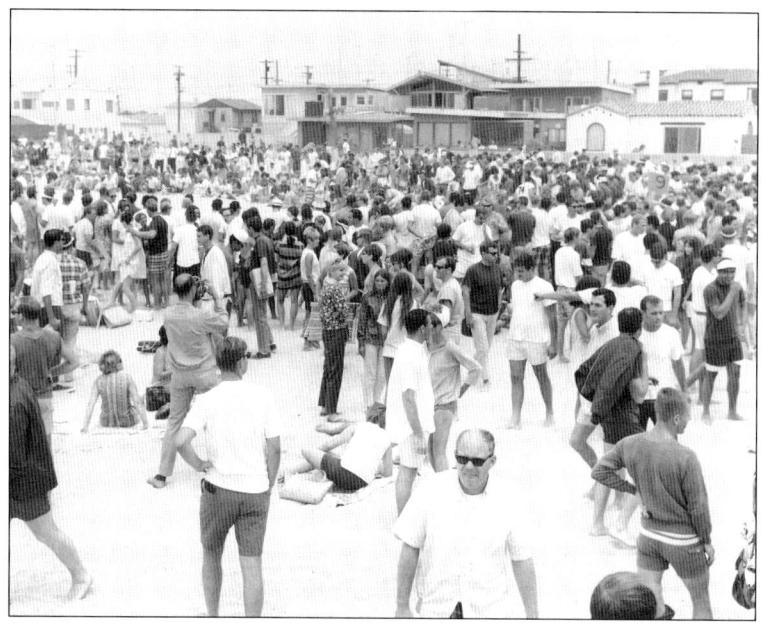

OMBAC's annual World Championship Over-the-Line Tournament has grown considerably since its beginning in 1954. The competition and the festive atmosphere attract thousands of spectators; everyone loves a good party. This c. 1965 photograph shows the beach at South Mission. (Courtesy of Dottie Simms.)

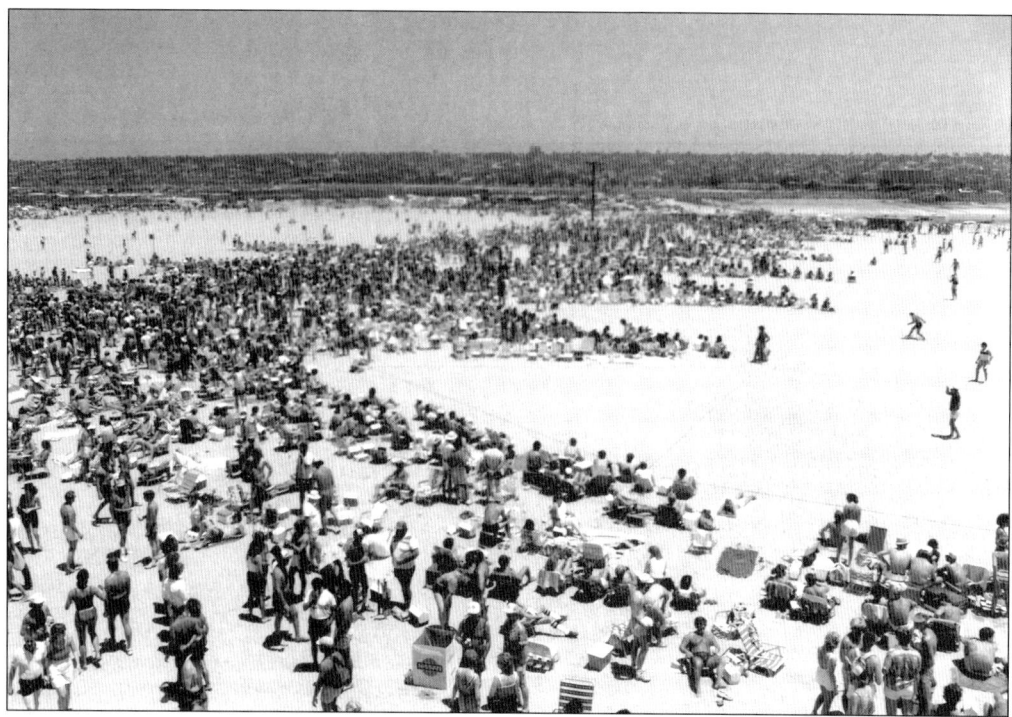

The Over-the-Line tournament has outgrown its beach venue and has been moved to Fiesta Island in Mission Bay. Today there are more than 1,300 three-person teams competing in several different divisions, sorted by gender and age. Players of both sexes range in age from 18 to 80. The world championships are held each year on the two middle weekends in July. (Courtesy of OMBAC.)

Every small town has its favorite watering holes, and Mission Beach is no different. South Mission is home of the Pennant and the Beachcomber bars, and locals and visitors alike can be seen rubbing and bending elbows is these establishments located at San Gabriel Place. Bicycles are a favorite means of transportation. Here Dottie Simms and Ray Hershman look for a spot to park. The pubs have become the place to have parties, wakes, wedding receptions, and business meetings. (Courtesy of Dottie Simms.)

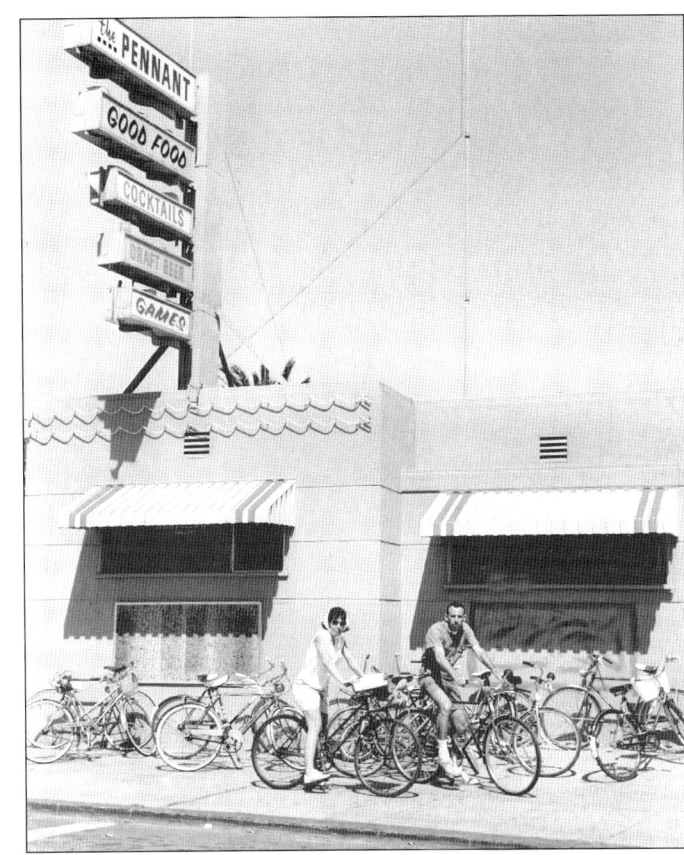

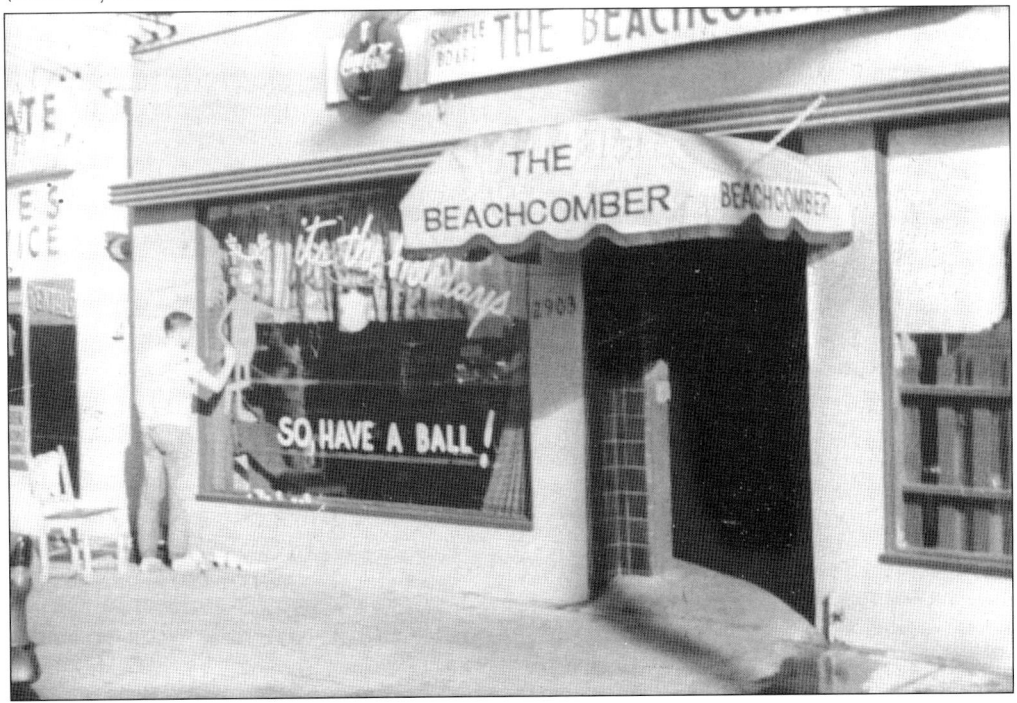

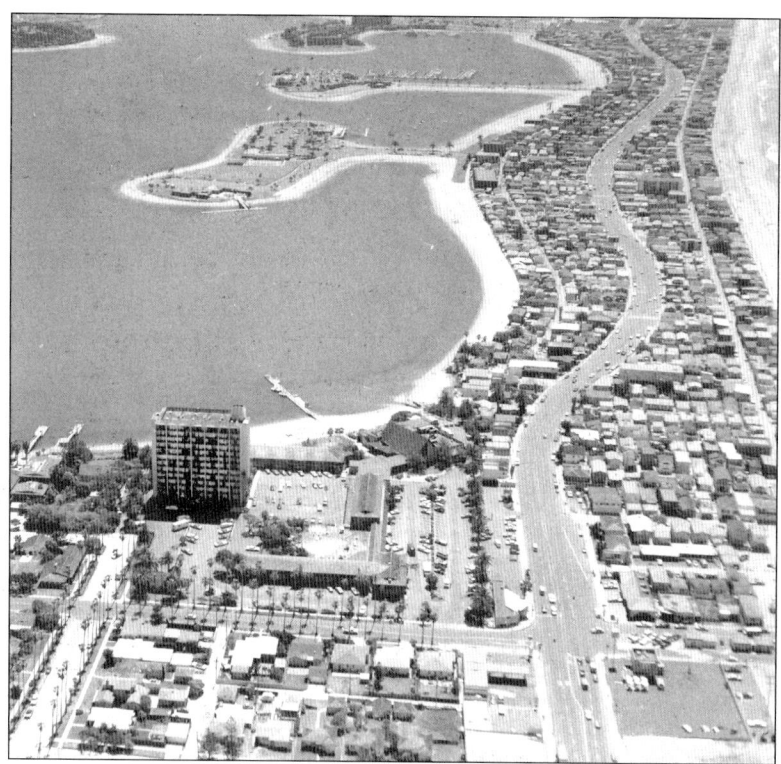

There are no vacant lots visible in this 1977 view. The Catamaran Hotel is the large building in the foreground. Santa Clara Point, El Carmel Point, and Gleason Point extend into Mission Bay. Santa Clara Recreation Center shares the point with athletic fields and boating facilities. El Carmel is the home of Mission Bay Yacht Club, and the Bahia Hotel occupies Gleason Point. (Courtesy of Ann Howe Mansfield.)

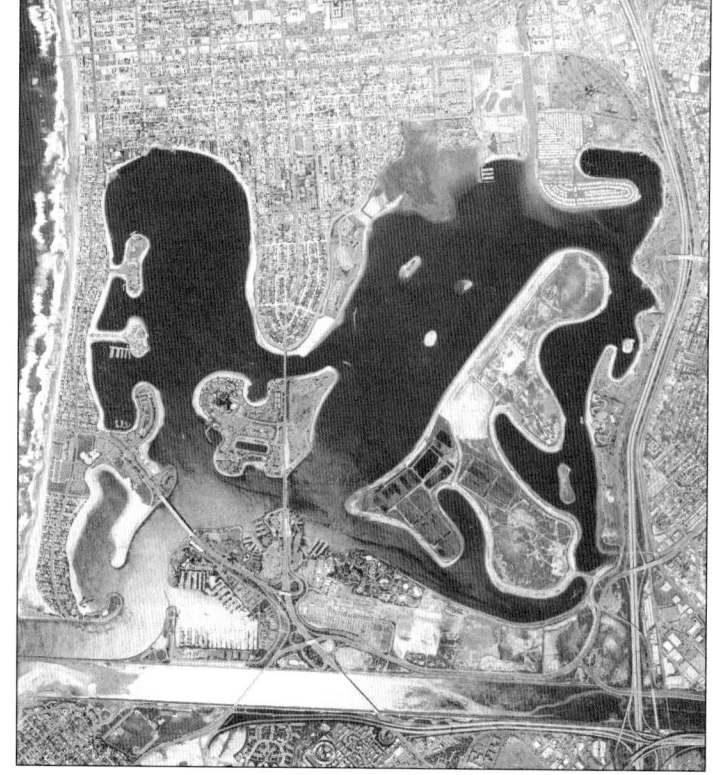

Looking down on paradise in 1980, Mission Bay has been transformed into a fabulous water park with something for everyone. There are several hotels, restaurants, and SeaWorld to serve visitors and locals alike. Mission Bay Channel is in the left foreground. The large island at center right is Fiesta Island, where the annual Over-the-Line tournament is held in the large sandy area. (Courtesy of Ned Huntington.)

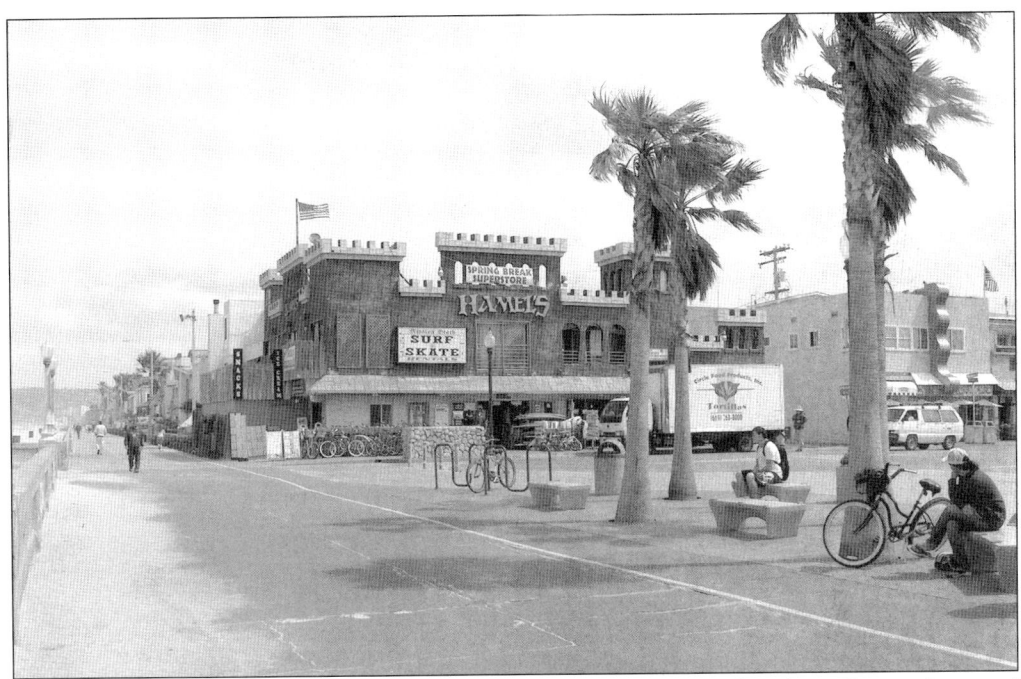

Hamel's has stood on the corner of Ocean Front and Ventura for decades, offering skate and bicycle rentals, beachwear, and accessories. Dan and Ray Hamel were very proud when they were awarded a "Stinky Onion" award for their building remodel when they created the castle. (Courtesy of authors.)

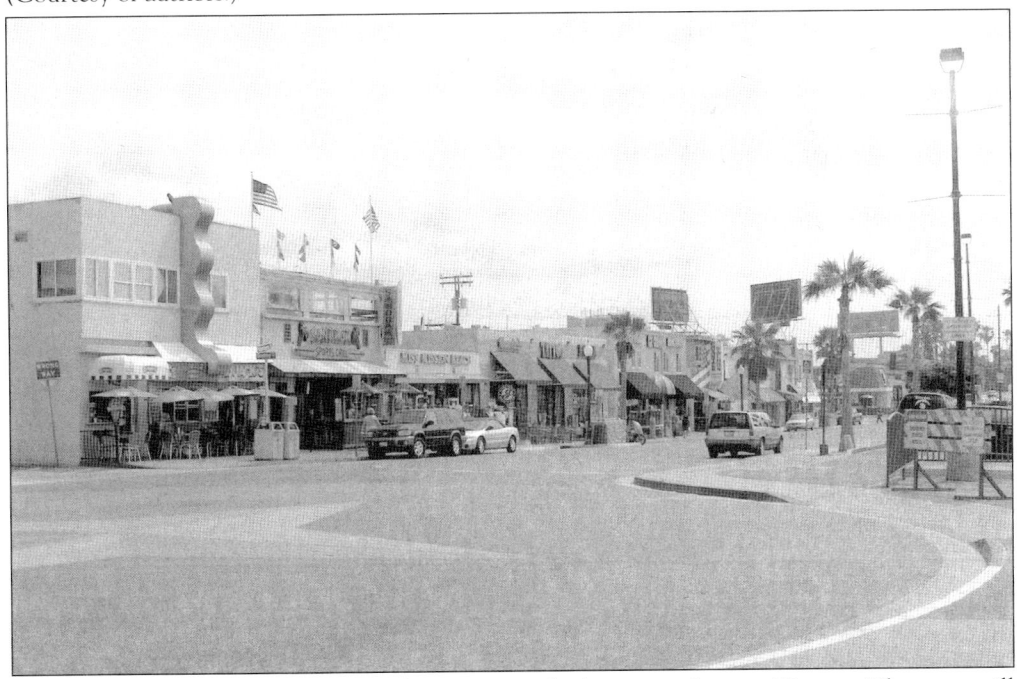

Looking east along Ventura in 2007 shows not much change in the past 70 years. There are still bars, T-shirt shops, souvenir stands, and fast-food places. The names of the business may have changed, but the selection and variety remains much the same. (Courtesy of authors.)

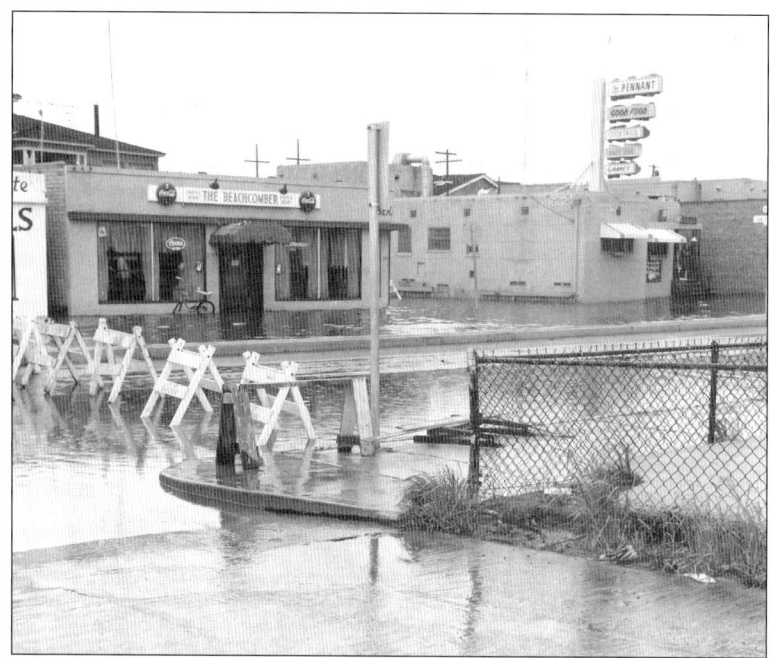

There doesn't need to be huge surf to cause street flooding. It seems that every time there is heavy rain and a high tide, the storm drain system is overwhelmed. If the flood gates are closed to prevent bay water backing up into the street, the rain water has nowhere to go, and usually, this is the result. This is the corner of San Gabriel and Mission Boulevard. (Courtesy of Dick Kovalcheck.)

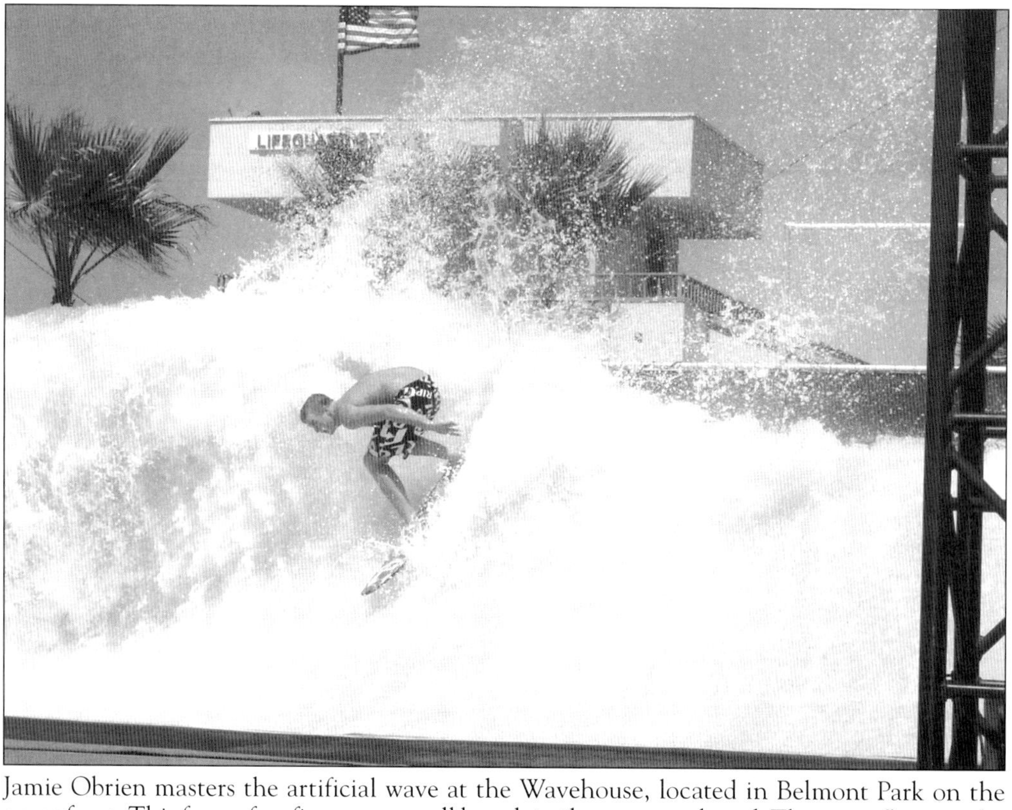

Jamie Obrien masters the artificial wave at the Wavehouse, located in Belmont Park on the oceanfront. This form of surfing uses a small board similar to a snowboard. The water flows up the slope to create the wave. Experts like Obrien make it look so easy. (Courtesy of Wavehouse.)

A large crowd is enjoying a great beach day and watching the surfers perform at the Wavehouse, which has provided a popular beach party atmosphere with outdoor bars and a restaurant. (Courtesy of Wavehouse.)

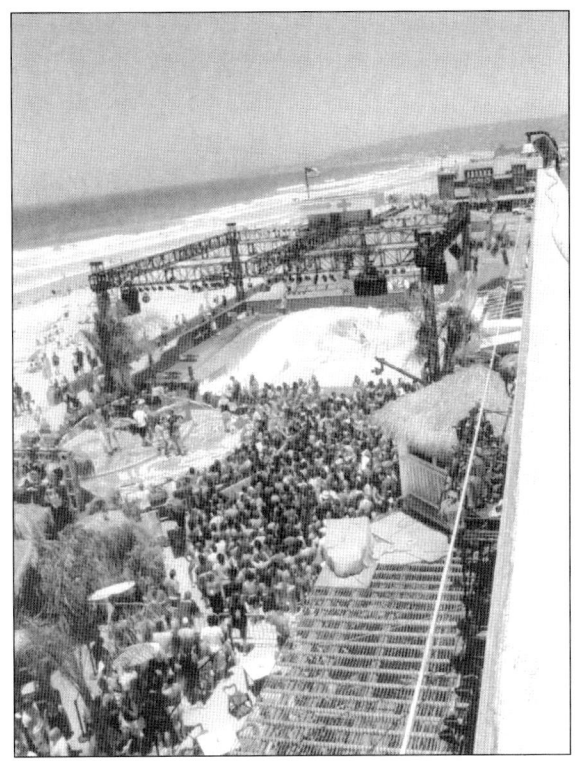

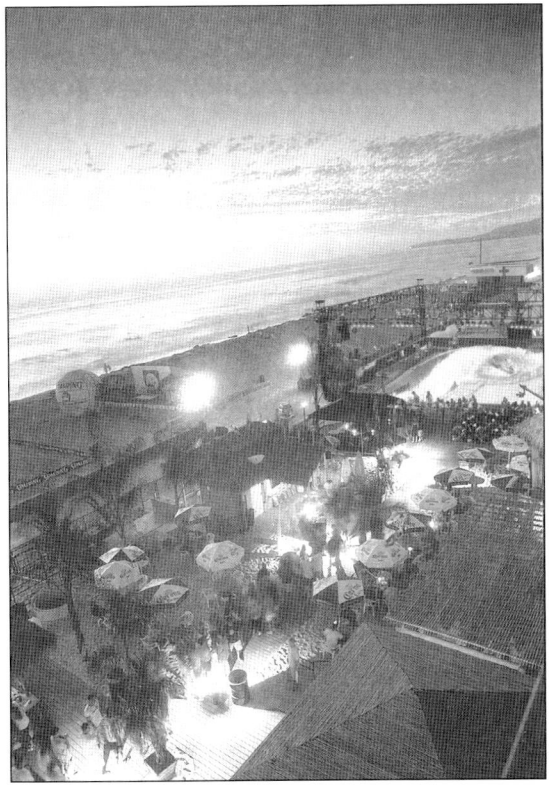

Night settles over the Wavehouse Restaurant in this final scene. A surfer still rides the wave, but the crowd has thinned. Mission Beach continues to be a special place to live and to visit, and the authors feel so very fortunate to have grown up here and to have been able to experience so many special times. (Courtesy of Wavehouse.)

ACROSS AMERICA, PEOPLE ARE DISCOVERING SOMETHING WONDERFUL. THEIR HERITAGE.

Arcadia Publishing is the leading local history publisher in the United States. With more than 3,000 titles in print and hundreds of new titles released every year, Arcadia has extensive specialized experience chronicling the history of communities and celebrating America's hidden stories, bringing to life the people, places, and events from the past. To discover the history of other communities across the nation, please visit:

www.arcadiapublishing.com

Customized search tools allow you to find regional history books about the town where you grew up, the cities where your friends and family live, the town where your parents met, or even that retirement spot you've been dreaming about.

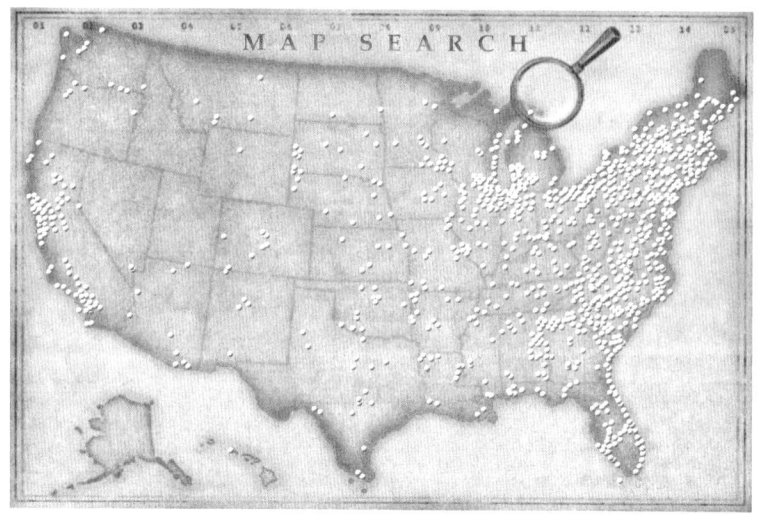